The ONE YEAR®

DEVOTIONS
FOR Men on the Go

STEPHEN ARTERBURN
AND
BILL FARREL

TYNDALE HOUSE PUBLISHERS, INC.
CAROL STREAM, ILLINOIS

Visit Tyndale online at www.tyndale.com.

TYNDALE, Tyndale's quill logo, *The One Year*, and *One Year* are registered trademarks of Tyndale House Publishers, Inc.

The One Year Devotions for Men on the Go

Designed by Beth Sparkman

Edited by Tracy M. Sumner

Published in association with the literary agency of Alive Communications, Inc., 7680 Goddard Street, Suite 200, Colorado Springs, CO 80920.

The Library of Congress has cataloged the first edition as follows:

Arterburn, Stephen, date.
  The one year book of devotions for men on the go / Stephen Arterburn with Bill Farrel.
    p. cm.
  Includes bibliographical references and index.
  ISBN 978-0-8423-5756-2
  1. Men—Prayer-books and devotions—English. 2. Devotional calendars. I. Farrel, Bill, date. II. Title.
  BV4528.2.A785 2004
  242′.642—dc22   2004007124

Printed in the United States of America

19   18   17   16   15   14   13
14   13   12   11   10   9   8

January

TO READ
James 4:1-17

How do you know what will happen tomorrow? For your life is like the morning fog—it's here a little while, then it's gone. JAMES 4:14

What's Really Important?

Pain in my chest . . . moving down my left arm . . . I think I'm having a heart attack! This is probably the last time I'll be able to eat a meatball sandwich!

My friend Rich was driving home one evening when this happened to him. The local sandwich shop was having a two-for-one special that month on meatball sandwiches—his favorite. So he bought a couple. He ate one on the way to pick up his wife, the other on the way to the hospital.

The doctor confirmed that Rich was indeed having a heart attack. After getting him stabilized and "out of the woods," the doctor put him on a restricted diet. But Rich felt like much more than his diet had been restricted. He was forced to ask himself some very hard questions.

After Rich survived the heart attack, he saw that he needed a more balanced and positive long-range life plan. He rediscovered who he really was and what really motivated him. He realized that he liked to help people, so he started looking for a career that would allow him to do just that. To his surprise, he found his niche in the funeral industry. Assisting others during their time of sorrow and transition brought clear answers to the questions in his own life.

Rich also discovered that the simple things in life—such as watching his kids' ball games—gave him real joy. He resolved to spend more time watching the kids play and less time being angry at the referees.

What things in life are really important to you? What gives your life joy and meaning? Think about decisions you can make today to keep you from missing out on those things tomorrow.

Lord, help me hold on to what's really important.

TO READ
2 Corinthians 3:1–4:16

All of us have had that veil removed so that we can be mirrors that brightly reflect the glory of the Lord.   2 CORINTHIANS 3:18

Almost

As I was growing up, my mother told me many times, "You don't have what it takes." Mom believed in reverse psychology, so she tried to motivate me by pointing out everything I would never accomplish.

Well, I set my mind to the task of proving my mother wrong. The only problem was that no man wants his mother to be wrong.

As a result, my twenties were characterized by the word *almost*. I *almost* ran a successful drafting business. I *almost* carried on a successful ministry. But whenever I got close to accomplishing my goals, I felt a strange need to change directions and do something else. Many times over, I *almost* finished the course—but not quite.

The final straw came when I almost lost the house I had spent a year building. I had dug and hammered and painstakingly given rise to the house that would be home to the most important people in my life. But after one year in the house, I was having trouble making the payments. When the foreclosure letter arrived in the mail, it stung. Waves of failure crashed down upon my heart. I desperately prayed for help.

A couple of weeks later, I was approached by a fellow pastor whose church was in a building program. They were looking for ways to cut their budget. He knew about my drafting background and asked if I would consider working with their architect to produce the final drawings. The church saved some money, and I earned enough extra income to keep up with my house payments.

What are the "almosts" in your life that cause you to despair? Help is only a prayer away.

Lord, don't let "almost" be the word that defines my day.

TO READ
1 Corinthians 9:24-27

Remember that in a race everyone runs, but only one person gets the prize. You also must run in such a way that you will win. 1 CORINTHIANS 9:24

Run for the Prize

Ron's hatred toward Ken consumed him. Ron was sure that Ken had been hanging around the preschool just to meet women, but why did it have to be his wife? Ron had been busy with his career, and his wife, Kathy, had been busy with the kids. But he never dreamed she would have an affair. He knew he hadn't been as attentive to her needs as he should have been, but he thought they had a stable relationship.

Ron hated Ken for stealing his wife's heart. He hated him for stealing his contentment. He hated him for complicating his life.

Ron hated himself too. He was losing his wife. In desperation he turned to the Bible. He read 1 Corinthians 9:24: "Only one person gets the prize." He remembered from a sermon he'd heard in church that this verse was a reference to the ancient Olympic Games, where athletes competed with one another and each race had only one winner.

In an instant, Ron realized that only one man was going to win Kathy's heart. But the other contestant, Ken, was increasing his lead every day because Ron's hatred was keeping him out of the race. If he was to have any chance at winning his wife back, he had to refocus.

That day Ron decided to get back in the race. Rather than dwelling on his anger and hatred for Ken, he would try to win Kathy back. By resuming the race, Ron rediscovered his love for her. In the race, he found his confidence again. In the race, his affection for his wife overshadowed his hatred for Ken. In the race, Ron found he had the advantage, and he won back his wife's heart. In the end, he won the prize of a stronger, more vibrant marriage.

Is there an area of your life where you feel like you are losing the race? If so, it may be that you need to refocus and start running like a winner.

Lord, teach me how to run as a winner and not a second-place finisher.

TO READ
Romans 6:15-23

Now you are free from sin, your old master,
and you have become slaves to your new master,
righteousness. ROMANS 6:18

Whose Rules?

There is a tendency for men and women to make up their own rules, regardless of the consequences. C. F. Kettering, father of the automobile's self-starter, has a story upholding the theory that ignorance is bliss.

> "We had a convention of household electric plant distributors in Dayton some years ago," he relates. "Each man was required to tell how much it cost him to wire a room. Finally one big breezy fellow named Bill, from Texas, got up and said, 'Why I can wire a room for half of what these fellows are talking about.'
>
> "The next day we took him to a room and told him to wire it his way. To our amazement he merely fastened the wire to the walls with staples.
>
> " 'But you can't put up electric wiring that way,' I said to him when he was done. 'It's against the fire underwriters' code.'
>
> " 'What's that?' asked Bill.
>
> "I gave him the code book of the underwriters and told him to study it overnight. The next morning he laid the book on my desk.
>
> " 'The more a fellow knows in this country,' he ruefully commented, 'the less liberty he's got.' "[1]

Of course, Bill's conclusion is ridiculous. The code was written to protect people from faulty wiring, and this electrician's renegade approach would have been disastrous. In the same way, following God's Word brings safety, direction, effectiveness, and confidence. In a word, you gain freedom when you follow his plan. When you ignore his plan and make up your own rules, things will eventually fail.

Whose rules will you follow today?

Jesus, thanks for the freedom truth brings to my life.

TO READ
John 6:34-58

"Sir," they said, "give us that bread every day of our lives." Jesus replied, "I am the bread of life. No one who comes to me will ever be hungry again. Those who believe in me will never thirst." JOHN 6:34-35

The Bread of Life

When people encountered Jesus, they realized almost immediately that he could provide everything they needed or wanted. The people had just witnessed him feeding more than five thousand people with just a few fish and five loaves of bread. They saw him provide for them that day, and the hope arose in their hearts that maybe he could provide even more for them. They were tired of the daily grind of providing for their families, and they were tired of being hungry. Perhaps if they just believed, Jesus would take care of all their needs.

But Jesus is never content to give us only material provisions. He intends to give us himself. He uses our various needs to help develop in our hearts a hunger for him. The people asked for bread so they wouldn't be physically hungry. But Jesus responded by offering to satisfy their deeper spiritual hunger: "I am the bread of life."

There are few lessons in life more important than this one. Jesus is the answer to your vital questions about life. Jesus is the solution to your pressing problems. Jesus is the food that satisfies the hunger in your soul.

The day you realize those truths will be one of the most important days of your life.

What need are you facing today? Are you allowing Jesus to use this need to give you more of a hunger for him? Are you prepared for him to meet your deepest need?

Lord, help me to learn that I need you more than anything else.

TO READ
John 8:31-35

You will know the truth, and the truth will set you free. JOHN 8:32

❋ Honest Questions?

My friend Van had lots of questions. He held back on making a decision for Christ because he wanted to be convinced. When I and another friend, Bob, met with Van, I thought we were there to answer his questions.

"What about all the people around the world who have never heard about Jesus?" Van asked confidently.

I shared my understanding of how God judges everybody by his or her reaction to creation. Bob interrupted me and said, "You don't really care about that question, Van. Just ask Jesus to come into your heart."

I was immediately irritated and wondered why Bob was ignoring Van's question. Van, however, seemed undaunted.

"How can the Bible say that the world was made in six days when science shows it has taken millions of years?" he asked.

Again, I jumped in and began answering Van's question, and again Bob interrupted me: "Van, you don't really care about that question, either. You are just using it to put off asking Jesus into your life."

Much to my chagrin, this same scenario took place several times. Van would ask a question, I would start to answer, and Bob would interrupt my answers and tell Van he needed to ask Jesus into his life.

I was about to confront Bob over his interruptions when Van said, "You know, Bob, you're right. I have been afraid to ask Jesus into my life, and I have been hiding behind these questions so I could ignore the real issue. I do need to ask Jesus into my life."

That day I learned something very important about people's questions, namely that they aren't always asked for the purpose of learning more about Christ but for trying to hide their real need: Jesus himself.

Lord, help me to see past people's questions to their need for you.

TO READ
Deuteronomy 34:9—
Joshua 1:9

Joshua son of Nun was full of the spirit of wisdom, for Moses had laid his hands on him. So the people of Israel obeyed him and did everything just as the Lord had commanded Moses. DEUTERONOMY 34:9

Stepping Out in Faith

After the death of Moses, God called Joshua to lead the people of Israel into the land of Canaan to claim it as their inheritance. They had the means to do it, and they were certainly motivated. They had been wandering in the wilderness for forty years, eating the same food, wearing the same shoes, and doing the same mundane things every day. They were bored and eager to do something purposeful.

To realize their goal of entering Canaan, however, the Israelites had to cross the Jordan—at flood stage. The river was overflowing its banks, and it looked formidable. Furthermore, nothing but obstacles awaited them on the other side.

If this venture was to succeed, it would require every bit of faith, every bit of energy, and every bit of determination Joshua and the people could muster. It would tax Joshua in every possible way, and there would be many battles.

But it had to be done because it was their calling.

What is your calling? What Jordan must you cross to fulfill your purpose? What battles has God called you to fight? Pursuing your calling will require every bit of faith, every bit of energy, and every bit of determination you can muster. And it will take courage. It will tax you in every possible way, but it must be done. If you go forward, depending fully on God, he will provide everything you need to succeed.

So don't be afraid! Have courage and take that first step.

Lord, help me never to fear the Jordans I must cross or the battles I must fight. Give me the courage to take that first step.

TO READ
John 6:16-29

They were three or four miles out when suddenly they saw Jesus walking on the water toward the boat. They were terrified, but he called out to them, "I am here! Don't be afraid." JOHN 6:19-20

❈ On Stormy Seas

The night was dark. The wind was blowing. The waves threatened the little boat in which the disciples traveled. They were hanging on for their lives.

Having grown up along the shores of the Sea of Galilee, the disciples were accustomed to storms rising unexpectedly. The fishermen in the group were used to the rigors of the sea. But this time it was different.

In the midst of this terrible storm, Jesus appeared to them—walking on the water. At first, Jesus' presence increased the disciples' fear. They did not expect him, and they had never seen anything like this. They thought they were seeing a ghost. But in the middle of a stormy sea of fear, Jesus called out, "I am here! Don't be afraid." He calmed the disciples' hearts and showed them that he was more powerful than the storm.

Jesus wants you to know that he will come to you in the midst of life's struggles, and he wants you to know that he is more powerful than even the mightiest storm. One of the most important truths God will teach you is that Jesus is bigger than the struggles in your life. His presence may scare you at first. He may surprise you at a time when you are so focused on your own struggles that you are tempted to look right past him. But when you encounter him and he speaks to your heart—"I am here! Don't be afraid"—you will never be the same again.

Next time you are caught in life's stormy seas, look expectantly for Jesus to meet you where you are, and depend on his power to calm your fears and anxieties.

Lord, teach me that you are bigger than any struggle or storm I will ever face.

TO READ
John 2:1-12

His mother told the servants, "Do whatever he tells you." JOHN 2:5

Simple Obedience

Mary had seen it all. She had watched Jesus grow up—feeding him, changing him, and teaching him how to speak Aramaic. When he was twelve, she had backtracked to the temple to retrieve him so she could take him home. She had watched him learn carpentry at Joseph's side. And now she was watching him begin his public ministry.

Mary knew Jesus' potential as only a mother can, and she could sense that he was about to do something very special. So she said to the servants at the wedding at Cana, "Do whatever he tells you."

It was such a simple introduction to Jesus' first public miracle. An insightful mother giving straightforward instructions. The servants were not aware that they were about to witness a miracle. They had no way of knowing that Jesus was about to transform jars of water into the best wine served that day.

In Mary's instructions we find an important lesson to learn. God has planned a life journey for you filled with surprises and opportunities for growth. He wants to provide for you beyond your abilities, and he wants to maximize your potential. He wants to put himself on display in your life over and over again.

The best way to live is to heed Mary's instructions: "Do whatever he tells you."

Lord, help me to hear your voice and obey your instructions.

TO READ
John 5:1-17

When Jesus saw him and knew how long he had been ill, he asked him, "Would you like to get well?"

JOHN 5:5

Would You Like to Get Well?

"Would you like to get well?" This is one of the most penetrating questions you could ever be asked. After all, wellness brings with it a lot of responsibility. If you're well, you have to be productive to the extent of your ability. If you're well, you need to work hard and discover your giftedness and use it to help others find their own potential in life.

Andy's father was hard to live with. He was harsh, demanding, and unrelenting. As a result, Andy's behavior became unpredictable. He was a gifted athlete and musician, but he often got into trouble. Andy wanted his dad's attention and tried everything from productivity to rebellion to get it. During his teen years, he experimented with sex and drugs to see if they would help.

Andy's life was one big search. A search for approval, a search for happiness and fulfillment, a search to get well. One day in the midst of this search, Andy met Jesus, who challenged him with some very pointed questions: "Would you like to get well? If you do, you will have to forgive your dad and let me be bigger and stronger in your life than he is. You will have to be willing to tell others about the work I am doing in your life. You will have to grow up and stop feeling sorry yourself. What do you think? Would you like to get well ?"

Andy took Jesus up on his challenge, and today he is running a successful youth ministry where he challenges students every week: "Jesus loves you and wants to make you well. Do you get it?"

What about you? Do you want to get well? Before you answer that question, remember that wellness brings with it great responsibility.

Lord, help me to understand that wellness comes with great responsibility.

TO READ
John 4:1-39

Many Samaritans from the village believed in Jesus because the woman had said, "He told me everything I ever did!"   JOHN 4:39

Unconditional Acceptance

Have you ever done something you wouldn't want to be made public knowledge? Is there something in your past that you believe disappointed God greatly?

In today's Scripture, we read of a woman who had done some things she no doubt wasn't proud to have on her track record. She was amazed that Jesus would even talk with her, because in her day respectable men didn't talk to such women. She was even more amazed when Jesus pointed out that she had been married five times and that the man she was living with was not her husband.

Jesus amazed this woman for two reasons. First, he knew all of this about her even though he had never met her before. Second, he was neither condoning nor judging her past. She knew he was calling her to a new life of excellence and that he was doing it with acceptance and encouragement.

After her meeting with Jesus, this woman went into town and told everyone she knew about this man who had known all about her. As a result, many realized that they needed the same kind of acceptance she had received from Jesus. Everyone who understood that God would bring excellence without judgment believed in Jesus that day.

Do you want that kind of acceptance and grace? Then tell Jesus about the things you've done that you are afraid have disappointed him. Once you have experienced his unconditional acceptance, tell someone else how he has worked in your life.

Jesus, lead me to excellence as you convince me of your grace.

TO READ
Acts 13:26-37

After David had served his generation according to the will of God, he died and was buried, and his body decayed. ACTS 13:36

Being What You're Made to Be

Who are you? I mean, who are you *really*? Everybody in your life probably has an opinion of who you ought to be, and they are only too eager to tell you their opinions. If you are the typical man, you have probably spent the majority of your life trying to be the person you think you are supposed to be just so you can compete in this world—and you silently resent having to do so.

Have you ever stopped to ask, "Who has *God* made me to be?" God knew exactly what he was doing when he made you and gave you the desires that are in your heart. But if you are like many men, you fumble around with the expectations others have put on you rather than courageously discovering who God has made you to be.

Think about the variety of ways God has made men. Moses was an impatient, soft-spoken man of miracles. David was an athletic champion who could write songs after winning battles. Jonathan was a loyal friend who was willing to give up his own success for God's bigger plan. John the Baptist was an unconventional street preacher. The apostle Paul was an uncompromising achiever, while his close friend Barnabas was a personal encourager of other men.

Some of God's great men look very successful, and some of them seem very unassuming. Others appear to have failed in their pursuits. But what they have in common is that they aggressively pursued what God put on their hearts to do with their lives.

Who do you think God has made you to be? Does that match the expectations of others? If not, whose expectations will you choose?

Dear God, thank you for making me the way I am. Thank you for giving me the desires I have. Show me how to live the way you have made me.

TO READ
Exodus 3:1-22

When the Lord saw that he had caught Moses' attention, God called to him from the bush, "Moses! Moses!"

"Here I am!" Moses replied. EXODUS 3:4

✳ Points of Change

God had chosen Moses from birth to be the deliverer of his people. He was miraculously protected as a baby and was privileged to grow up in the finest home in the land. He received the best possible education and had all the benefits of wealth. As a result, he became proud and believed everything would come easy for him. As a forty-year-old man, Moses concluded it was time for him to live out his destiny as the rescuer of Israel.

It was a disaster! The very people Moses was called to lead didn't appreciate him or accept him as a leader. Moses' education was only half finished and he didn't realize it. Concluding he had failed, his confidence plummeted and his vision shifted. He disappeared to his uncle's homeland to lose himself in herding sheep and raising a family. For the next forty years, he learned to live quietly and contentedly and to work hard and expect little. He figured he would die in obscurity with a dream of what might have been.

Then Moses encountered the burning bush. Speaking from the bush, God called him. Moses was changed again. He was humble this time but determined to do what God made him to do. His education was complete. Now he was a man with authority, not just aggression. His vision was clear because there was no pretense in it. He was ready to lead the "sheep" of Israel through a wilderness journey.

Moses was not doing what men are naturally inclined to do. He was doing what his Creator had called him to do.

God has called you and is training you for a purpose. There will be key moments along the path that are necessary to shape you into the man for the job. Those moments might seem like failures or like great achievements. Either way, the key question is this: Will they change you?

Lord, use key events in my life to make me the man you want me to be.

How do you benefit if you gain the whole world but lose your own soul in the process? MARK 8:36

✤ *Partnership with God*

Mike was soaring in his career. He was energetic, creative, highly productive, and by all accounts very successful. And he was empty. He could sell anything, but he couldn't sell himself on the idea that he was fulfilled.

One day Mike's boss invited him to attend his church. Mike admired his boss because of his work ethic and his effective risk-taking, so he decided to take him up on it.

When the pastor read the words, "How do you benefit if you gain the whole world but lose your own soul in the process?" Mike's soul was stirred. He realized he had the ability to "gain the whole world." God had made him strong and full of energy. Mike knew how to soar, but he had nowhere to land. He had no spiritual foundation, so all his pursuits were ultimately empty. He finally realized that his efforts at work would influence a large number of people but his life would have no eternal impact.

Mike gave his heart to Christ that day and found a relationship with God that filled his entire life. His energy level stayed high, but he found a new purpose in his work. He discovered he could use his business skills to help people in more meaningful ways. From then on, he was able to make a profit and find satisfaction at the same time.

Since the day Mike entered into a partnership with God, he became not only a better businessman but a better man altogether.

Do you want to be a better man? Not just a better businessman, not just a better husband, not just a better father, not just a better friend, but simply a better man? Then make your partnership with God your number one priority.

Lord, make me a better man by helping me keep our partnership strong and growing.

"No," Peter protested, "you will never wash my feet!" Jesus replied, "But if I don't wash you, you won't belong to me." JOHN 13:8

A Picture of Servanthood

At the time of Jesus' earthly ministry, people wore sandals everywhere they went, and their feet got very dirty. When visitors arrived at a friend's house, it was the custom for one of the servants to wash their feet. It was dirty work, so it was reserved for those at the bottom of the social list. Jesus shocked his friends when he chose to wash their feet. After all, their Master should not be doing servant's work. If anything, the disciples should have been washing his feet! But Jesus knew his disciples were going to be servants and that they needed an unforgettable picture of the type of servanthood they were to live out.

Peter didn't understand what Jesus was doing, so he vehemently declared, "You will never wash my feet!"

Peter thought that protesting his Lord's actions showed that he understood who Jesus was and who the disciples were. But he needed to be reminded that God's ways are not our ways, and he also needed to see what being a true servant looked like. Jesus immediately put Peter in his place when he said, "But if I don't wash you, you won't belong to me." It was a lesson Peter never forgot. This picture of his Savior, humbly serving, set the course for the rest of his life.

Jesus' example of humble servanthood was an important one for the disciples to see, and it's equally important for us to read about. It not only shows us that Jesus is the one who washes us completely, but it shows us that no matter how important we think we are, we should always strive to serve others.

Lord, thank you for your example of servanthood. Help me to follow that example in everything I do.

TO READ
Matthew 9:1-13

As Jesus was going down the road, he saw Matthew sitting at his tax-collection booth. "Come, be my disciple," Jesus said to him. So Matthew got up and followed him. MATTHEW 9:9

Come, Be My Disciple

Matthew had developed complicated procedures for collecting taxes, and they ensured him a healthy profit. He had devised sophisticated formulas for assessing the value of other people's property, and he had built himself a reputation. He had learned that you had to be tough to be successful and that good business did not always make for good friends. He was committed to success. He was skilled in negotiation, and he knew how to close the big deals. Many people disliked him, but everyone feared him. He was self-sufficient and hardened by the realities of life. He believed he had found the necessary balance of life and was content to live out his successful but lonely existence.

Then he met Jesus. There was no fanfare; there were no lectures. Jesus didn't point out the misalignment of his priorities or argue with him over the bankruptcy of his inner life. He simply said, "Come, be my disciple."

Matthew had never heard anything so simple and so profound. If Jesus had confronted him, he could have fought back. If Jesus had argued with him, he could have defended himself. But Jesus simply said, "Come, be my disciple." There were no defenses and no schemes. Matthew was left with nothing to do but get up and follow him.

When Jesus calls us to follow him and be his disciples, we don't need to defend ourselves or our past actions, and we don't need to tell Jesus why it might not be a good idea to call people like us to follow him. We just need to get up and follow.

Lord, help me every day to obey your call to follow you.

TO READ
Isaiah 2:1-17

The arrogance of all people will be brought low. Their pride will lie in the dust. The Lord alone will be exalted!   ISAIAH 2:17

Nothing to Lose

Glenn prided himself on having a higher energy level and a more positive attitude than the average person. But three failed marriages and the death of his only son at the age of thirteen had drained him. The pain and emptiness of his daily existence was dulled only by the numbness in his heart.

Glenn probably could have kept up the facade if one of his associates, Judy, hadn't asked him the question, "Why don't you give Jesus a chance? What do you have to lose?" The question brought the disappointment and confusion of his life rushing to the surface. He couldn't sleep. He couldn't concentrate. He couldn't escape the haunting reality that he had nothing to lose because he had gained none of what he really wanted in life.

One quiet night, he asked Jesus to forgive him and come live in his heart.

As Glenn was praying one day, a thought stuck in his heart. *I need to go back to school and get my teaching credentials.* It seemed to him a crazy thought for a man in his fifties, but he enrolled anyway because he had nothing to lose.

Glenn never dreamed that he would discover his real purpose in life through the interviews at the end of the teaching program. His move to Colombia to teach English-speaking students turned out to be the door to the only career he ever loved and the path to the only woman who truly captured his heart.

Glenn found his life when he realized he had nothing to lose.

Are you trying to decide whether or not to give your life to Jesus? Then don't hesitate to do it! After all, you have nothing to lose and everything to gain.

Lord, meet me today and show me that I have nothing to lose in giving my life to you.

TO READ
John 4:46-54

Jesus told him, "Go back home. Your son will live!"

JOHN 4:50

✳ *Taking Jesus at His Word*

The man took Jesus at his word and departed. He was not used to taking people at their word like this. Usually he needed more proof. But this was his moment of greatest need. His son was deathly ill, and the doctors could not help him. His last resort was to turn to Jesus and plead for his help.

"Lord," he pleaded, "please come now before my little boy dies."

The way Jesus said "Your son will live" changed this man's life on the spot. There was such conviction in Jesus' voice, such authority and confidence that the man immediately believed him and went on his way.

He didn't need to see the results to believe, because the Son of God had spoken them. He didn't need the opinions of others, because the author of creation had spoken. The simple word of God calmed his heart in the most dire situation he had ever faced.

This is what happens when you encounter the Word of God. It rings in your soul and inspires your faith. It supersedes all other opinions and banishes all doubts. It addresses your heart's fears and sets you back on course for the adventure of your life.

In what areas do you need to hear the simple and clear word of God? What situations in your life need God's insight? Ask God to provide his wisdom in these areas, and then read the Bible expecting to hear from him.

God, I need to hear from you. Give me the faith to believe what you tell me, just as the man whose son was deathly sick believed.

<table>
<tr><td>

TO READ
Genesis 39:1-6

</td><td>

The Lord was with Joseph and blessed him greatly as he served in the home of his Egyptian master.

GENESIS 39:2

</td></tr>
</table>

❁ *God Is with You!*

Joseph was living in a foreign country separated from his family. He was the slave of a man named Potiphar, a good man but a man who every day reminded Joseph that he was not home. Each task reminded Joseph that his own brothers had rejected him and that his own family had turned him away.

Joseph had a long list of reasons to feel sorry for himself, but he had one reason for hope—a reason bigger than anything else he faced: the Lord was with him.

The pressures of life discouraged Joseph, but the presence of God brought him hope. His responsibilities were heavy, but the presence of God brought success. Life had been a circumstantial and emotional roller coaster, but the presence of God brought the kind of stability that allowed Joseph to prosper in the midst of the unpredictable.

One of the most important moments you'll ever experience in your life is the one when you realize the presence of God is greater than everything else combined. When you believe that God is with you, you can't help but prosper. When you understand that God is with you, life is always doable. When you embrace the fact that God is with you, you can flourish in any circumstance.

Lord, remind me today that you are with me no matter what my circumstances look like.

TO READ
Proverbs 20:1-30

The purposes of a man's heart are deep waters,
but a man of understanding draws them out.

PROVERBS 20:5, NIV

Changing Fatherhood

I was incredibly proud of my eldest son the day he graduated from high school, but I still found that I thought of him as a child. All that changed one day when my son showed me he had become a man.

Not long after his graduation, I asked him to speak in our church about what had helped him get through his high school years. I just wanted him to talk truthfully about what the church had meant to him growing up.

I asked my son if he wanted my help in preparing himself to speak. I expected him to gladly accept my offer, but he didn't.

As much as I wanted to challenge him and get him to show me his notes, I knew this was a part of his "rite of passage." I knew that he wanted to show me and the rest of the adults in his life that he was becoming a man.

He did a wonderful job. He told the congregation that three things had prepared him for the challenges of high school: (1) constant exposure to and memorization of the Bible; (2) the church's youth ministry, which challenged him and gave him a place to belong; and (3) the encouragement he received from older adults every week.

At that moment, I knew my son had become an adult. He would still need my help from time to time, but in a different way. I could tell that he was up for the change—but I wondered if I was.

Are you ready for the changes that are sure to come as your sons and daughters become men and women? As the "waters of their heart" deepen, are you prayerfully and carefully drawing them out?

Lord, prepare me to be a good father even after my children become adults. Help me to understand that my role will change even though I will always be "Dad."

TO READ
John 1:43-50

"How do you know about me?" Nathanael asked. And Jesus replied, "I could see you under the fig tree before Philip found you." JOHN 1:48

✳ Jesus Knows All about You!

Nathanael was a thinker. He was astute to the world around him and paid attention to the trends of his day. When Philip told him that Jesus was from Nazareth, his response was "Nazareth! . . . Can anything good come from there?" (John 1:46). He understood the reputation of the inhabitants of Nazareth. At that time, nobody wanted to be known as being from Nazareth. So when Nathanael came to Jesus, he was skeptical. He came to check him out and scrutinize him.

From Nathanael's perspective, no thinking man would just accept that Jesus was the Messiah. So he went to Jesus, not with faith but with a head and heart full of doubt. Then Jesus rocked Nathanael's world. Before they had ever met, Jesus knew all about him. He knew what Nathanael was doing. He knew what he was thinking. He knew where he had been. When Nathanael realized that Jesus knew everything about him, he was stunned.

"How do you know about me?" he asked (v. 48).

It wasn't really a question as much as a declaration of wonder. Nathanael instantly realized that Jesus knew everything about him because he had been an eyewitness to his entire life.

The realization that Jesus knows and sees everything is either frightening or enlightening. If you are frightened, you will attempt to hide from him. But if you are enlightened, you will declare like Nathanael, "You are the Son of God" (v. 49) and follow him every day for the rest of your life.

Jesus, teach me to fear you without being frightened by the fact that you know everything about me. May the realization that you know all about me motivate me to follow you more closely.

TO READ
Isaiah 6:1-7

In the year King Uzziah died, I saw the Lord. He was sitting on a lofty throne, and the train of his robe filled the Temple. ISAIAH 6:1

❀ *The Need to Speak*

Isaiah saw the Lord. What he saw was spectacular! The train of God's robe filled the temple. Angels flew about shouting praises: "Holy, holy, holy is the Lord Almighty! The whole earth is filled with his glory!" they sang over and over (Isaiah 6:3). The glory of the Lord filled the whole sanctuary.

Isaiah's first reaction was to admit his inadequacy. "My destruction is sealed, for I am a sinful man and a member of a sinful race," was his personal summary of his life (v. 5). But in the midst of this wondrous, awesome experience, one of the angels touched his tongue with a burning coal and pronounced him clean and forgiven before God.

Then Isaiah could no longer remain quiet. Once he had seen the glory of God, he had to speak. He had no choice but to speak about God's glory and grace. He had to speak about God's judgment. He had to speak about the blindness of mankind. He had to speak about eternity. He had to speak about his own amazement that God had chosen him.

When the glory of God becomes a reality for you, when God himself pronounces you forgiven, you cannot keep quiet. You have to tell someone your story. You are compelled to describe to others the wonderful works of God so that they will not miss out on the glory.

Lord, keep me quiet about the things that don't matter and keep me talking about your glory.

TO READ
John 11:1-15

Then [Jesus] told them plainly, "Lazarus is dead. And for your sake, I am glad I wasn't there, because this will give you another opportunity to believe in me. Come, let's go see him." JOHN 11:14-15

God's Faith-Building Work

Sometimes it's a good thing you don't get what you ask for when you ask for it. Sometimes it's a good thing when you have to wait.

Lazarus was dead, and the people at the scene knew that had Jesus been there, he could have healed Lazarus and prevented his death. They felt defeated, and they grieved.

But Jesus was grooming his disciples for the task of reaching the world for him after he returned home to his Father. In order to do this, he had to teach them to rely on the power of God within them. Jesus knew that the great commission (Matthew 28:18-20) could not be accomplished through human means, so he needed to build memories for the disciples that would demonstrate the effectiveness of God's power.

That is why Jesus said to them, "For your sake, I am glad I wasn't there, because this will give you another opportunity to believe in me."

As far as the disciples were concerned, there were no options. Lazarus was dead, and it was too late to do anything about it. But that wouldn't do for Jesus. He knew that the power of God gave him options. The disciples did not understand this truth, and Jesus knew that simply telling them was not enough. They would have to see it in action for it to sink in.

So Jesus waited and let his friend die. But when he raised Lazarus from the dead, the power of God was transformed from theory to reality in the disciples' minds.

The same could be true for you today. Some of God's best work in your life requires him to make you wait, sometimes to the point where things appear hopeless. When he works that way on your behalf, you will learn that nothing is hopeless for those who know him.

God, keep anticipation alive within me as I wait on you.

TO READ
2 John 1:1-13

How happy I was to meet some of your children and find them living in the truth, just as we have been commanded by the Father.   2 JOHN 1:4

He's Honored to Be Your Dad!

As he was growing up, Stan heard only harsh demands and criticisms from his father: "You're too slow"; "You aren't smart enough"; and "Why do you have to be so uncoordinated?" Those words stung Stan to his very core, and they never left him. Even as a young adult, he felt unlovable and worthless.

Stan's confidence was shaken, and his sense of what it means to be a man was shrouded in confusion. He had considered finding a mentor, an older man of God, but he didn't know if he could trust anyone enough.

One evening at a church retreat, a group of men were sitting around talking about their dads. Stan told the group that his father had been a big disappointment for him. An older man by the name of George said, "I would be honored to be your dad!" Stan tried to ignore his thoughts and feelings about the offer, but his desire to believe George was almost overwhelming.

With fear in his heart, Stan approached George to talk with him about his offer. He was prepared to insulate himself emotionally if George did not convince him that he had meant what he had said at the retreat. But when George repeated his offer, Stan instantly wanted to trust this man. Despite his fears, he asked George to start meeting with him.

From the time he began meeting with George, Stan could feel confidence and clarity building within him. He began to realize that not all men are like his dad; there are some who would accept him and not criticize him unfairly. But even more importantly, because of George's vote of confidence, Stan believes today that God considers it an honor to be his heavenly Father. Is that what you believe?

God, thank you for using others to show me that you feel honored to be my Dad!

TO READ
1 Thessalonians 4:1-8

God has called us to be holy, not to live impure lives.

1 THESSALONIANS 4:7

✼ *"New" Priorities*

Prior to the events of September 11, 2001, Roger McMillan was living with Ganelle Guzman, the last survivor found among the rubble of the World Trade Center. They loved each other and enjoyed their lives together. But something was missing in their relationship.

Roger and Ganelle had attended the Brooklyn Tabernacle a couple of times. They felt inspired each time they went but weren't ready to commit to the lifestyle a relationship with Christ would require of them.

After the terrorist attacks, Ganelle was trapped in the rubble of the World Trade Center. During her time in captivity, both she and Roger did a lot of soul searching and a lot of praying. Both of them came to the conclusion that they needed God, and they both asked Jesus to come into their lives.

After twenty-six hours, Ganelle was rescued. During her recovery in the hospital, she made some decisions concerning her priorities as a new believer. She told Roger, "If we are going to stay together, things are going to have to change. We have to stop living in sin. And we are going to the Brooklyn Tabernacle every week."

Roger agreed. Without hesitation, he got down on one knee and asked Ganelle to marry him. The sudden realization that he could have lost her made life seem less casual. Roger began to see what was important in life. For Roger, expressing his love for Ganelle and doing it in a noble and godly way became an instant priority.

Life in Christ requires us to live lives that are different from those in the world around us. How does your relationship with Christ affect your priorities and how you live them out?

Lord, help me to set the priorities you would have me set and live them out in the way you would have me live them out.

Since I know it is all for Christ's good, I am quite content with my weaknesses and with insults, hardships, persecutions, and calamities. For when I am weak, then I am strong. 2 CORINTHIANS 12:10

When We Feel Helpless

John was supposed to be at the World Trade Center in New York City for a company meeting on September 11, 2001. The other senior officers were there in person, but John was in San Francisco with the company's president, taking part in the meeting by conference call.

As John and the president listened in on the meeting, the first plane of the terrorist attack crashed into the tower that housed the company's New York office. Almost immediately, city officials began evacuating the building.

John desperately wanted to help, but there was nothing he could do. He wanted to be there to help rescue his coworkers and others, but he was twenty-five hundred miles away. He wanted to help carry the wounded to safety, but he was only connected through the phone line from his own safe office building. The moment he felt most helpless was when he heard his friend's final words on the phone as he plummeted to his death.

On that horrible day, John had to live with his feeling of helplessness. He hated being on the phone when people needed heroes in person. At that moment there was nothing he could do except pray. So pray he did—more fervently than he had ever done before.

In a time of horror and helplessness, John realized that prayer was the most aggressive, most effective thing he could do. Indeed, it was the only thing he could do.

How do you respond when life has you feeling weak and helpless? As men, we want action. We want to do something. But we need to realize, like John, that our most strategic assignment in the battle of life is prayer.

Lord, when I feel weak and ineffective—even helpless—please remind me that prayer is the most aggressive and effective thing I can do.

> **TO READ**
> Psalm 127

Children are a gift from the Lord; they are a reward from him. . . . How happy is the man whose quiver is full of them! PSALM 127:3-5

A Blessed Moment

Twenty-four hours of labor and still no baby. The last six hours were the scariest because of what the doctors called fetal distress. I couldn't help but wonder if the baby was going to be all right. I watched my wife agonize through each contraction. At the same time, I watched my unborn son's heart beat at half its normal rate.

I was already nervous enough about being a dad because I had no previous experience with kids. I was still in school and made no money to speak of. On top of that, I had grown up in a dysfunctional home and didn't know how I was going to raise a family of my own. I knew there was no turning back, but how was I supposed to go forward?

After we were ushered into the operating room for an emergency cesarean section, the first thing I saw was my wife, sedated and lying on her back, her arms strapped down as if she had been tied to a cross. When the doctors pulled my son out, he was very blue from lack of oxygen. It only took a few seconds to get him breathing, but it seemed like hours.

When they placed my son in my arms, something inside me changed. Any hesitation I had about being a father evaporated as my heart melted in love for my boy. It didn't matter anymore what it would cost to raise him. It didn't matter how much of my life I might have to sacrifice. It didn't matter that I still had no idea what it would take to be the head of a healthy family. I was a dad now.

Lord, thank you for blessing me with children. And thank you for giving me the strength to be a dad.

TO READ
Proverbs 12:1-16

Fools think they need no advice, but the wise listen to others. Proverbs 12:15

Get in the Game

"You have got to get in the game!" the pastor exclaimed.

"What do you mean by that?" the man asked in frustration.

"Your wife was designed to be loved in a certain way, and you are trying to make up your own way," his pastor answered. "You cannot just make up your own rules and expect them to work."

The man didn't like hearing his pastor's words, but because he did not want to lose his wife, he listened. He had tried confronting her, pointing out her inconsistencies, and feverishly arguing with her, but none of those things had worked. He knew that his old ways were leading his relationship to disaster. He also had two daughters, and he was afraid he might alienate them too. He knew he had to make some changes.

Get in the game. Those words inspired the man to think differently. He didn't know exactly what to do, so he tried listening to his wife—really listening. Before, he had been in the habit of listening just long enough to correct her. But now he began listening until she got to the end of her thinking. It didn't feel like it would work at first, but he kept listening. It made him feel more passive than before, but he continued to listen. It was hard work holding back his thoughts, but he made up his mind just to listen. Amazingly, his wife began to respond.

The man still can't explain why listening worked, but he will tell you that one of the greatest days of his life was the day his wife said, "At first I stayed because of the kids, but I am actually falling in love with you again. You are definitely back in the game!"

Do you feel the need to "get in the game" when it comes to your marriage and family? Then try listening! You will be amazed at the results.

Dear Lord, show me how to listen well.

Then the man said, "Let me go, for it is dawn." But Jacob panted, "I will not let you go unless you bless me." GENESIS 32:26

Real Blessings

Jacob had had enough of his own manipulative, conniving, and deceptive ways. He had prospered indeed, but he had complicated his life in the process. All of his most important relationships were entangled in hurt and confusion. And now he was about to see his brother—the brother from whom he had stolen the birthright and blessing of their father. He did not know what to expect from his brother, but he knew he could not continue to take advantage of others for his selfish purposes.

Jacob knew he needed to change. He knew he had to find a new way to live. So he would wrestle with God until the Lord changed his heart. He was not looking for a solution for his meeting with Esau; he was looking for change. He wasn't looking for a way to smooth things over in his family; he was looking for change. It wasn't enough just to *feel* different; he needed to *be different. And he would not let go of God until the change had taken place.*

"I will not let you go unless you bless me."

We are all like Jacob in some way. We have schemes we hope God will bless. We have ways of defending ourselves, many of which are unhealthy for us and for the ones we love. We have self-absorbed priorities that dictate our behavior. But we each get opportunities to face these patterns and change our behavior. If we use those opportunities simply as a means to feel better, the negative patterns of behavior just lie dormant until a time in the future when we think they can benefit us. But when we desperately and earnestly seek God and ask for real inner change, the healing begins.

Which would you rather have: temporary relief from your struggles, or the real transformation that comes from seeking God until he blesses you?

Lord, never let me settle for relief from the pain in my life when real inner transformation is what I really need.

TO READ
1 Corinthians 11:1-34

You should follow my example, just as I follow Christ's. 1 CORINTHIANS 11:1

A Real-Life Jesus

I was at a camp with my family, and we were attending a meeting with a public speaker who was giving the evening Bible lesson. My preschool-age son, Brock, had become fidgety, to say the least. He was not going to settle down and sit still, so I took him outside for a walk.

During our exploration of the camp, we sat down for a quick rest on the stairs to the dining hall. As we rested, my son began explaining to me how to have a personal relationship with Christ. He had been watching the *JESUS* film the past couple of months, and he had become familiar with the invitation at the end of the movie. Brock told me that if you recognized you were a sinner and asked Jesus to come into your heart, he would save you.

I was very excited at what I was hearing. This was my first son, and I thought to myself, *This is the big moment! I have been praying he would want to know Jesus, and it is going to happen tonight!*

"Brock, do you want to ask Jesus into your heart?" I eagerly asked.

My son thought about the question for a few moments, then very matter-of-factly said, "No."

I was disappointed and a little bewildered. I wondered why Brock was talking so much about asking Christ into his life if he really didn't want to do it. Then he made a statement that has become the theme of my entire ministry:

"As soon as Jesus gets out of the Bible, I will ask him into my life."

That is the Jesus all of us need to know. He's the real-life Jesus who is more than a character in the pages of the Bible; he's a Jesus who makes a real difference in our lives here and now.

Lord, teach me how to get you off the pages of the Bible and into the flow of my everyday life.

TO READ
Genesis 39:7-23

About this time, Potiphar's wife began to desire [Joseph] and invited him to sleep with her.

GENESIS 39:7

Temptation: A Moment of Choice

Temptation, particularly sexual temptation, is powerful in the life of any man. Sex is one of the greatest gifts God has given us, but inappropriate use of that gift is also one of the greatest struggles we men face, even when we're not "looking for trouble."

Joseph was not looking for trouble; it came to find him. He was busy working when Potiphar's wife aggressively offered herself to him. She was desperate and willing. She had the time, the motivation, the means, and the authority to protect him, so it was conceivable that he could have gotten away with it.

That is the nature of temptation. At first it appears to be harmless and doable. The problem with temptation, however, is that it causes you to choose between two difficult courses of action.

In Joseph's case, if he gave in to temptation, he would live under the tyranny of Potiphar's wife. He would hand her control of his life, and she could demand anything she wanted of him from that time forward. On the other hand, if Joseph refused to give in, she would despise him and make his life miserable.

Once temptation presented itself to Joseph, there was no way he could avoid the struggle between two difficult courses of action. He could either give in and give up control, or he could choose God's will and suffer the rejection of those who did not value a relationship with God.

The same is true for you. Temptation can be an opportunity to give up control, or it can be an opportunity to endorse God's value in your life.

Lord, help me remember that you are far more attractive than any temptation.

February

TO READ
Genesis 41:1-57

"It is beyond my power to do this," Joseph replied. "But God will tell you what it means and will set you at ease." GENESIS 41:16

✳ *God of the Impossible*

Every once in a while, God asks each of us to do the impossible. Part of our development as men is learning to face the impossible, knowing that the power of God, and only the power of God, can accomplish it.

Without conquering the impossible, we are merely guys fumbling through life. But when we conquer that which only God can conquer for us, we ourselves rise to a level worthy of partnership with God.

Others had tried to do what Pharaoh asked Joseph to do—interpret the meaning of his dream—but, as Pharaoh told Joseph, "None of these men can tell me what it means" (Genesis 41:15). Those other men had proven that interpreting the dream was a human impossibility, thus setting the stage for Joseph's finest moment.

Joseph was aware of his inadequacy but was confident in God's power working within him.

Anonymity would have been easier for Joseph at that point, but that was not God's plan for him. As soon as Joseph committed himself to partnering with God, the Lord went into action and made the impossible happen—he gave Joseph the interpretation of Pharaoh's dream.

At some point, God will ask you to do the impossible. It may not be something as dramatic as interpreting a dream, but it will be something equally beyond your abilities. He knows how little you can do on your own and how much he can accomplish through you. He longs for the day when you will step past the barriers that hold you back and step forward with his ability to do the impossible. He applauds when you take your eyes off your own abilities and put your trust in him for what he can do.

Are you ready?

Oh God, prepare me for the day when you do the impossible through me.

TO READ
Genesis 45:1-15

"Come over here," he said. So they came closer. And he said again, "I am Joseph, your brother whom you sold into Egypt." GENESIS 45:4

Aggressive Forgiveness

Every man will encounter times when he needs either to forgive or to be forgiven. The average man's life is marked by events that never should have happened. Often there is no good explanation for why bad things happen, no way to make up for those things, and no way to forget them. In cases like these, forgiveness is the only effective course of action.

Joseph had plenty of reasons to be angry at his brothers. They had sold him into slavery, and he had spent much of his adult life in prison as a result. They had also lied to their father and therefore denied Joseph the privilege of his father's influence.

Now Joseph had the opportunity to treat his brothers however he chose. He had the resources to bless them extravagantly or punish them severely. He had complete authority to direct the outcome of their lives. He could terrorize them, or he could embrace them.

God had been in the process of redeeming the self-centered acts of Joseph's brothers for the better part of two decades. He was using them as part of his plan to save an entire family and an entire nation.

It all came down to this moment. Had Joseph chosen to give in to bitterness, the plan would have failed, his family would have remained alienated, and his entire nation would have suffered. But because Joseph chose to forgive his brothers and be reunited with them, God blessed Joseph, his family, and his nation.

We need to remember that forgiveness always sets us free—free to respond to others in love, free to enjoy closeness with God, and free to receive his blessing.

Lord, teach me to aggressively forgive others, no matter how "justified" I may be in my anger.

TO READ
Genesis 37:1-20

One night Joseph had a dream and promptly reported the details to his brothers, causing them to hate him even more.   GENESIS 37:5

❋ The Certainty of God's Promises

God communicated clearly his blueprint for Joseph's life. Speaking to him through dreams, God delivered the plan with such clarity that Joseph felt compelled to tell his brothers and father about it.

Joseph's dreams and his decision to tell his family about them marked the beginning of the hardest journey of his life. The message of the dreams was very clear, but it wasn't what his family wanted to hear. God had shown Joseph special favor, and his brothers, who hated Joseph anyway, did not like it. They betrayed him, sold him into slavery, deprived him of numerous well-deserved rewards.

The dreams clearly showed Joseph that he would rule over his family—in that culture, a privilege reserved for the oldest son.

But since the dreams were from God, there was no way that circumstances could stop them from becoming reality. The world said that Joseph was underprivileged—his family was made up of shepherds, not kings. The world treated him like a victim, not a ruler. Joseph's life circumstances turned from bad to worse, but the dream was still clear.

The message of Joseph's dreams was clear because it had come directly from God. The circumstances of his life, on the other hand, had come from the world. God's plan would ultimately win out over the circumstances.

While the circumstances of your life may not always seem to line up with God's plan, nothing on earth can compete with a God-given promise.

The path to making your dream a reality may be dark and strenuous, but you can rest assured knowing that God has a plan for you and that he always keeps his promises.

God, give me the will to trust you.

TO READ
Genesis 40:1-23

Pharaoh's cup-bearer, however, promptly forgot all about Joseph, never giving him another thought.

GENESIS 40:23

When You Feel Forgotten

Joseph was the secret of the royal cup-bearer's success. The cup-bearer had offended Pharaoh, who sent him to prison—the same prison where Joseph was incarcerated. While there, the cup-bearer had a dream, which Joseph interpreted for him: The dream meant the cup-bearer would be restored to his former position. That dream came true.

Without Joseph, the cup-bearer probably would have remained confined to prison, lost in self-pity. But because of Joseph's insight, his hope was restored. When he received another opportunity to serve the Pharaoh, his countenance was cheerful and his performance superb. Without Joseph's prophecy, he probably would have remained hopeless.

But the cup-bearer forgot about Joseph. He didn't just overlook Joseph or forget to reward or recognize him; he completely forgot about him. Not one thought of Joseph ever crossed his mind again.

Joseph deserved to be remembered. But the cup-bearer forgot him, and it would be a couple of years before opportunity would come Joseph's way.

Bitterness or betterment—those were Joseph's choices. He could dwell on the forgetfulness of the cup-bearer and foster bitterness, or he could continue building the character that had seen him through to this point.

When was the last time you were forgotten? Did you fail to get the credit you believed you deserved? Did someone else get the rewards you worked hard to earn? Your reaction to such a slight makes all the difference. If you take matters into your own hands, God may leave you to reap your own rewards. But put your future in God's hands, and he will give you his reward in his time.

Lord, help me not to focus on the times I have been forgotten or slighted, and give me the courage to wait for your reward.

TO READ
Genesis 37:21-36

So when the traders came by, his brothers pulled Joseph out of the pit and sold him for twenty pieces of silver, and the Ishmaelite traders took him along to Egypt. GENESIS 37:28

✽ *What Would You Do If . . .*

Talk about dysfunctional families! Joseph's plight was unfair, undesirable, and unthinkable. His own brothers—the people who were supposed to love him and look out for him—sold him to foreign slave traders.

Where was God in all of this? What was Joseph supposed to think?

It was one of those moments in life that nobody wants but that so many need. The kind of moment that shows us where we really are with God. The kind of moment that truly defines us.

After Joseph was sold into slavery, he rode with the Ishmaelites to Egypt. He later served Potiphar with integrity but in obscurity. We don't know how long he lived in this oblivion, waiting for God to do something. We just know how Joseph responded.

In the midst of his own crisis, Joseph concluded that God was in control and that he would somehow work things out. He couldn't tell when, and he certainly couldn't say how, but Joseph refused to define God based on his life circumstances. Rather, in the midst of tragedy, he chose to believe that God had a purpose for his life.

Life crises don't just build our character, they confirm it. When trials and tragedies come at us, our understanding of God is put on display for all to see.

How do you respond when your life circumstances aren't what you think they should be? Do you become angry at the world and angry at God? Or do you rest in the simple and wonderful fact that no matter what you are going through and no matter who or what caused it, God is in total control?

Lord, help me to always believe your promises, especially when circumstances are not what I had expected or hoped for.

TO READ
Genesis 41:25-36

[Joseph said,] "My suggestion is that you find the wisest man in Egypt and put him in charge of a nationwide program." GENESIS 41:33

When You Are the Answer

What do you do when you are the answer to your own advice? Joseph was the only one who could interpret Pharaoh's dream. He knew what Pharaoh needed to do to ensure that his nation would survive the coming famine, and he clearly laid out the plan of success for the entire land of Egypt.

Pharaoh was looking for answers, and Joseph had them. The challenge for Joseph was that *he* was the answer. The people of Egypt needed a man with the kind of discernment Joseph had, the kind of wisdom he had, and the kind of clarity he had. In short, they needed Joseph.

God had invested thirty years preparing Joseph for this moment, so Joseph was ready when the time came for him to provide clear, wise answers.

Accepting the challenge of being the answer means a lot of work, sometimes hard work. It means others will look to you for wise decisions. It means those around you will expect you to understand a situation or problem better than they do. It means an increase in your influence but a decrease in the amount of sleep you get. And sometimes it means the growth of your legacy and a rise in the stress in your life.

How do you respond when you are the answer to the challenge in front of you? Do you shrink away in fear, or do you step up and accept the task for which God has called you?

At some point in your life, God will call you to be the answer. The question you need to ask yourself now is, "What am I doing today to make sure I'm ready?"

God, give me wisdom to know when I am the answer and the strength and humility to be the kind of answer you want me to be.

TO READ
Joshua 4:10-13

About forty thousand armed for battle crossed over before the Lord to the plains of Jericho for war.

JOSHUA 4:13, NIV

Made for a Purpose

God made you for a special purpose. He gave you a unique collection of talents and desires. He made you the way you are so you can fulfill your purpose as he has defined it.

Joshua ordered the men of Israel to conquer the land of Canaan while their wives and children remained behind to settle their families.

No doubt the men fighting under Joshua's command wondered what their leader had in mind for them. Here they were, dedicated family men, being taken away from their wives and children to answer another calling.

Some of us are faced with those same kinds of questions today.

When the United States Marine Corps called Carl to leave immediately to serve in Operation Desert Storm, he wondered what God had in mind for him. He was a good and dedicated marine, but he also had a very effective ministry in his local church.

Rather than seeing his situation as a choice between serving his country and serving God, Carl decided on the way to Kuwait City that he would lead a daily Bible study for anyone in his platoon who wanted to attend.

God blessed Carl's efforts. In the face of danger and potential tragedy, everyone in Carl's platoon attended his Bible study every day.

Carl had been called to defend his country, but he continued to carry out the purpose God had called him to fulfill by providing comfort to a group of young men and helping them come to grips with their need for God.

No matter where life places us—whether we work as soldiers, accountants, pastors, or anything else—we need to ask ourselves daily what we are doing to carry out the purpose God made us to fulfill.

Lord, give me the insight to live out your plan for my life, no matter where circumstances place me.

TO READ
Hebrews 10:19-25

Think of ways to encourage one another to outbursts of love and good deeds. HEBREWS 10:24

❋ *Time for a Change?*

All Ken could do was blame Ann for their marital problems. Indeed, she had been difficult to live with and had grown distant over the past few years. But Ken made the situation worse with his constant correcting and demanding that she be more responsive to his needs. They constantly accused one another, and they even began talking to their children about who would live with whom after the divorce.

In the midst of this turbulent time, Ken went golfing with his best friend, Dave. Throughout the first two holes, Ken complained about Ann.

By the third hole, Dave had heard enough. He grabbed Ken by the arm, kneeled at the bench by the tee, and prayed: "Lord, we claim this marriage for you. Humble Ken and show him that he is as much the problem as Ann. Open Ann's heart to see the value of this relationship. Do whatever you need to do to help them take back their marriage."

When he had finished praying, Dave turned to Ken and said, "Okay, now you pray." Then he bowed his head and waited.

Ken struggled to get out even a few words, but he prayed: "Lord, I guess Dave's right. Help us."

Ken was amazed that Dave would do something like that for him and his family. It made a difference too. Ken left the golf course with a different perspective. His heart had been turned around, and he was ready to do whatever it would take to heal his marriage.

When we humble ourselves, seek God, and ask him to change our hearts, he is willing to do wonders in our lives. Are you willing?

God, help me to humble myself so that you can do amazing things in and around my life.

TO READ
1 Corinthians 9:19-23

I do all this to spread the Good News, and in doing so I enjoy its blessings.   1 CORINTHIANS 9:23

Keeping Your Message Clear

Billy Graham is one of the most remarkable men ever to represent the cause of Christ. He will long be remembered as a great evangelist who introduced innumerable people to our Savior, Jesus Christ.

We may be tempted to think of Dr. Graham as a man who stands out among his peers because of his immense talent. But it is not talent that sets him apart. Rather, it is his commitment to keeping his message clear, even in the ordinary things.

Two stories that illustrate this truth about Billy Graham stand out to me. Once a clothier offered to provide at no cost the finest suits available for Dr. Graham to wear as he preached. But when people began accusing Billy Graham of spending donated money on expensive clothes, he went to his clothier and humbly told him he could no longer accept the free suits because it was causing people to miss the real message.

On another occasion, Billy Graham stepped off a plane and was greeted with an innocent hug by a woman who supported his ministry. The press got a picture of the event, and some of Dr. Graham's critics used it to question the evangelist's motives with women. Immediately, Dr. Graham adopted the policy that he would no longer hug any woman except his wife and daughters.

Some people might look at these stories and say that Billy Graham over-reacted to two seemingly harmless situations. But no one can say he hasn't been careful to do everything he could to keep his message clear.

Are you doing all you can to make sure your message about Christ is clear? What do you need to do—or stop doing—so that no one misses your message?

Lord, show me what I should do to make sure the message of my life is clear.

TO READ
Joshua 1:5-11

I will not fail you or abandon you. JOSHUA 1:5

A Promise We Can Count On

At first glance, today's verse seems to be a promise of shelter from danger. It sounds like the words of a father offering his young child comfort. But in reality, it is the battle cry of a God who wants to do great exploits in the life of a man named Joshua.

Joshua was preparing for his finest hour. He was about to miraculously cross the Jordan River, victoriously face the most barbaric people of the earth, and walk the nation of Israel through the complicated task of settling in a new land. The promise that "I will never fail you or abandon you" is God's commitment to go with Joshua on the journey ahead of him.

There was no escape or back door for Joshua to go through, only the seemingly insurmountable challenge ahead for him to face down. History was counting on it, and God's plan included a guarantee of his success. That guarantee was the very presence of God himself.

This is what a man's life is about. It's about recognizing the challenges God places before you and meeting those challenges head-on, knowing that he is with you. Without challenges, a man's life is just a list of chores; but with challenges, life is a humble pursuit of doing what is beyond our own ability, only because God is with you.

What seemingly insurmountable challenge is God calling you to face today? Whatever that challenge is, your only guarantee of success is God himself and his promise: "I will never fail you or abandon you."

Lord, constantly remind me that your presence guarantees that I can accomplish your will.

TO READ
Hebrews 3:7-13

Be careful then, dear brothers and sisters. Make sure that your own hearts are not evil and unbelieving, turning you away from the living God.

HEBREWS 3:12

The Danger of Distraction

Distractions can undermine the success of a leader. Take Moses for instance. He could have led the people into the Promised Land, but his anger was a costly distraction that led to sin (see Numbers 20:1-12).

Tragically, distractions can do the same thing to today's leaders. Stuart was a sad example of the dangers of distraction.

Stuart had an unusual talent for relating to teenagers. He was energetic and outgoing. He could laugh with teens one moment and challenge them to take their faith in Jesus seriously the next. Young men and women flocked around Stuart and hung on his every word. He conversed with them effortlessly, and his up-front presentations were engaging. Everyone who knew Stuart understood that he was unusually gifted when it came to influencing the next generation.

But Stuart got distracted. His passion for people was replaced by an interest in pornography. Soon that sinful distraction developed into a sexual relationship with a young lady who worked with him on his church's volunteer youth staff.

Stuart would have been one of the most influential young men of his generation if he hadn't gotten distracted. Sadly, the distraction that overtook Stuart turned his life into a story of what might have been.

Do you want to be certain that you will never have to look back on "what might have been" when it comes to God's calling on your life? You can avoid distractions by remaining focused on Jesus.

Lord, make my love for you and your calling stronger than the distractions that I face.

TO READ
2 Timothy 4:5-8

I have fought the good fight, I have finished the race, and I have remained faithful. 2 TIMOTHY 4:7

Believing and Finishing Strong.

With one minute left in the game, the players on my son's high school football team were stunned. They had just come back from a seven-point deficit by scoring a touchdown and a two-point conversion. They had a one-point lead—until the opposing team scored a touchdown. My son's teammates blocked the extra point, but they still trailed by five points. Murmuring could be heard throughout the stands and the sidelines.

My son, Brock, the team's quarterback, rallied his teammates. "Hey, guys," he shouted, "this is when it gets fun. This is what we play for."

After my son's team returned the kickoff to the twenty-five-yard line, the offense came in and quickly began moving the ball downfield. Play after play moved them closer to their goal, and with five seconds left in the game, they were at the opposing team's twenty-yard line. Brock went back to pass, spotted an open receiver in the end zone, and threw the ball. The pass landed in the receiver's hands, and for a moment we could taste the sweetest victory of Brock's high school football career. But just as suddenly, the receiver dropped the ball, and the game was over.

I have relived that play many times because it illustrates the two greatest lessons I have learned in my life as a Christian. First, you really can do anything you believe God has called you to do. And second, if you want to do it, you have to finish well.

You see, my son's football team moved the ball downfield during the final minute of that memorable game because they believed they could. But in the end, they couldn't finish what they had started.

In the Christian life, just as in football, how you start is important. But even more important is how you finish.

God, grant me the perseverance to finish well.

Boldly and without hindrance [Paul] preached the kingdom of God and taught about the Lord Jesus Christ. ACTS 28:31, NIV

Movin' Out

Frank set out on his motorcycle with about four hundred other men and women on bikes for a one-week journey to "ground zero" in New York City to commemorate the events of September 11, 2001.

Frank is a member of the Christian Motorcycle Association (CMA), and although the CMA didn't sponsor the event, Frank knew God wanted him to go wearing his CMA colors. He decided to watch and see how God moved. When God moved, Frank was ready to follow.

Each night of the trip the group of bikers stopped in a different town, where they participated in memorials to the events of 9/11. One night Frank was asked if he would publicly address the group and honor the heroes who had emerged from the disaster. Frank agreed to speak, and through his efforts, he gained the trust of many of the riders.

On the fourth day of the trip, one of the riders had a heart attack and was rushed to a local hospital. The group immediately turned to Frank and asked him what they should do. He contacted the victim's family, made arrangements to care for his motorcycle and personal effects, and then made his way to the hospital. As Frank sat in the man's room, he had the opportunity to tell him and his family how God had worked in his life and how they too could have a personal relationship with God through Jesus Christ.

This story is a beautiful example of what can happen when one man boldly steps out in obedience and lifts up the name of Jesus. And it's a reminder that when you see God moving, it's time to move out and follow him.

God, orchestrate my day, and grant me the courage to move out and follow you where you lead.

TO READ
Joshua 1:10-18

Go through the camp and tell the people to get their provisions ready. In three days you will cross the Jordan River and take possession of the land the Lord your God has given you. JOSHUA 1:11

Getting Ready

The people in Joshua's generation were about to enjoy one of the greatest moments of their lives. In just three days, they would see the Jordan River part so that they could cross over it on dry land. It would be a miracle they would never forget. They could not make the miracle happen on their own, but if they did not prepare themselves, they would miss it altogether.

Preparation was essential for the Israelites to see a miracle, and it's true for us today too.

I regularly do premarital counseling as part of my ministry. The goal of this kind of counseling is to equip couples as they prepare for marriage. I know that the real secret to a great marriage is the presence of God in the relationship, and I also know there are certain skills couples can practice to give God free access to their lives. One of those "skills" is regular prayer.

A recent survey by Harvard University discovered that although the divorce rate in America is around 50 percent, the divorce rate among those who pray together on a daily basis is less than one percent. This is evidence that when couples pray, God adds his strength to the relationship, and it tells us that God gives real power only to those who pray.

In marriage, prayer is one way of "getting your provisions ready." In business, getting an education and mastering the skills your career requires is another. Our personal discipline when it comes to getting our provisions ready gives God the opportunity to create moral excellence and prepare us for success.

Most of life is preparation. And when we master preparation, we give the Master free reign in our lives.

Lord, show me what I need to do today to prepare for the work you call me to do.

TO READ
Joshua 1:12-15

Occupy your own land. JOSHUA 1:15, NIV

❀ *A Land to Occupy*

When did you first realize that God had a plan uniquely and specifically designed for you? God showed the nation of Israel a specific plan. He had given the people land to occupy. Each tribe had its own specific borders, each family its own specific portion.

The apostle Paul pointed out that each believer in Christ is called to "occupy your own land," or to honor God in a specific way, when he wrote, "We are God's masterpiece. He has created us anew in Christ Jesus, so that we can do the good things he planned for us long ago" (Ephesians 2:10).

A man named Buster was one of the greatest influences in my life, but he probably doesn't realize how much he did to show me the importance of "occupying your own land." I dated Buster's daughter for a period of time. I enjoyed spending time with her, and I especially enjoyed the friendship with her father that dating her allowed me to have.

Buster talked with me about his relationship with God and my relationship with his daughter. He shared with me the joys and struggles of his life. I watched him on his journey as his wife succumbed to cancer. I saw him grieve and ask hard questions. I then watched him recover and rediscover love in his life.

Through each of these points along Buster's journey, I saw a man of action, a man who understood what God wanted from him. His example encouraged the maturing of my faith.

Buster taught me something that is important for all believers to understand: Never underestimate the value of your influence, for it is your land to occupy.

Lord, give me strength to occupy the land you have for me and to live my life with excellence.

TO READ
Joshua 1:12-18

Stay with them. JOSHUA 1:14

Working Together

Two and a half of the tribes of Israel could take possession of their land without fighting. God had given the Reubenites, the Gadites, and the half-tribe of Manasseh the land east of the Jordan, where the Israelites were already camped. It would have been easy for those Israelites to stay behind and take care of their own homesteads, but their work was not done. Although they had their land, God called them to go with the other tribes who hadn't taken possession of their land, help them conquer it, and stay with them until the job was finished.

This biblical story is an illustration of something very important to God: he wants people who are committed to helping and cooperating with one another to accomplish what he has called them to do.

I remember well the day this really hit home for me. I was standing in our new church building while it was still under construction, when a mother and her two young daughters arrived to take a look at the progress. As I talked with the three of them, one of the young ladies asked me, "How many people will it take to clean up all this dirt on the floor?"

It occurred to me that it was going to take all of us doing our part to get the work done. In order to build a church that could reach our entire community, we were all going to have to give of our time, talents, and treasure as we worked together to see the project through to its completion. The lesson from that little girl's question has stuck with me ever since.

How many people do you think it will take to win our world for Christ? More importantly, in what ways can we as God's chosen people work together to accomplish that task?

Lord, give me strength and courage to help my brothers in Christ who are attempting to do the things you have called them to do.

TO READ
Joshua 2:1-5

The two men set out and came to the house of a prostitute named Rahab and stayed there that night.

JOSHUA 2:1

❋ *Simple Boundaries*

The old saying "There is strength in numbers" is a timeless truth, and it is well represented in the Bible.

The task of the spies Joshua sent out was strategic but risky when they stayed at the home of Rahab, a known prostitute. Their success was partially dependent on the repentant heart of the prostitute, but it was even more dependent on their accountability to one another. If one of the spies went into Rahab's house, his reputation would be, at the very least, questioned. So they both went.

Much of the really significant work we do on earth today is also risky, simply because we live in a world full of sin and temptation. For that reason, we need to be careful to set solid boundaries. I learned that when a woman in our church asked me to counsel her. This woman looked like she could be my wife's sister, so I wanted to send her to someone else for counseling. However, no one else was available.

I wanted to help this woman, but I wanted to do it safely. I told her, "If you can find three friends who will come with you to every meeting and hold you accountable to your homework, I will meet with you."

I assumed I would not hear back from her, but three weeks later she called and said, "I have my three friends. When can we get started?"

As I counseled her, she got better faster than anyone I had previously counseled.

This story demonstrates two important facts about boundaries: First, they keep us safe from even the appearance of impropriety. Second, they can produce huge results.

Lord, help me set the kind of boundaries that enable me to safely and effectively live out your calling on my life.

"Who told you that you were naked?" the Lord God asked. "Have you eaten the fruit I commanded you not to eat?" GENESIS 3:11

The Sad Results of Rebellion

One of the hardest facts of life to accept is that rebellion always leads to death. In some way and to some degree, our every act of rebellion produces death: the death of our emotions, the death of our decision-making ability, the death of our relationships, and sometimes physical death.

Adam and Eve didn't realize they were changing the entire course of human history when they ate the forbidden fruit. Randy didn't know he was ruining his life when he first tried drugs. Bill didn't know that his first beer at seventeen years of age would result in a lifelong struggle with alcoholism.

Steve didn't realize that giving in to one temptation would result in the death of his family relationships. Steve was frustrated with the way his wife made decisions and felt he couldn't really communicate with her. When he met a woman named Joan, he thought he had found the deepest friendship of his life. He didn't think his relationship with her would progress any further than a friendship, but when the opportunity came for him to be more than friends with her, he didn't resist.

Steve didn't think about the hurt his rebellion would cause his family. And he didn't hear his youngest daughter's request during a Sunday school prayer time: "Please pray for me. Another family stole my daddy."

Rebellion will always hurt. It hurts the man who rebels, and it hurts those who are close to him. Worst of all, it hurts his relationship with God.

When you are tempted to rebel—and you will be tempted—ask yourself if giving in to that temptation is worth bringing death on yourself and on your loved ones. Then ask yourself if it's worth doing the same to your relationship with God.

Lord, keep me from any hint of rebellion, for rebellion always brings death to me and to those I care about.

TO READ
Joshua 2:1, 22-24

"Spy out the land on the other side of the Jordan River, especially around Jericho." JOSHUA 2:1

The Look of Success

What do you think success looks like? A big bank account? A nice house and car? A thriving ministry?

Joshua sent two spies to check out the Promised Land. God had promised to give the land to Israel. But what did the spies find in Jericho? A city full of hostile people who wanted to take them by force.

I think I know a little something about how those spies must have felt.

When I arrived at the church where I now serve as senior pastor, it was a small congregation of good-hearted but wounded people. But it was not easy. About two months after we arrived, we were standing in the worship center just fifteen minutes after the end of the service. As we looked around, we realized that we were all alone. Everybody had left.

I turned around in the eerie silence, looked at my wife, and asked, "What have we done?" I had come from leading a youth ministry of 250 students who loved to be together and who had a dynamic impact on their campuses. Now I had arrived at a church afraid of influence and suspicious of newcomers.

This looked to me like anything but success.

But God had called us there, so we stayed. We continued pushing forward, doing the things we knew God wanted us to do within the congregation. Our perseverance and commitment paid off. Years later, it is the largest evangelical church in our city.

What's your "Jericho"? Maybe your situation doesn't look like a success right now, but if you are where God has put you, be patient and keep working. God is about to do something good for you.

Lord, help me to stay on your path of success for my life, regardless of how it looks right now.

TO READ
Psalm 27:1-14

Wait patiently for the Lord. Be brave and courageous. Yes, wait patiently for the Lord.

PSALM 27:14

Wait!

Waiting is definitely the hardest command God ever gave to men on the go. We love to be productive. But we agonize over waiting.

Before David could take his place as the king, he had to wait for Saul's reign to end. Before the apostles could experience the power of God in their lives, they had to wait for Pentecost. Even Jesus waited until he was thirty years old to begin his public ministry.

I know from experience how frustrating it must have been for some of those people to have to wait.

When I was twenty-one years old, I asked God to put me in full-time ministry, but he said, "Wait. Finish college."

When I was twenty-four years old, I asked God to put me in full-time ministry, but he said, "Wait. Go to seminary."

When I was twenty-eight years old, God asked me to leave youth ministry and begin pastoring a church. My first reaction was, "Wait. I am not old enough." But God said, "Go!"

When I was thirty years old, I asked God to make my church bigger, but he said, "Wait. I want you to build deeper rather than bigger."

When I was thirty-five years old, I asked God to make me wiser. He said, "Now you are starting to catch on." Since then, the church I pastor has been growing steadily—in numbers and in depth.

As men, it is in our nature to want to go and do—right now! Today, however, the most important thing God may ask you to do is wait. Are you willing to do that?

God, give me enthusiasm for whatever you have planned for me today, even if it is just waiting.

<table>
<tr><td>

TO READ
Ephesians 3:14-21

</td><td>

Now to him who is able to do immeasurably more than all we ask or imagine, according to his power that is at work within us, to him be glory.

EPHESIANS 3:20-21, NIV

</td></tr>
</table>

Beyond Imagination

Every once in a while, God does something to show you that your life is bigger than you. We are all capable of accomplishing so much in life, but we could use reminders of our need for God and his surpassing resources for doing things we can only dream about.

I saw an example of this when a friend of mine, Brent, went to serve his country in Operation Desert Storm. He was not a pilot dropping smart bombs from a safe distance. He was a foot soldier, marching on the sand into Kuwait City.

One morning Brent was in a bunker with his buddies when they heard the ominous sound of tank treads. Three Iraqi tanks were moving into position around their bunker with their turret guns pointed directly at them. Brent and his comrades were sure they were going to die. Each of them quickly reviewed their lives and asked hard questions about whether they had finished the course they were made to run. They prayed fervently and pleaded with God for mercy.

So Brent and the men with him were utterly surprised when the hatch of each tank opened up and the Iraqi soldiers piled out with their arms held high above their heads. They were desperately tired and hungry. All they wanted was to surrender so they could eat and get some rest.

In a sudden turn of events, disaster was transformed into triumph. God had provided a victory that could not be orchestrated, manipulated, or invented in human terms. He had done what no one had even thought to ask for.

What is going on in your life today that needs God's intervention?

Lord, when things look bleak in my life, teach me to expect blessings from you beyond what I can even imagine.

TO READ
1 John 5:1-5

This is love for God: to obey his commands. And his commands are not burdensome.   1 JOHN 5:3, NIV

✳ *Flexible Obedience*

One recent weekend, I was watching my oldest son playing quarterback for his college football team when I gained a whole new perspective on what it means to be obedient.

As Brock ran his team's offense, he did what his coach commanded him to do. The coach called the plays, and Brock ran them.

Brock's obedience, however, was not robotic or blind. The kind of obedience Brock had to demonstrate required every ounce of strength he could muster and every bit of talent he possessed. He could not just blindly follow the plays the coaches had drawn up that week; he had to constantly adjust to the struggle around him. He had to follow the script the coach had laid out for him, but he had to do it in the environment in which he was competing.

Sitting in the stands at that football game, it hit me that this is what everyday obedience to God looks like. In the Bible, God has given us clear directions for living. Obedience to those directions requires every bit of talent and energy we can muster, but often it also requires us to have the wisdom to know how to adjust to the environment in which we obey. In short, obedience to God sometimes means flexibility on our part.

God never called us to be like mindless robots; he just called us to obey. And just as my son's ability to adapt and adjust helped him to be a success on the football field, so our ability to adapt and adjust helps us to be successful in our walk of obedience to God.

Lord, show me how to be flexible and adaptable when it comes to obediently applying the truth of your Word in every situation I face.

TO READ
2 Thessalonians 3:6-13

I say to the rest of you, dear brothers and sisters, never get tired of doing good.

2 THESSALONIANS 3:13

✤ Don't Give Up

Our church was one month away from moving into a brand-new building. The financing was in place, we were completing the finishing stages of construction, and we were planning the celebration. Then we got word that the lender was changing the financing plan, which meant we had to come up with $100,000 in one month. Everyone had already sacrificed so much to get into this building. We had all given diligently and prayed diligently, and we had been so close to our goal. The news left us stunned.

We gathered together for a week of prayer meetings to seek God's answer to this unexpected obstacle. It was on the third night of praying that Frank, a hardworking man faithful in his walk with Christ, came and asked if some men could help him bring something in from his car. Two men followed him out, and they came back with a huge bottle filled with coins. Then Frank told his story.

As a reward to himself, Frank collects his pocket change in a five-gallon water bottle throughout the year. When it comes time for vacation, he uses the change as his play money. He generally ends up with several hundred dollars in change each year. In the course of praying for guidance in our church's current crisis, Frank came to the conclusion that God wanted him to give his "pocket change" to the building fund.

Frank's selflessness launched a wave of hope and determination in the church that was nothing short of remarkable. Everybody began praying for God to use them too. Almost everybody found a new way to give. Within a month, the church raised the $100,000. The pocket change of one diligent man changed our church. In what ways are you diligent?

Lord, work in my heart so that I never get tired of doing what is right.

TO READ
Philippians 2:3-13

It is God who works in you to will and to act according to his good purpose.

PHILIPPIANS 2:13, NIV

Called to Lead

Jake had a promising future. I could see his potential, but I could also see a hesitancy that didn't match his ability. I made a commitment to help him develop his skills.

At first Jake's goals seemed small and unimaginative. I asked him to take some time to set some new goals. The next time we met, Jake's goals were different but still shortsighted.

I asked him, "Why do you have such small goals? You are a talented, natural leader. Don't you want to influence other people?"

Jake lowered his head and said, "No, I really don't."

"Why?" I exclaimed.

"Because I am afraid they might actually want to follow me."

Then Jake humbly told me his fears. "My dad was a leader in our church. He taught Sunday school. He led more people to Christ than anyone I know. Then he had an affair and divorced my mom and left a huge number of people disillusioned. I'm capable of doing the same thing."

Over the next few months, Jake focused on this struggle. He believed that his dad's influence was greater than the influence of Jesus. Jake had to decide which of those influences would dominate his life.

Jake finally chose to believe that God's work in his life could overcome his heritage. A young man recently told me, "I am so glad I met Jake. Spending time with him has changed my life and helped me discover God's purpose for me." What do you believe about God's ability to work in your life?

Lord, help me trust you as I lead others.

TO READ
Acts 7:2-8

God told him, "Leave your native land and your relatives, and come to the land that I will show you."

ACTS 7:3

A Different Path

A few friends, two of my sons, and I traveled to Baja, California, to a place called the Bay of Los Angeles. It is one of those places you never get to by accident. After an eight-hour drive from the border of California on paved roads, we had to drive another three hours on a dirt road.

We were hot and tired when we first got to the bay, so we piled out of our vehicles and headed for the water. As we approached the shoreline, we saw what appeared to be a red line bordering the edge of the water. Thousands of baby crabs had crawled to the edge of the water and were apparently resting. They parted to allow us to pass, and then they quickly filled in behind us. Living in San Diego, I had seen many of these red crabs at the beach, but I had never witnessed anything resembling this type of behavior.

The next day we went out in a sixteen-foot boat to try our hand at catching some fish. As soon as we anchored and put our lines in the water, we were astonished to see a whale bigger than our boat surface within fifty yards of our position. We were all a little nervous because we instantly recognized that the whale could easily overwhelm our boat. My oldest son was afraid the whale would take his bait, so he reeled it in just as fast as his ten-year-old arms would allow him. As he was frantically reeling, he cried out, "I don't want the whale to get my bait!"

Our time at the Bay of Los Angeles was a memorable time full of relaxation, fun, and laughter. And it was full of the wonders of God's creation, wonders none of us had ever before seen.

On what memorable paths has God taken you? Are you open to his leading?

God, open my eyes to the new paths you have for me.

TO READ
Hebrews 11:6-10

So, you see, it is impossible to please God without faith. Anyone who wants to come to him must believe that there is a God and that he rewards those who sincerely seek him. HEBREWS 11:6

The Healthy Kind of Fear

Steve and I were talking about the building program our church had undertaken. Our conversation had a nervous tone to it because the project was bigger than anything the church had ever done. I was the pastor, so I had a lot at stake in this. Steve and his family had been attending the church for seven years and were deeply involved in it, so he had much at stake as well.

On paper, Steve and I knew we couldn't afford the project. On paper, it would require everyone in the church to buy into the program at a level deeper than ever before. On paper, we were planning to triple the size of the church. But in my heart, I knew God was leading us in this direction.

Steve looked me in the eye and asked me, "Aren't you scared of doing this?"

The best answer I could offer him was, "Yes, I am scared. But the only thing that scares me more is not doing it."

We men often live with just this kind of fear. When we have an intimidating challenge ahead of us, if we think about it enough, we can muster up enough fear to walk away from it. But we know we can't back off. We know it's something we must do. And sometimes the only thing that keeps us moving forward is the conviction that not doing it is more frightening than doing it.

Is there something God wants you to do that scares you—enough that you are considering backing away and not doing it? If so, fix your mind on the fact that God has promised to be with you in everything he calls you to do. Then watch your fear melt away.

Lord, make my fear of not doing your will stronger than my fear of doing it.

TO READ
Joshua 2:8-12

[Rahab said,] "Now swear to me by the Lord that you will be kind to me and my family since I have helped you." JOSHUA 2:12

God's Ambassador

Rahab the prostitute recognized that the two spies of Israel were powerful and influential men. She had heard about how God had worked in their lives, and because of that, she acknowledged the awesomeness of their God. She had come to realize that her only chance of survival in a time of war was through the mercy of their God and the kindness of their nation.

To Rahab, these two men were more than spies; they were ambassadors for the one true God. For that reason, she begged them to show her and her family kindness.

We are to the people around us what those spies were to Rahab: ambassadors of the almighty God who can show them kindness, who can say and do things to let them know he cares about them too.

I have been coaching youth basketball for nine years and have found it to be my most effective tool for showing my community the kindness of God and for establishing myself as his ambassador in my neighborhood. Many of our neighbors have begun attending our church because of the relationships my coaching has helped build between them and my family. Many of these families have asked me to perform either weddings or funerals for their loved ones, and one of my close friends in our neighborhood even allowed me to help him come to grips with his long-term addiction and his eternal need for Jesus Christ.

You may not be an international spy or even a youth basketball coach. But wherever God has put you, you are Christ's ambassador to the world around you. Remember: your friends, neighbors, coworkers, and others need what you have!

God, establish me as your ambassador to those within my sphere of influence.

TO READ
Joshua 2:13-21

If they go out into the street, they will be killed, and we cannot be held to our oath. But we swear that no one inside this house will be killed—not a hand will be laid on any of them. JOSHUA 2:19

❈ The Importance of Obedience

Sometimes obedience can mean the difference between life and death.

The spies had given Rahab simple instructions: She and her family were to stay in the house. If they obeyed, they would be spared. If, however, they ventured outside, they would be slaughtered along with the rest of the city of Jericho. It was their obedience that would save their lives.

As a teenager, I saw an example of this from up close. As I was learning to drive, I was told, "When you start out at a green light, always look to the left and right before you take your foot off the brake." When I first heard these instructions, I thought they were silly, but I got in the habit of looking left and right simply because I was taught to do so.

One night a few years later, I was driving home from a youth function. I stopped at a red light and waited. When the light turned green, those words came back to me: "Look left and right." The impression was strong enough that I did so, even though I felt foolish. Just as I turned my head left, a police car—with no lights on—came ripping through the intersection, fast enough to catch air and send out sparks as it scraped the pavement on the far end of the intersection.

If I had ignored that reminder to look left and right, I would probably have been severely injured or even killed.

Obedience is important when you are driving, but it's absolutely essential when you want to live a victorious, thriving life in Christ. What is God calling you to do today? Whatever it may be, your obedience to that calling will make all the difference in where you are headed tomorrow.

God, help me understand the importance of simple obedience, and let my life reflect that understanding.

March

TO READ
Proverbs 16:1-16

We can make our plans, but the Lord determines our steps. PROVERBS 16:9

Following God's Directions

Jesus, I am only twenty years old. I have no education and no job. I believe you called me to serve you in ministry. I know how these things work out. I get married, Pam gets pregnant, I work at a job I don't really like to provide for my family, and we all feel miserable. Why would you want me to get married now?

As long as I was in this frame of mind as I prayed, my stomach was knotted up and stress was lodged in my neck. But when I changed my heart and prayed, *Okay, God, I will marry her,* peace swept over my body. My stomach unwound and my neck relaxed. But as I thought again about what God wanted me to do, it seemed too hard for me, and stress returned.

This argument with God went on for two hours as I drove home to my parents' house for the summer. Pam and I were not going to see each other for a couple of months, and we had agreed to spend this time apart praying about our relationship. As I made the journey home, God was making it clear to me that he wanted me to marry Pam.

I was sure I would be in God's will if I accepted his direction, even though it looked scary. But I also knew that my life would be simpler if I walked away from my relationship with Pam—except that I would have to justify ignoring God's clear leading.

Pam and I have been married twenty-four years. I now realize that God called us together early in our lives because he wanted to "rebuild" us together since we both grew up in dysfunctional families.

Since I married Pam, I have finished two college degrees and am in full-time ministry today. The very things I feared neglecting if I got married were energized by the relationship I once hesitated to embrace.

Lord, teach me never to fear the direction you clearly reveal for me.

TO READ
Ecclesiastes 4:7-16

A person standing alone can be attacked and defeated, but two can stand back-to-back and conquer. Three are even better, for a triple-braided cord is not easily broken. ECCLESIASTES 4:12

Building a Team

As of this writing, I have been the leader of our church for fourteen years. I have gotten used to being the one to make the important decisions. When it is time to put things on the line and make tough choices, the people look to me. When it is time for a vision to move forward and take bold steps, I'm the one the people come to.

But I have come to the realization that the church cannot grow unless I change my approach, allowing others to make decisions and live with the results. In a span of two weeks, three people told me, "Bill, you are just going to have to back down and leave these decisions in the hands of other people." They were right!

It seemed so simple, but I was amazed at the questions that flooded my mind. *Will they really follow through? Do they understand the vision well enough to make wise decisions? If they mess up, does it mean that I failed? At what point do I jump back in? Where is the line between skilled leadership and control?*

I am learning that walking by faith sometimes means letting other people take the lead. Even though trusting the team may slow things down from time to time, I know that it makes the team stronger in the long run.

Sometimes successfully and obediently following God's direction for your life means giving up some personal control, learning to trust others, and building a team. When you do that, you will find that the collective results far outweigh your individual efforts.

Jesus, teach me to trust the people you have put in my life.

TO READ
Matthew 4:17-20

Jesus called out to them, "Come, be my disciples, and I will show you how to fish for people!"

MATTHEW 4:19

✳ A New Kind of Fishing

Peter and Andrew knew fishing. They had been fishing their whole lives. They knew how to fish when the weather was nice and when the weather was stormy. They knew how to read the conditions of the sea and sky. They knew when and where to catch fish.

Peter and Andrew had planned their entire life around fishing. But then Jesus came along. He redefined the thing they knew best. From that day on, they would fish for people. Jesus would take everything they knew about fishing and transform it so that it would have an eternal impact.

The amazing thing about this story is that Peter and Andrew could no longer rely on their own knowledge of the thing they were best at. They knew how to harvest fish, but they knew nothing about the harvest of souls. They could repair their boats and nets, but they had no idea how to repair broken hearts. They were responsive to the changing weather conditions, but they had no experience at getting people to respond to the One who created everything.

If Peter and Andrew's new fishing venture was going to succeed, it would only be because they learned from the Master and because the power of God had energized them. What is the best you have to offer Jesus? God wants the very best you have to give, but only if you will let him transform it and make it useful for the work he calls you to do.

Jesus, take what I do best and make it work for you by teaching me and energizing me through your Holy Spirit.

TO READ
Deuteronomy 34:1-12

Moses, the servant of the Lord, died there in the land of Moab, just as the Lord had said.

DEUTERONOMY 34:5

The Role of a Mentor

God was undeniably strong in Moses' life, and that turned out to be a great encouragement to his successor, Joshua. Just as God had been strong in Moses' life, he would be strong in the life of Joshua as Joshua took over the reigns as leader of the nation of Israel.

Joshua was going to be in charge of taking God's people through one of the most challenging transitions of their history. They had to transition from being wanderers for the past forty years to being warriors in a hostile land. Joshua had to transform the mentality of the people from that of survivors to conquerors. To ensure Joshua's success, God promised to be with him just as he had been with Moses, who was not only a deliverer but a mentor in the life of Joshua.

We all have mentors. Some we deliberately ask to play that role in our lives. But others mentor us through their example. We see God doing great works in their lives, and we are inspired to pattern our lives after theirs. These "mentors by example" possess the skills and the confidence that stir our hearts and challenge us to greater effectiveness in our walk with Christ.

Years ago I asked Jim Conway to be my mentor because he had done many of the things I wanted to do. He had pastored a church, written books, and spoken at Christian conferences. I admired Jim Conway greatly. In fact, he was just the kind of man I wanted to be.

God is always looking for men to work through and to set examples for others. When you find that kind of man to mentor you, you can be confident that God will be just as active in your life as he has been in the life of your mentor.

Lord, help me to remember that you desire to be just as strong in my life as you have been in the lives of the men I admire most.

TO READ
Luke 10:1-12

The harvest is plentiful, but the workers are few. Ask the Lord of the harvest, therefore, to send out workers into his harvest field. LUKE 10:2, NIV

Passing of the Mantle

The passing of the mantle is a normal activity in the plan of God. Moses passed the mantle to Joshua. Elijah passed the mantle to Elisha.

The first year that I was a senior pastor, I spent a few months leading worship. I wanted to set an example for others who would lead worship, but I am not especially gifted in that area. It was important to me that we started the service with high energy, so I made a habit of enthusiastically welcoming everyone to church.

One morning I stepped up on the platform, smiled, and with great exuberance said, "Welcome this morning to church. I am thrilled that you have chosen to join us. Now, please stand and worship me this morning!"

I only forgot the one little word—*with*—but it completely changed the meaning of my sentence and the atmosphere of the church. The crowd just froze and stared at me for a second with shocked looks on their faces. I am sure some of them were thinking, *What is up with this young pastor? Is he really this proud?* At that point, I realized what I had done and began to laugh. I knew there was nothing else I could do. What was I going to do—explain what I really meant? Once I started laughing, everyone else joined me.

After a couple of minutes, I tried to start the service again, but we erupted into laughter again. It took us a full twenty minutes to recover from that one silly misstatement.

In all our imperfection, we are Jesus' ambassadors. We are the ones to whom he has passed the mantle. He has entrusted us with the most important message on earth. He trusts us, not because of our talent but because he has put his Spirit in us.

Lord, show me what legacy I am to pass on to others.

TO READ
John 8:1-11

Then Jesus stood up again and said to her, "Where are your accusers? Didn't even one of them condemn you?" "No, Lord," she said. And Jesus said, "Neither do I. Go and sin no more." JOHN 8:10-11

Motivated to Change

Grace is a great motivator. Most of us, however, think that the way to get people to change their behavior is through confrontation. Most of us live with the mistaken notion that people will repent if we point out their sin and condemn them for their actions.

That is exactly how the story in John 8 began. A group of influential men in the community publicly accused a woman of adultery and were ready to condemn her. They brought the woman, whom they had caught in the very act of adultery, to Jesus to find out what he had to say about the situation.

Jesus didn't angrily send these men away, and he didn't give them a "rubber stamp" approval for what they wanted to do. Instead, he gave them the go-ahead to condemn her—but with one condition: The one among them who had no sin in his life should be the one to cast the first stone. Jesus brilliantly silenced all of them because he pointed out the undeniable fact that they too were sinners deserving condemnation and in need of forgiveness.

But what Jesus did next was even more remarkable. He offered this sinful woman forgiveness, giving us his greatest lesson on motivating people with grace. Jesus knows that people who understand they are forgiven will live a life pleasing to God. His is not the cheap forgiveness that says "What you did is no big deal," but he offers a free and complete forgiveness that challenges us to "Go and sin no more."

How do you respond to those who need forgiveness? Do you confront and condemn them like the religious leaders who wanted to stone the woman caught in adultery? Or do you lovingly reach out and show them the free forgiveness Jesus offers?

Lord, help me to show those who need Jesus' forgiveness what it really looks like, and help me to do it without a hint of condemnation.

TO READ
Psalm 145

Let each generation tell its children of your mighty acts. PSALM 145:4

A Moment of Clarity

"Those who want to lead others must set goals for themselves. . . . A leader is someone who knows where he is going and invites others to join him. . . . Leadership begins within an individual and is then expressed in his lifestyle." The conference speaker went on and on. I was sitting in the audience taking notes, although I had heard the information many times before.

But then the speaker said something that got my attention: "It is not clear where the next generation of national Christian leaders will come from. The men and women who are currently national spokespeople are getting old, and we cannot tell at this time who will take their place."

I was sitting among hundreds of other people, but it seemed as if this statement was spoken directly to me. Before that moment, being a public speaker had never been a dream of mine. In fact, I had always been embarrassed to talk about my life in front of others. I knew that if I were to "go public," I would have to be open about both my victories and my struggles.

Hesitation gripped my mind, but conviction gripped my heart. I knew instantly that God was calling me. I knew that somehow, some way, I would communicate with thousands of people and represent the cause of Christ at a national level.

Since that time, I have become the pastor of a church, written books, been on radio and television, and spoken at conferences all around the country. As it turns out, the very thing I thought would embarrass me-public speaking—has turned out to be the most comfortable part of my life.

Keep your ears open to what God may be telling you. Today may be the day you hear the statement that clarifies your life calling.

Lord, give me ears to hear your voice in the midst of my everyday life. Make your purpose for me clear.

TO READ
John 3:1-21

"What do you mean?" exclaimed Nicodemus.

JOHN 3:4

Understanding Truth

Nicodemus was a teacher in the synagogue in Jerusalem. He had grown used to having the answers and liked being the expert. He had taught hundreds of people the truths from the Scriptures.

But Jesus' teaching confused him.

Nicodemus was not accustomed to being stumped. It was highly unusual for him not to understand a simple statement about God. But Jesus' words "Unless you are born again, you can never see the Kingdom of God" puzzled him. As soon as Jesus said it, Nicodemus knew it was true, even though he didn't fully understand what it meant. He was in a crisis of faith, the kind where you can't fully understand what you know to be true.

Nicodemus longed to be able to explain Jesus' words, but he just couldn't grasp them. It was at once humiliating and stimulating for him. So he decided to simply ask Jesus what he meant, then just listen.

Jesus began to describe the words of life. Nicodemus's heart stirred while Jesus talked. For the first time in his life, he began to understand what knowing God really meant. It was no longer about the Law and "getting it right." It was now about life and loving God. He didn't know all the implications of following Jesus, but he knew that he needed to follow him from this day forward. His heart was ignited with the desire to know the things Jesus knew and to tell them as simply as Jesus told them.

What do you do when God shows you a truth that you don't understand? Do you run away from his truth, or do you run to it?

Lord, show me your truth in a way that is simple enough for me to understand it.

TO READ
Genesis 6:11-22

God said to Noah, ". . . Make a boat from resinous wood and seal it with tar, inside and out. Then construct decks and stalls throughout its interior."

GENESIS 6:13-14

A Life of Faithfulness

Things had gotten bad on earth—really bad. Evil had become the norm, and people's lives were corrupt in every way imaginable.

Noah's family was in danger, but his obedience to God would be the path to safety for all of them. It would require long-term obedience. The ark could not be built overnight, and it couldn't be built in a single act. The future of Noah's sons and their families was in his hands.

The command to "make a boat" was given very quickly, but it would require a lifetime to accomplish. In one short command, God had called Noah to a life of faithfulness.

Often a single decision can lay out the path for the rest of your life. God wants to meet you on the path of your career. He understands that your career decisions have lifelong implications. He understands that you must set your heart to do your work well and that you must put in a lifetime of days to make that happen.

If you have already made your career choice, ask yourself how God wants to meet you in the midst of your work. When you respond to him, God will transform your faithfulness into the care and safety of those you value most. Your financial contribution will provide opportunity for their growth. Your example will teach them the diligence they need for their future. Your stability will become the norm for them.

If you haven't made your career choice yet, ask God to reveal his plan for you. Ask him what career he wants your faithfulness in so that you can provide a safe future for those you love and a platform from which to serve him.

In short, don't just work a job, "make a boat."

Lord, in the midst of my career, show me the value of faithfulness to you.

TO READ
James 3:2-12

Sometimes [the tongue] praises our Lord and Father, and sometimes it breaks out into curses against those who have been made in the image of God.

JAMES 3:9

The Power of Words

I was watching the NBA all-star weekend's slam dunk contest with my sons, who were ages twelve and ten at the time. That year Anthony "Spud" Webb was in the contest and was spectacular.

After the contest, Zachery, my ten-year-old, asked me, "Dad, how tall is that guy who was slam-dunking?"

"His name is Spud Webb, and he is five feet seven inches tall," I answered.

I knew I was in trouble when I heard the inevitable follow-up question: "How tall are you, Dad?"

"I am five feet eleven."

"Well, how come you can't slam dunk? Are you too fat?"

I was about to respond when Brock, my oldest son, chimed in, "Zachery, Dad is not too fat; he weighs the same as Michael Jordan."

For a brief moment, I thought I was raising a genius. But then he added, "Dad isn't too fat. He's just too old."

In a strange and humorous way, I learned the value of words that day. The interaction between my sons and me was truly funny. We had a good laugh about it then, and we've often laughed about it since. But at the same time, my sons' words have haunted me. I've wondered how my kids really view me. Do they see me as too fat? too old? I've wondered if I will always be able to laugh at myself or if I will begin taking myself so seriously that I become overly self-conscious.

Words can bring great blessings, but they can also cause great pain. How will you use your words?

Lord, remind me to choose my words carefully.

TO READ
John 9:1-5

"It was not because of his sins or his parents' sins," Jesus answered. "He was born blind so the power of God could be seen in him." JOHN 9:3

✹ When You Can't, Jesus Can

Because he was born blind, his career choices were extremely limited. In his day people didn't have much use for blind people, so his only real option was to beg for a living. It was humiliating. Most people who saw him assumed that God was punishing him, either for his sins or for his parents' sins. He knew he had done nothing to deserve this, but that didn't change the fact that he had no options in life.

The truth is, neither the blind man's sin nor his parents' sin had anything to do with his condition. On the contrary, his condition was a matter of divine appointment. In other words, the course of this man's life was designed to intersect with the life of Jesus.

Jesus used the blind man's plight to display his own power. Healing really got people's attention, and he often used it to put his power on display and to show people that he had the authority to forgive sins. That was exactly what was going to happen the day this blind man met Jesus.

The man's blindness caused people to ask why it happened. But the miracle of his restored sight caused even more people to ask, "Who is this man who caused your healing?"

If you are willing, Jesus can use your deficiencies and setbacks to put himself on display in your life. Your physical shortcomings, your emotional scars, and your lack of ability are all areas where Jesus can make himself known.

When you cannot, Jesus can. When you are weak, Jesus is strong. The thing you may wish was different about your life may be the very thing Jesus wants to use in order to do his greatest work.

Lord, help me see the value of my life, especially in the areas that don't work the way I think they should.

TO READ
James 1:9-21

Your anger can never make things right in God's sight. JAMES 1:20

The Folly of Anger

"I can't believe she left."This became Ben's mantra in the months after his wife of fifteen years walked away from their relationship. She told him that his anger was the cause of their marital problems, but he couldn't see it.

About three months after Ben's wife left him, he became consumed with crazy thoughts of how to get even. He never would have imagined that he could hurt his own children in order to get back at his ex-wife. But one night he sat in his bedroom thinking up a detailed plot to kill his kids and then take his own life—just to show her how badly she had hurt him.

In the midst of his despair, the words "Your anger can never make things right in God's sight" echoed within Ben. He had heard that Bible verse but had never understood what it meant. Now it haunted his thoughts.

Ben's mind ping-ponged back and forth between "I'm so angry" to "I can't be this angry" until he was completely exhausted. In desperation, Ben cried out—first to God, then to a counselor in the New Life Ministries network. He logged on to www.newlife.com and found a counselor in his area. He met a therapist who allowed him to be brutally honest and who helped him develop a strategy for emotional healing.

Ben has traveled a long, difficult road since that dark day his wife left him, but today he has found there is more power in forgiveness and peace than there is in anger.

Do you believe there is more power in anger than in forgiveness and peace? Or do you believe God when he tells you that hanging on to your anger will never makes things right with you, with those around you, or with him?

Lord, please control my anger before it controls me.

TO READ
John 14:1-7

There are many rooms in my Father's home, and
I am going to prepare a place for you. If this were
not so, I would tell you plainly. JOHN 14:2

Your Own Eternal Home

In today's Bible verse, the word *prepare* literally means to make something
fit for a specific use. The idea here is that Jesus is using his time and expertise to make you an eternal home that perfectly meets your particular needs
and desires.

In preparing this everlasting home for you, Jesus is putting action behind
his love. He is a living example of this truth: When you love someone, you
go the extra mile for that person.

In 1990 I built a home for my family. It was a long year of hard work.
There were countless details to oversee and endless tasks to accomplish in
order to create the right place for my family to live. That year I held down
a job and built a house. It meant long hours of work, but it didn't matter
to me. All that mattered was my family. I loved my wife and children, and
I knew they needed a home. But I also knew that they were not capable of
building one on their own, so I committed myself to providing it for them.

Likewise, Jesus loves you and knows you need an eternal home to live in.
He also knows that you are not capable of building this home yourself, so he
has made a commitment to provide it for you. He is taking great pains to
prepare it. He is watching over the countless details and joyfully assigning
the endless tasks required to give you an eternal dwelling place that is perfectly suited for you.

Oh Master Builder, thank you for preparing the perfect place for me
to spend eternity with you.

TO READ
Ephesians 5:21-33

You husbands must love your wives with the same love Christ showed the church. He gave up his life for her. EPHESIANS 5:25

❋ *Prove It!*

Andy loved Sheri, but Sheri wasn't sure she could trust him. Andy was an outgoing, energetic young man, but to those who knew him, he appeared to be self-absorbed. Andy knew about his reputation, and he knew about Sheri's misgivings.

It was obvious to everyone who knew this couple that Andy was in love with Sheri. Andy had been trying to get Sheri's attention for months, and he finally decided to take the direct approach.

"Sheri, I really care about you and I want you to spend some time with me," Andy said. "I want you to know that you can trust me."

Sheri's response echoed in Andy's heart: "Prove it."

"What do you mean?" Andy asked.

"If you say I can trust you, prove it!" she repeated.

Andy decided that Sheri was worth the challenge. He knew he wanted to marry this young lady, so he set out to show her over and over again that he could be trusted. When she was upset, he listened. When he was supposed to meet her somewhere, he showed up—on time. When he had to change their plans, he called to let her know. When he disappointed her, he apologized without making excuses.

Sheri finally decided that Andy had proved himself worthy of her trust. She said yes to his proposal of marriage. Today Sheri is secure in his love because he had proved it. Andy is confident in their relationship because he had proved his trustworthiness.

Do you want a marriage and family in which your loved ones are secure in your love? Then don't just tell them you love them—prove it!

Lord, give me the courage to prove my love every day to those who matter most to me.

TO READ
Leviticus 11:41-47

After all, I, the Lord, am your God. You must be holy because I am holy. LEVITICUS 11:44

Understanding Holiness

Holiness is hard for us to understand. That's because we too often view holiness through the lens of our standards and our society's standards.

In his book *The God Who Hears*, Bing Hunter describes God's moral purity as "his inherent personal righteousness and holiness . . . symbolized in Scripture as light: blinding, unending, undiminishing, dazzling whiteness."[1] He also applies the issue to our daily lives:

> Another reason why holiness is so hard to understand is that Christians are like fish, living in a fluid medium (society) which has become so morally murky that "light" seems abnormal. We were born in dirty water and have gotten used to it. Mud and murk are normal; clean and light are threatening. We can see rotten things on the bottom, but assume we cannot get stuck in the muck if we keep moving. And besides, we generally swim (in circles) higher up in the pond. We have learned to live comfortably with unholiness and see lots of others wearing Ichthus pins who do too. . . . It is little wonder sin grieves the Holy Spirit who lives in us (Ephesians 5:30). Yet the greater and more astounding wonder is that sin grieves us so little.[2]

What is making your water murky? What is making it hard for you to understand God's holiness? What sin used to upset you before but now makes you yawn? Take a good look at God, and then look at him again. That should help you see things more clearly.

Give me sense, Lord, to see through the murkiness of my own life and the society I live in so I can understand your holiness.

TO READ
1 John 1:5–2:2

If we say we have no sin, we are only fooling ourselves and refusing to accept the truth.

1 JOHN 1:8

Painful, Courageous Honesty

What will you say when your children ask you the really tough questions about your life? Will you be honest, or will you try to hide your mistakes?

I recently counseled a man and his seventeen-year-old son. The father wanted to know how to better communicate with his family, and he wanted to start with his son. I told him that he would need to be honest and vulnerable about his own life at his son's age.

The three of us had a great time talking about the father's first car, his first fishing trip without his dad, and the girlfriends in his life. When I asked him if there was anything he would have done differently, he said, "Yes. I would not have had some of the friends I had. They were exciting and fun to be around, but every time I was with them, I got into trouble."

When the father was finished, I asked the son if he had any questions for him. His first question was, "Did you ever do drugs?"

Courageously, the dad answered, "Yes, I did. First it was alcohol. Then it was marijuana, and eventually I did cocaine. I wish I hadn't, but I did."

"Why did you stop?"

"I got caught. I was out with my friends, and we were driving on the railroad tracks when the police stopped us and arrested us. That night I decided I didn't need it anymore."

Sometimes being vulnerable and honest with those you love means telling them about the things you aren't proud of. But if you tactfully and truthfully answer their questions, God can redeem even your worst mistakes and use them for your benefit and theirs.

Lord, prepare me to answer tough questions truthfully.

TO READ
Joshua 3:1-6

In the morning Joshua said to the priests, "Lift up the Ark of the Covenant and lead the people across the river." And so they started out. JOSHUA 3:6

❋ *Who's Number One?*

I recently saw a series of comic strips that portrayed different episodes of history as if they were sporting events. The one that really caught my attention depicted a band of soldiers excitedly huddled together in front of the camera with their right index fingers held triumphantly in the air, announcing to the world that they were number one and could not be defeated. The problem with the scene was that it was *before* the battle and the leader of this particular band of men was General Custer.

This comic illustrated the danger of following the wrong leader into the wrong battle.

God constantly communicates to us men the message that we need to allow him to go out ahead of us in everything we do.

Israel was at the threshold of crossing the Jordan River and moving on to conquer the land God had promised them. If the men of Israel were like most of the men I know, they were tense, nervous, excited, and ready to go and do great things for their God.

The temptation at times like this is to rely on our own strength and enthusiasm. But just to remind the Israelites who was really leading, God had the priests go first, carrying the Ark of the Covenant. The men who were about to charge into battle had to follow the ones who represented them before God.

Do you want success and blessing in the things God has called you to do? Then slow down and let him go out before you, knowing that he has promised you victory.

God, teach me to get behind you as you go out ahead of me in the battle of life.

TO READ
Luke 18:18-30

"There is still one thing you lack," Jesus said. "Sell all you have and give the money to the poor, and you will have treasure in heaven. Then come, follow me." But when the man heard this, he became sad because he was very rich. LUKE 18:22-23

One Huge Decision

Life had been good to this rich young leader. He had a successful career and a strong reputation. He was used to being treated with respect and having what he said taken seriously. He had every advantage money could buy.

Then he encountered Jesus. He knew every important person in his community, so he wanted to know Jesus too. He knew Jesus' reputation for wise teaching, so he asked him what he had to do to make his life complete. When Jesus told him to live a life of integrity, the rich young man confidently told Jesus he was already doing that. Then Jesus pulled the rug out from under him when he said, "Sell all you have and give the money to the poor."

That didn't sit well with this young man. He was used to being rich. He liked being self-sufficient, and he liked the advantages prosperity gave him. How could he give it all away? How could he trust a man who had no earthly possessions? How could he ever explain to his friends what he did and why he did it?

But then again, how could he refuse to say yes to the greatest man who ever lived?

This was the defining moment of the young man's life. Sadly, he decided that the price of following Jesus was too high, and we never hear about him again. With this one decision, his journey toward God appeared to be over.

When Jesus asks you to do something, remember that your decision will go a long way in determining your legacy with him.

Lord, help me to make decisions that enhance my legacy with you.

TO READ
John 9:39–10:19

When he said these things, the people were again divided in their opinions about him. JOHN 10:19

A Defining Moment

Sometimes division over the words of truth can become the most defining moments of our lives.

As an eighteen-year-old college freshman, I felt pretty cocky about my faith in Christ. I honestly believed that I could persuade anyone to respond to the call to know Jesus personally.

I made an appointment with my boss so I could tell him about my faith and give him the opportunity to give his heart to Christ. But I hadn't counted on my boss being a devout Buddhist. I shared my testimony with him, and he told me about his own religious experience. He spoke with great conviction in his voice. He told me that during his journey to the Orient—where he immersed himself in meditation—he had reached his state of peace.

What my boss told me had my head spinning. I knew there was something wrong in what he had said, but I couldn't tell what it was. I knew that the Bible was true and that the resurrection of Christ was the dividing point in all human spirituality. But for the first time since I had asked Jesus into my life, I had doubts. I could not fit it all together.

This division between my boss's beliefs and mine launched me on a journey of discovery. Over time I learned that the Resurrection could be researched and validated historically. I also learned that my boss's spiritual discovery could not be adequately explained, researched, or validated.

This was a defining moment in my life of faith. I realized that I was not willing to base my eternal destiny on something that could not be validated. And as I studied and learned more about my faith in Christ, I became humbly confident in my ability to explain and defend that faith.

Lord, give me a confident faith that I can boldly share with others who may not believe the way I do.

TO READ
1 John 4:1-6

You belong to God, my dear children. You have already won your fight with these false prophets, because the Spirit who lives in you is greater than the spirit who lives in the world. 1 JOHN 4:4

Peace in Christ

When I was sixteen, I thought I had the world by the tail. I had starting positions in two sports at my high school, and I had a girlfriend I thought I was in love with. In addition, I had learned how to lie to my parents effectively enough that I could do pretty much whatever I wanted.

When I went with my best friend and his father to see the movie *The Exorcist*, I thought I could handle it. I was "scared to life" that night.

My friend thought of the movie as a comedy and spent the night laughing as he rehashed different scenes. To me, however, it was no joke.

What I saw on the screen was not just a movie but a horrifying portrayal of a spiritual world I knew nothing about. What really scared me was that I couldn't see any difference between myself and the demon-possessed girl in the movie. I was haunted by the thought, *If that could happen to her, why couldn't it happen to me?*

I went home the next morning a shaken young man. I turned to the Bible in a desperate attempt to find some relief from my fear. For the next thirty days, I was up five or six times each night looking for relief from my fear.

One night I read 1 John 4:4, which says that "the Spirit who lives in you is greater than the spirit who lives in the world." At that moment, the light came on, and I realized I would be safe if I just had Jesus inside me. That night I prayed and asked Jesus to come into my life.

For the first time in a month, I slept peacefully all night.

We live in a world full of all kinds of spiritual influences. But when we put our faith in Christ and allow his Spirit to live within us, he will give us safety as well as peace.

Lord, help me trust that you are greater than anything or anyone in the world today.

TO READ
Job 1:1-22

In all of this, Job did not sin by blaming God.
JOB 1:22

A Brush with Greatness

William Randolph Hearst built an empire. He was the leading newspaperman in the country, and he had power to make and break lives. He acquired treasures from around the world. He owned a castle on California's central coast that housed his impressive collection of antiques and art.

Hearst had everything the powerful people of the world want, but he was deeply in debt. He had leveraged everything he could to amass his fortune, which he believed would last forever. But his empire eventually crumbled. His treasures were sold at auction and his newspapers were distributed to others. By the end of his life, he was broke. The only thing he had left was a magnificent but heartbreaking memory of what could have been. His own summary of his life was this: "I am a man who could have been great but wasn't."

In contrast to Hearst is Job. He worked hard, planned strategically, and lived with integrity. His character was formidable enough to be considered for a special mission. God volunteered him for a spiritual confrontation that would serve as an example for every generation. Job spent a significant portion of his adult life suffering at the hands of Satan, but he refused to give in to mediocrity or self-destruction. In the end, God chose to reward him with twice as many blessings as he had before his struggle.

The key difference between William Randolph Hearst and Job is that while Hearst boldly did things his own way, Job courageously followed God's plan. Because of that, Job was a man who could have been great and was!

Does your life resemble Hearst's? If so, seek God and his plan for your life, and commit yourself to following his plan with all your strength. God always blesses that kind of obedience.

Lord, open my eyes to see the greatness you have planned for my life.

| TO READ | The next day John saw Jesus coming toward him and said, "Look! There is the Lamb of God who takes away the sin of the world!" JOHN 1:29 |
| John 1:19-34 | |

The Passing of the Baton

Jesus thought very highly of John the Baptist, so highly that he called him the finest man who ever lived (see Matthew 11:11).

God sent John to deliver a profound message to humankind. John had great insight as well as great passion for telling others about the coming of the Messiah.

But John's life purpose was not complete until he saw Jesus. When he did, he was able to point out to others that Jesus himself was the one they had been waiting for, their Messiah.

As always happens when a man meets Jesus, nothing about John's life was the same after seeing his Savior.

John was popular and sought after during the time he was preparing people to see the Messiah. He was in the forefront of the religious scene of his day. But when Jesus arrived, John began slipping into the background. He had fulfilled the purpose for which God had prepared him. His leg of the race was finished, and it was time for him to pass the baton to the one he had been called to announce all along.

In every man's walk with Christ there is a time to rise up and be counted and a time to step back and give up the stage to others. When it is your turn to hand off the baton, will you do so willingly, or will the next generation need to tear it out of your hands?

Lord, give me a sure grip on the baton during my leg of the race and a sure pass to the next person when it is finished.

TO READ
Psalm 61:1-8

Lead me to the towering rock of safety, for you are my safe refuge, a fortress where my enemies cannot reach me. PSALM 61:2-3

A Passion for Our Priorities

Life can be dangerous. Many people who have survived brushes with death have learned the important truth that the only truly safe place on earth is in the presence of God. They also learn something about the importance of their priorities.

On the morning of September 11, 2001, Brian Birdwell was coming out of one of the Pentagon restrooms when Flight 93 crashed into the side of the building just four windows away from his office. He was knocked unconscious as jet fuel and flames engulfed him, covering 60 percent of his body with second- and third-degree burns.

Brian is certain that if he had been in his office at the moment that jet hit the Pentagon, he would have died instantly. Since the terrible events of that day, he has searched his heart and asked himself many wrenching questions:

"Why was I one of the survivors?"

"Is there some special purpose for my life?"

Today Brian admits that there have been many times when he wished that he had died rather than have to endure so much physical and emotional pain. But he pushed forward. And during his painful journey to recovery, Brian has struggled to find answers to the questions that have haunted him.

While not all of his questions have been answered, Brian has made some changes concerning his priorities in life. He says, "I still have the same priorities: God, my wife, and my kids. I am just more intense about them now."

What are your priorities? How have the hard times of your life caused you to view these priorities differently?

Lord, help me to set the kind of priorities that I can be passionate about.

TO READ
2 Corinthians 9:6-14

God loves the person who gives cheerfully. And God will generously provide all you need.

2 CORINTHIANS 9:7-8

Honoring God through Giving

"This is Juan," the pastor explained, pointing to the picture on the screen. "He lives in San Salvador. For just a few dollars a month, we can make sure that Juan has clothes and food and gets an education. Please pray about what part God would have you play in helping Juan."

When Steve got home from church that afternoon, Malachai, his six-year-old son, approached him.

"Dad, we need to get my piggy bank out," Malachai said with urgency.

"Why, Son?"

"I want to give the money to Juan," he announced.

"But you have been saving that money for the toy you want to buy," Steve countered. "You have almost five dollars saved. Once you get to five dollars, you'll be able to go buy it."

"I know, Dad," Malachai answered. "But Juan needs the money."

Steve and Malachai emptied the piggy bank and took the coins to the church office. They explained that the money was to be used to help Juan.

Three days later, Malachai received a letter in the mail from his grandmother. But there was more than just the letter. Inside the envelope was a check for five dollars. Malachai read his grandmother's letter. She told him that she loved him and that she had been thinking about him and wanted him to have a little money to spend.

Steve was changed that day. He saw in his six-year-old son what his son should have seen in him: the kind of faith that inspired him to honor God and give everything he had for the good of others. And Steve saw something firsthand about God too: He honors those who honor him.

Jesus, I want to honor you with everything I have, knowing that you honor those who honor you.

TO READ
Isaiah 55:8-13

Just as the heavens are higher than the earth, so are my ways higher than your ways and my thoughts higher than your thoughts. ISAIAH 55:9

Yes, Lord!

As a pastor, I'm supposed to desire more than anything to be involved in people's lives. But when I was asked to perform a wedding for a certain couple, I balked. I didn't know the couple very well, and I had not met any of their family members.

I knew in my heart that God wanted me to perform this wedding, but it was a mystery as to why. I soon found out.

At the rehearsal I was surprised to recognize the groom's best man, a man named Wes. I knew Wes and his father, who would also be at the wedding, and I had been praying for months for an opportunity to minister to them. Neither of them knew Jesus, and they had become something of a personal mission for me.

The next day I was able to spend more time with Wes and his father at the reception than I had been able to in the previous three months. As best man, Wes had to give the toast for the bride and groom, but he was very nervous and didn't quite know what he was going to say. He approached me and asked me to help him put his thoughts into words, which I gladly did.

Two wonderful things came out of my willingness to do the wedding. First, Wes did a wonderful job giving the toast. Second and more importantly, a new mutual appreciation developed between Wes and me, and that allowed me to minister to him and his father more easily.

The irony of this story is that in calling me to do a wedding I didn't want to do, God gave me the opportunity I had been praying for. Once again, I was reminded that when God speaks to my heart and asks me to do something, the only answer that should come from my mouth is, "Yes, Lord!"

Lord, give me the confidence to obey you.

TO READ
John 13:32–14:1

Don't be troubled. You trust God, now trust in me.

JOHN 14:1

Strategic Warnings

It is hard to find anyone in history who had more passion or abandon in his dedication to the Savior than Peter. He was the first to speak, he was the only one to get out of the boat when Jesus walked on water, and he honestly believed he would give his life for Jesus if necessary. There was no way he could have predicted what he would say and do when confronted by a lowly servant. It was impossible for Peter to conceive of the possibility that he would deny knowing Jesus, not just once, but three times.

But Jesus knew. He knew that Peter loved him as much or more than anyone else loved him. He knew that Peter's curiosity would draw him close to the trial. He knew that Peter would rashly deny knowing him. He knew that Peter's heart would break when he realized what he had done. So he told Peter and the other disciples, "Don't be troubled."

I recently received information that a very good friend of mine has been diagnosed with cancer. He is a godly man with an important ministry. His health challenges now make it impossible for him to have the active ministry he has had in the past. I find it very interesting that God has been systematically simplifying his life over the last three years. My friend didn't understand why his opportunities were being limited until the doctor told him he was going to have be focused on his recovery. Suddenly, the new lifestyle made sense.

You may have to face some dark moments in your life. That doesn't mean, however, that you should be looking over your shoulder, waiting for the darkness to fall. Jesus will faithfully prepare you for what is next.

Lord of heaven, give me ears to hear your warnings as well as your words of comfort.

TO READ
1 Corinthians 10:14-33

Whatever you eat or drink or whatever you do, you must do all for the glory of God.

1 CORINTHIANS 10:31

❊ Doing It God's Way

Shane had been in my office before. The first time he had been very angry because we encouraged his live-in girlfriend, Marjie, to move out. Shane couldn't understand why we would encourage her to leave him. He had convinced himself that he was good for Marjie, even though he was verbally abusive and had cheated on her numerous times.

Marjie's absence left Shane feeling lonely and empty. Without her to come home to, he became desperate to fill the void. He tried more sex with more women, but it didn't fill the void. He tried working more, but that didn't help. He tried drinking, but that, too, left him empty. Everything he did reminded him of his difficult, painful childhood.

Shane's parents had been involved in the sexual revolution of the 1960s, and Shane himself had begun using pornography at the age of thirteen. As a teenager, he asked Christ to be his Savior, but he never really took his faith seriously. As a result, there was no real change in his life.

That day in my office Shane was a broken man ready to make changes. The first thing out of his mouth was, "Okay, we'll try it God's way."

Almost instantly Shane lost his appetite for alcohol and for sexual conquests and gained a desire for the adventure of seeking out God's will.

Shane began finding joy in relationships based on respect rather than sex. And he became so engrossed in the Bible and in the things of God that he got involved with a youth group as a discussion leader, helping young people avoid the mistakes he had made.

Are you struggling with an emptiness that the things of the world can't seem to fill? Like Shane, are you willing to try it God's way?

Lord, help me to remember that your way is always the best way.

TO READ
John 6:61-69

Then Jesus turned to the Twelve and asked, "Are you going to leave, too?" Simon Peter replied, "Lord, to whom would we go? You alone have the words that give eternal life." JOHN 6:67-68

A Crisis of Faith

For the twelve disciples, following Jesus had become more and more difficult. There was an escalating price to pay. Following him had become unpopular, and most people had decided that it wasn't worth it. Then Jesus created a crisis of faith in their hearts when he pointedly asked, "Are you going to leave, too?"

We will all face a crisis of faith sometime. One day I spoke with a young man who was having one of his own.

Jason was a troubled young man who lived with bitterness in his heart toward his abusive father. Jason felt justified in hating his father, and he began rebelling. He started dressing in dark clothes, and he mistreated his mother, even though he desperately wanted her to love him.

"Jason, I think I know what is really wrong," I told him. "It's your bitterness toward your dad. You put up this rough exterior, but I think you are just hiding behind all of that."

Jason's gaze went to the floor, and for an instant his heart softened. In a flash of vulnerability he admitted that I was right. But then his expression hardened, and he defiantly told me, "I can never forgive him."

That day Jesus asked Jason the same question he asks each of us: "Are you going to leave, too?" Sadly, Jason walked away from his chance to know Christ at that time in his life. For him, the price of walking with Jesus was forgiving his father, and that was too high a price to pay.

Daily following Jesus means paying a price—the price of faith, the price of perseverance, the price of obedience, the price of forgiveness. Ask yourself, "Am I willing to pay that price?"

Jesus, may I always walk with you, no matter what the price.

TO READ
Matthew 4:18-22

He saw two other brothers, James and John,
sitting in a boat with their father, Zebedee. . . .
And he called them to come, too. They immediately
followed him, leaving the boat and their father
behind. MATTHEW 4:21-22

Leaving and Following

James and John were helping their father run the family business. Commercial fishing required a lot of hard work from all three men, and that day they were mending nets. But in the middle of a busy workday, Jesus called the two brothers to follow him. He never asked their father for permission, never asked them to check their schedules, and never gave them time to find replacement workers. He just called them to follow.

For James and John to fulfill their calling, they had to leave their father to work by himself. They could not follow Jesus *and* help their father or help their father *and* follow Jesus. It was one or the other. Their purpose in life was to follow Jesus, and the time to follow was that very moment.

Because James and John chose to leave their father and the family business and follow Jesus, they enjoyed a special relationship with him. Along with Peter, they formed the "inner circle" of apostles. As such, they were allowed to take part in experiences with Jesus that the other disciples missed out on. For example, they saw the Transfiguration (Mark 9:2-3), and they were invited to pray with Jesus in the garden of Gethsemane (Matthew 26:36-38).

When Jesus calls you to follow him, he wants your undivided attention. That's serious business, so serious that you must turn away from anyone or anything that competes for your attention. It may mean disappointing someone, and it may mean giving up a part of your life that you truly enjoy.

Are you willing to leave everything and everyone behind to follow him?

Lord, make me willing to leave behind anyone or anything that would distract me from following you.

TO READ
Hebrews 4:12-16

Let us come boldly to the throne of our gracious God. There we will receive his mercy, and we will find grace to help us when we need it.

HEBREWS 4:16

A Bold Prayer

"Nick, are you sitting down?" The doctor's tone indicated that something was terribly wrong. Nick's stomach was suddenly overrun with nausea.

"Your wife has been badly hurt," the doctor hurried on, leaving Nick no opportunity to interrupt him. "We think she is going to live, but she may not be able to take care of herself and will probably never walk again."

Janet had been the glue that held the family together. Nick never had to worry about his behavior or his character because Janet had always fixed things for him. But suddenly she was a quadriplegic. Now everything was up to Nick.

The weeks that followed the accident were agonizing. There were hospital visits, talks with doctors, and endless questions from friends and family.

In the midst of the agony and turmoil, Nick prayed differently than he ever had before. After particularly difficult days, Nick would slump down and pray, "God, do whatever you want with me. I'm too tired to figure out my life anymore."

Much to Nick's surprise, an uncommon peace took up residence in his heart. The more he aggressively talked to God about his present situation, the stronger this peace grew.

Nick will never tell people that Janet's accident was a good thing in their lives, but even she says with amazement, "My accident made Nick a better husband than I ever thought I would have."

If you are facing a difficult situation right now, boldly talk to God. He will give you peace and grace to see you through.

Lord, when I want to run away, help me instead to run to you in prayer.

TO READ
Hebrews 13:1-7

Remember your leaders who first taught you the word of God. Think of all the good that has come from their lives, and trust the Lord as they do.

HEBREWS 13:7

Stepping Up

Remembering the men who mentored me in my faith has always been easy for me. As a young man I received quality training when it came to the things of God. And I needed that training! You see, my father was a great man, but he certainly was not the best when it came to teaching me about spiritual matters. Therefore, I needed other older and wiser men to step up and take an interest in me if I was to run my life course as God had mapped it out.

Recently a young man approached me and asked, "Bill, would you mentor me this summer?" As I considered his request, it suddenly occurred to me that this young man saw me as older and wiser, and he wanted to know what I've learned on my journey of faith. It also occurred to me that for this young man to run God's course for his life, he needed to be mentored.

I already understood the value of being mentored, but this young man's request made me see the value of being a mentor. He was asking me to be a vital link in his life, believing that he would grow spiritually if he spent time with me.

I realized that it was now my turn to step up and play the same role others had played in my life. And I realized that investing my time and energy in him might make the difference between wandering through life and being focused in his walk with Christ.

But mentoring looked different from the "giving" end. It felt a lot like responsibility. I even thought of others who might be better mentors. In the end, however, I decided to do it.

Will you step up and give to others the way others have given to you?

Lord, motivate me to invest myself in those who need mentoring the way others invested themselves in me.

April

TO READ
Romans 13:1-10

The authorities do not frighten people who are doing right, but they frighten those who do wrong. So do what they say, and you will get along well. The authorities are sent by God to help you.

ROMANS 13:3-4

Real Heroes

Those who serve the public are the real heroes in life. They faithfully carry out their everyday duties and regularly prepare to do heroic deeds when needed. They look out for those of us who are doing right and protect us from those who are doing wrong.

And every once in a while, they get the honor they deserve.

An article in the September 11, 2002, edition of *Time* magazine tells the story of a father and his eight-year-old son leaving a New York Mets baseball game at Shea Stadium. They approached an intersection where a New York City police officer was directing traffic. He stopped the cars and motioned to the father and son to cross. When they were right in front of the officer, the little boy stopped and held out his baseball glove and asked, "Will you sign this for me?"

The policeman was stunned. He bent down to eye level with the boy and asked him, "Don't you want the autograph of a ball player or a coach? Why would you want a cop's signature?"

The boy looked up at the officer with deep admiration and said, "Because you helped save the world."

The events of September 11, 2001, should challenge all of us men to be courageous, even courageous enough to be that kind of hero when it's needed.

God calls all men to be real heroes in their own worlds. While that may not mean saving lives or protecting the public, it does mean making a difference in the lives of people around us.

Lord of courage, build in me fearless faith today so I can accomplish your will tomorrow.

TO READ
John 11:38-46

Jesus responded, "Didn't I tell you that you will see God's glory if you believe?" JOHN 11:40

Responding to a Miracle

The crowd gathered around to see what Jesus would do with Lazarus. It was obvious from the things Jesus had said to Mary and Martha that something dramatic was going to happen. Word spread, people came, and the curtain rose on one of Jesus' greatest miracles.

First the men in the crowd moved the stone inch by inch out of its place at the mouth of the cave that served as Lazarus's crypt. Then Jesus prayed loudly enough so that all would know that the power of God was going to be put on display that day. Finally he called out those now-famous words: "Lazarus, come out!" (John 11:43).

As the wide-eyed crowd looked on, Lazarus, wrapped head to toe in burial cloths, shuffled out of the tomb to greet his friends.

The glory of God was undeniable.

This miracle required a response from everyone who was there. Some of those who witnessed it instantly believed in Jesus, while others despised what he did and ran to the Pharisees to stir up trouble.

Whenever you encounter the glory of God, you are forced to respond. When God does something great in front of you, the condition of your heart is laid bare and you are forced to either make a commitment or turn away.

How will you respond to the glory of God when it breaks out around you?

God, move my heart toward you every time I see you act in my life.

TO READ
Hebrews 3:1-13

As the Holy Spirit says: "Today, if you hear his voice, do not harden your hearts."

HEBREWS 3:7-8, NIV

Just One You

You were made for today! There is only one you, and there will never be another. God designed you to be one of a kind. There are paths that only you can walk. And those come to you one at a time.

God designed Moses to deliver Israel out of bondage in Egypt. He designed Joshua to lead the nation of Israel into the Promised Land. Samuel was designed to lead the nation and ordain its first two kings. The apostles were designed to get the church on earth started. Each of these men were the right age, had the right abilities, the right experiences, and the right training. Each was the right man for the job, the only man God wanted for the job.

It's a sad thing when a man loses sight of who God created him to be. That's what happened to Dan. We all tried to get him to stay with his family and work on his marriage. We pointed out to him that leaving his wife and children for his girlfriend was only going to complicate his life. But Dan wouldn't acknowledge the purpose for which God had designed him—to be a good, faithful husband and father.

I wish Dan could have been there when his daughter talked to my wife and me about the pain he had caused in her heart. She said to us, "My dad used to love my mom. I hope he doesn't 'used to love' me too." We tried to encourage her, but we knew that nobody could take her dad's place. Only Dan could convince her of his love.

Where has God designed your feet to walk? Only you can be a husband to your wife and a father to your children. Only you can have an influence on the people God has placed in your life. Only you can be in the place where God has uniquely designed you to walk.

Lord, may I walk the paths you have designed me to walk with dignity and exuberance.

TO READ
James 4:4-10

Humble yourselves before the Lord, and he will lift you up. JAMES 4:10, NIV

A Divine Endorsement

God does not choose people based on their talents or experiences or their vision or organizational skills. He chooses people who humble themselves and are willing to depend on him rather than their own schemes. Jack is a perfect example of this.

Jack was not your typical pastor. He didn't have a clear vision for his church. He attended a few conferences on church growth because he was told that he should. He would grow so nervous before a conference even started that he would pack his bags and head back home. Yet his church's attendance averaged around fifteen hundred people a week.

I worked on Jack's staff for four years. One day another staff member and I asked him, "Jack, what is the vision of our church?"

He responded, "Everybody knows what it is."

I said to him, "I'm sure that's true, but maybe you could put it in your own words."

Without hesitation he said, "Have church and get people saved."

"Is that it?" I asked.

"Yep," he said triumphantly, as if he had just explained everything.

One reason for Jack's success was God's favor. But there was another thing Jack did that impressed everyone who knew him. He walked through his church's auditorium every week before the service and prayed over each seat.

The real secret to success in Jack's life—and in your life—is God's endorsement. The only thing you must add to that endorsement is your faithfulness.

Dear Lord, please give me your endorsement as I follow you and attempt to do great things for you.

TO READ
Joshua 3:9-13

Joshua told the Israelites, "Come and listen to what the Lord your God says." JOSHUA 3:9

Reliable Words

It is one thing to perform a miracle, but it is quite another thing to announce it ahead of time to an entire nation.

Joshua explained to the people of Israel what was about to happen. He told them that the priests would go first into the water of the Jordan River, carrying with them the Ark of the Covenant. He told them that while the rest of the people waited and watched from the bank, God would cause the waters of the Jordan to wall up, creating a path of dry land for them to cross the river.

Throughout history, God has been in the habit of announcing his miracles ahead of time. He told Joseph there would be seven years of prosperity in Egypt followed by seven years of famine. He told Moses he would deliver Israel from Egypt, the most powerful nation on earth. He announced his resurrection ahead of time in such detail that guards were placed at his tomb in an attempt to prevent it. And he has promised eternal life to all who believe in him, and wisdom to all who seek him.

Time and time again, our God has proven that his words are the most reliable words ever spoken.

The only requirements Israel had to fulfill to experience a great miracle was take God at his word, wait for him to do what he had promised, then claim a victory that would have been unthinkable in their own power.

Are you facing something today that is impossible to handle in your own power? Does victory in your situation seem unthinkable? If so, take the Lord your God at his word, then wait for him to act on his own word. Just wait and "listen to what the Lord your God says."

Lord, show me today that you are absolutely reliable. Then give me a victory that would be unthinkable in my own power.

TO READ	Now it was the harvest season, and the Jordan was
Joshua 3:14-17	overflowing its banks. But as soon as the feet of the priests who were carrying the Ark touched the water at the river's edge, the water began piling up.

JOSHUA 3:15-16

God's Best Work

Have you ever noticed how God does some of his best work when the floods of life are raging? For example, he instructed the people of Israel to cross the Jordan River at flood stage, not when the waters were low, simply because he wanted them to realize that it was his power, not their own efforts, that allowed them to taste victory.

I once had the chance to counsel a couple in a situation very much like the one the people of Israel faced that day.

Peter and Stephanie were in a desperate situation. They were angry at each other. They had been in constant conflict over how to parent their blended family. Peter was unwilling to deal with his dependence on alcohol, and Stephanie was unwilling to face her bitterness. Finally, when their conflict reached "flood stage," they asked me if I could help their marriage.

After listening to them for an hour, I concluded that they didn't just need help with their marriage; they needed a miracle. I told them, "You don't need help. You need to be transformed. My best advice is that you start meeting together every day and begging God for a miracle."

Eight months later, after much prayer and hard work, the transformation took place. I received a call from Peter. "You were right," he said. "We have been praying for a miracle, and it's working. I have actually quit drinking. Stephanie is not angry at me all the time. The other day she even told me she loved me. I guess God likes to work when things look hopeless. Thanks."

When the floods of life rage around you, turn to God. He works best in "flood" situations.

Lord, teach me to depend on you when the floods of life rage.

Meanwhile, the priests who were carrying the Ark of the Lord's covenant stood on dry ground in the middle of the riverbed as the people passed by them. They waited there until everyone had crossed the Jordan on dry ground. JOSHUA 3:17

❁ *The Discipline to Stand in the Middle*

Discipline is a big part of life, especially when God calls us to faithfully "hold down the fort" for the benefit of others.

The priests of Israel showed discipline when they were asked to stand in the middle of the Jordan River holding the Ark of the Covenant while everyone else passed by. The priests were the first ones in the water, the first to see the water pile up and stand still, and the first to the middle of the river. But they were the last ones out.

I know a man who has served God for decades with the same kind of self-discipline.

Mel helped get our church started. He was there for the first ground-breaking ceremony and for the very first service. Since then, he has served under every pastor the church has ever had, and for thirty-five years, he has taught a class for adults.

Mel's faithfulness in serving has produced amazing results. His son is well known in the world of Christian camps. People Mel has taught have written books, started ministries, recorded music, and traveled the world for the cause of Christ.

Through it all, Mel has had the discipline to "stand in the middle," serving faithfully while others passed by to live out their callings.

God may call you to lead a conquest, or he may call you to faithfully "stand in the middle" while others lead the charge.

Either way, you will need to have the discipline to make sure you do your part in seeing that God's will is done.

Lord, help me to love the place of service you have for me and give me the discipline to "stand in the middle," if that's where you want me to serve.

TO READ
John 5:1-15

"Who said such a thing as that?" they demanded.

JOHN 5:12

What's Your Story?

The most useful, influential tool you own is the story of your life.

The man who was asked the question in today's verse had been sick for thirty-eight years. He had been immobile for so long that it became normal to him. He had never accomplished anything noteworthy. Everybody knew him, yet nobody wanted to be like him.

When this man encountered Jesus, his entire life changed. In an instant, he was healed. He could walk! He suddenly had a story he couldn't keep to himself. What Jesus had done for this man left him no choice but to tell the story. Everybody who heard his story asked questions. "Who did this for you?" "Where is he now?" No doubt some who heard this man's story were also forced to ask some hard questions about their own lives.

In some ways, your life story is no different from the story of the man Jesus healed that day. You are the only one who can tell your life story. You are the only one who can tell others about how you met Jesus, where he has taken you, and what he has done for you. You are the only one who can tell of your struggles and accomplishments in your walk with him.

You need to tell your story over and over again, because when you do, somebody will be blessed and encouraged. Besides, you are the only one who can tell it.

Lord, remind me daily that the story of my walk with you is of great value.

TO READ
Psalm 37:23-40

The steps of the godly are directed by the Lord. He delights in every detail of their lives. PSALM 37:23

Redeeming the Negatives

As I was growing up, my mother was afraid of many things in life. She had grown up in an unpredictable, alcoholic home, and as a result, she carried many emotional scars. Those scars caused her to work hard to control her environment. When she was afraid, part of that control came out as lecturing.

It was not uncommon for my mother to lecture me for two or three hours at a time. If I didn't pay close attention or if I so much as smirked at Mom during one of her lectures, it would last longer. I learned at a very young age to be a good listener. You could say that listening was one of my survival skills early in life, and it was something God knew I would need later on.

I have often asked God why I had to grow up with a mother who was afraid of people, afraid of my siblings and me growing up, afraid of life. While I have never received what I would consider a satisfactory answer to that question, I can see in hindsight that God has used my mother's fear for good in my life. He redeemed her fear and used it to help motivate me to live by faith so that fear would never be the defining factor in my life. He redeemed Mom's lecturing and used it to help me develop good listening skills, which have since proved extremely useful in my ministry.

Looking back on my time growing up, I can see that even before I met God, he was at work in my life, turning what could have been negative into good.

When you look back as far as you can in your own life, can you see instances where God was at work? He was using negatives to build positives when you weren't even aware of what he was doing. How has he done that specifically? Have you taken the time to thank him for doing so?

God, thank you for redeeming what could have been negatives by using them for good.

TO READ
John 5:18-46

The Jewish leaders tried all the more to kill him. In addition to disobeying the Sabbath rules, he had spoken of God as his Father, thereby making himself equal with God. JOHN 5:18

Who Is Jesus?

The most important question in the life of every man is this: Who is Jesus?

Jesus spoke with confidence and authority about his true identity because he knew he was telling the truth. Some hated him for speaking that truth. The Jewish leaders of his time became angry when they heard who Christ claimed to be. They were incensed that Jesus called himself the Son of God and referred to God as his Father.

I recently talked with a young man who, like those Jewish leaders, struggled to accept Jesus as the Son of God and the Savior of humankind. I talked to him about the biblical evidence of who Jesus is, but he just couldn't accept it. I pointed out the evidence of Christ's resurrection and how he had announced ahead of time that it would happen, but the young man couldn't believe it. Instead, he tried to explain away the evidence of Christ's identity, saying that the Bible is just another religious book. When I asked him what he based his beliefs on, he did not have an answer.

Finally I asked this young skeptic, "You are deciding your entire future on conjecture, aren't you?"

Sadly, his response was, "Yes. I think that is what we all do."

How do you answer the question, who is Jesus? On what do you base your answer? What you believe about the identity of Jesus will make all the difference in how you live your life and where it is headed. And how you answer questions about the identity of Jesus may make a difference in the lives of others.

Jesus, thank you for showing me that you truly are the Savior of the world.

TO READ
Joshua 4:1-8

These stones will stand as a permanent memorial among the people of Israel. JOSHUA 4:7

Remembering God's Goodness

One of the most strenuous but most rewarding events my family has gone through was the construction of our home. Our entire family and a lot of friends were involved. Even my sons, who were only six and four years old when we started, wanted to do their part. They took their turns swinging hammers and acting like they were "big boys."

When we finished the building of our home, it seemed only fitting that we mark the completion of the task with something that would last forever. So my boys put their handprints in the concrete driveway. My sons are teenagers now, but every time I pull into our driveway, I remember that our house is not just a building in which we live but a home full of memories.

Some things in life should never be forgotten.

The nation of Israel's crossing of the Jordan River was a miracle that would never be repeated. God did it to show his people that he supported them in the extremely important task of settling in the land of Canaan. Their entire future hung on the success of their conquest, and God wanted them to know that he was fully invested in what he had called them to do.

To ensure the people of Israel would never forget God's faithfulness and power, they built a memorial of stones to commemorate their river crossing.

God has done things in your life he wants you to remember. He's provided for you, done miracles for you, and given you salvation through the work of his Son, Jesus Christ. What can you do today to make sure you never forget these events?

Lord, remind me often of the events in my life that have shaped who I am in you.

TO READ
Joshua 4:8-24

They took twelve stones from the middle of the Jordan River, one for each tribe, just as the Lord had commanded Joshua. They carried them to the place where they camped for the night and constructed the memorial there. JOSHUA 4:8

The Importance of Your History

God is writing a unique story of your life. He chose your history for you. He chose your parents, and he chose the time and place of your birth. He chose the unique features you possess. These are the things that "represent" who you are today.

In the same way, God wanted the nation of Israel represented by twelve stones, "one for each tribe." Each Israelite was born into a certain tribe. Each had a unique history God had chosen for them. God was weaving the events of each of their lives into a unique and dramatic story of influence, power, and victory.

My own history includes a father who loved his job. Dad was an aerospace engineer who spent his entire adult career designing rocket engines. His role was to figure out how to start them, accelerate them, decelerate them, and finally shut them down. "I can't believe they pay me to do this," Dad often told me. Like most men of his generation, he had evaluated his career options on the basis of what he really wanted to do for the rest of his life. It was an easy decision for him because he still had a youthful enthusiasm for working with rockets.

Only God fully knows why I grew up with a father like mine. I have realized, however, that growing up with Dad led me to follow his example and find a career that I loved and that would give me fulfillment.

How has the story God has written for your life brought you to where you are now? Have you thanked God for those events in your history?

Lord, thank you for the things in the story of my life that have molded me and put me where you want me.

TO READ
Acts 1:1-8

On one occasion, while he was eating with them, he gave them this command: "Do not leave Jerusalem, but wait for the gift my Father promised, which you have heard me speak about." ACTS 1:4, NIV

A Time to Wait and Watch

Steve Young was one of the greatest quarterbacks ever to play in the National Football League. But for years he had to wait and watch from the bench as Joe Montana—who many think was *the* greatest quarterback ever to play the game—set passing record after passing record for the San Francisco 49ers.

Another quarterback, Frank Reich, had been a backup his entire career. All he had done was wait and watch as starter Jim Kelly led the Buffalo Bills to victory. Then it came time for Frank to step up in a 1993 wildcard game in Buffalo. He led his team to the greatest comeback victory in NFL playoff history, overcoming a 32-point deficit to defeat the Houston Oilers 41 to 38.

There is a time to wait and watch, and there is a time for action.

The Bible contains many examples of men who had to wait and watch until God called them to action. Elisha waited for years while he watched Elijah perform miracles. And John the Baptist waited and watched as Jesus' ministry grew and his own following dwindled.

Before the apostles could experience the birth of the church, they had to wait. One of the greatest days in the history of the world was about to take place. The Holy Spirit was on the verge of taking residence in the lives of believers and empowering them to do great works for Christ. But first they had to wait!

Sometimes God will call you to wait and watch as others do great things for him. When that happens, you need to be content to serve behind the scenes. But you also need to keep yourself ready, for you never know when God will call you to step up.

Lord, give me as much enthusiasm for waiting and watching others do your will as I have for doing it myself.

TO READ
Ephesians 4:1-6

Be humble and gentle. Be patient with each other, making allowance for each other's faults because of your love. EPHESIANS 4:2

✤ *It's Worth It*

One day my wife, Pam, called me because she'd encountered an unexpected situation and needed my help.

"Bill, I ran out of gas. Can you come rescue me?" She told me where her car was. "I am going down the road a couple of blocks to my appointment. Can you take care of my car and meet me there?"

Wanting to be a good guy, I decided to do the noble thing. I grabbed a gas can and drove to the place where Pam had told me she left the car. But when I arrived, the car was gone. I knew it couldn't have been stolen because it was out of gas! I found out that the car had been towed and impounded. As I drove down the street to where I needed to pick up Pam, I was thinking, *I can't believe this is happening. Pam is so intelligent, and she has such a great impact on other people. Why can't she remember simple things like getting gas? So, how am I going to respond to this? I want to be mad at her. I guess I need to just bear with her on this.*

As we drove to the impound lot, Pam started running herself down. "I can't believe I did this. I do things like this too much."

I realized that she was being hard enough on herself for the both of us! So I decided to be the heroic one.

"Pam," I interrupted, "if this is all it costs me to be married to you, it is well worth it."

The atmosphere suddenly lightened up. By the time we got Pam's car back, that "tank of gas" had cost me $148—but my friendship with Pam took a big step forward.

Who are the people in your life that most need you to bear with them?

God, give me strength to value people over convenience.

TO READ
Ezra 3:1-13

Despite their fear of the peoples around them, they built the altar on its foundation and sacrificed burnt offerings on it to the Lord, both the morning and evening sacrifices. EZRA 3:3, NIV

Getting Past Fear

Brad made some very poor choices when he was in college. One night he went to a party, drank too much alcohol, and got on his motorcycle to ride home. But he never made it home that night. He lost control of his bike and slammed into a telephone pole. When he woke up the next morning, his left leg had been amputated just below the knee, and his left arm had been amputated just below the elbow. To say the least, he was disillusioned with life.

Brad grieved the loss of his abilities for months. In his shame, he humbly turned his heart to God and pleaded with him to restore his hope and give some new direction to his life.

In the course of his recovery, doctors asked Brad if he wanted to try an athletic prosthesis. The thought turned something on inside him. He loved to water ski and snow ski but hadn't believed he would ever be able to do either one of those again. He was afraid to even get his hopes up. But despite the fear, he said, "Yes. Let's give it a try."

Getting used to the new leg was awkward and painful at first. The spring that was built into the leg to make it more responsive to athletic activity also made it harder to control. The process of "learning" how to move with this device was agonizingly slow and frustrating. But he pushed on.

When I met Brad, he was a member of the U.S. Handicapped Ski Racing Team. He competed in the downhill, slalom, and giant slalom. When I asked him how he did it, his response was, "The hard part was getting over the fear. Once I decided to move forward despite my fear, it all came together."

What fear do you need to push past in order to accomplish God's will?

Jesus, help me to never define my life by what I fear.

TO READ
John 1:1-7

God sent John the Baptist to tell everyone about the light. JOHN 1:6-7

What's Really in a Name

John the Baptist was a man of destiny. Before John was born, God had chosen him to announce the coming of the Messiah. He was different from other people. He lived in the wilderness, dressed in rough clothes, and ate an unconventional diet of locusts and honey. He was bold in his message of repentance yet humble as he baptized Jesus. He knew his role, for he pointed to Jesus, "the lamb of God who takes away the sin of the world" (John 1:29). John was willing to take a back seat when it was Jesus' time to shine.

John is a common, simple name. But when it refers to John the Baptist, it's a name that means something, a name that brings to mind a picture of one who was willing to do great things in the name of his God.

When my oldest son was born, the realization hit me that this young man would carry my name his entire life. I wondered if he would be proud to do so. I wondered if my name had a heritage worth emulating. Would he look others in the eye and confidently say, "I am proud to carry my father's name"? Or would he see my name as a burden and feel the need to recover from carrying it?

As my son was growing up, I knew he wasn't thinking about what it meant to carry my name. He was too busy enjoying life as a child. But even then I wanted the fact that he carried my name to mean something. So one day I looked him in the eyes and said, "Hello, partner. Together we are going to discover manhood. Let's make our name mean something."

Having your children grow up bearing your name will mean something. What do you want it to mean to them?

Lord, may I live in such a way that my name inspires those I care about most.

TO READ
John 1:8-18

John himself was not the light; he was only a witness to the light. JOHN 1:8

❋ The One True Hero

When I was growing up, my favorite cartoon characters were the super-heroes. But I didn't just *watch* those characters—I *was* those characters. I flew with Superman, swam with Aquaman, and climbed buildings and swung through the city with Spiderman. In a childlike but very real way, it was my dream to do something heroic with my life.

As children, it was acceptable for us to have dreams of being superheroes, but society tells us that as we grow up, we are supposed to develop a more mature approach to life. I thought I would eventually out-grow my desire to be a hero, but today that longing is just as strong as it has always been. It drives me as a father, because I want my kids to see that they are worth the effort I put into raising them. It adds to my motivation as a pastor, because I want my ministry to give people real help in their lives. And it pushes me in my relationship with my wife, because I want her to always have "that look" in her eyes when she sees me.

But I have to come to grips with the fact that there is really only one perfect hero, and his name is Jesus.

John the Baptist was a great and godly man, but he was not the hero the world had been waiting for. Rather, he was the one who would shine some light on the true hero so that the world could see him.

We are all capable of some pretty remarkable accomplishments, some of which might be considered heroic. But none of us can ever be the hero the world needs. Our job is to shine our light and point people to the one true and perfect hero—Jesus.

God, use my life to steer people toward you so that they can have a real hero in their lives.

TO READ
John 1:35-44

Andrew, Simon Peter's brother, was one of these men who had heard what John said and then followed Jesus. JOHN 1:40

❋ *Only the Best!*

Andrew had been part of a very successful religious movement led by John the Baptist. At the time, nobody was bigger news than John. He was well-known, influential, and young. There appeared to be no end to his ministry. The men who had chosen to follow him were enjoying God's blessing every day.

Then came Jesus. He was bigger news than John the Baptist. He was unknown at first, but his presence was undeniable. John was doing awesome work, but there was something more about Jesus. He spoke with authority, walked with determination, and performed with power unlike anything John's followers had ever seen.

Andrew had to choose. If he stayed with John, he would have a life of God's blessings. But when Jesus confronted Andrew, he realized this man was offering something more.

When I first met Jesus, I was enjoying a good life. I was getting good grades, competing successfully in sports, and enjoying the respect of my teachers and peers. But Jesus offered me something none of these things could provide. I knew that money, personal achievement, and popularity with people could never compare with Jesus.

I realized that good is only good enough until you find something better. And I found more than "better"; I found the best in Jesus.

Are you in a place in your life where you are settling for "good" or striving for "better," when you should be seeking the best? Nothing this world has to offer can compare with the best God has to offer, and that's Jesus Christ.

Jesus, never allow me to settle for the good when I can have the best in you.

TO READ
John 2:1-11

Jesus and his disciples were also invited to the celebration. JOHN 2:2

✳ *Lord of the Ordinary*

So much of what God does in our lives takes place against the backdrop of ordinary events. In following Jesus, the disciples had to attend what they no doubt considered an ordinary, everyday event: a wedding.

I have never met a man who really looks forward to weddings. He goes because they are important to others. He goes because of friendship. He goes because his family expects him to. But he doesn't go to weddings for the sheer joy of it. To the average man, a wedding is an ordinary event— one he would skip if he could.

I can only imagine what the disciples were thinking when Jesus told them they would be going to a wedding: *Oh, great! We get to go to a wedding. I wonder if Jesus really likes weddings or if he feels he needs to attend. How much pull does his mother have in his life?*

But at the scene of this ordinary event, the disciples, along with the other wedding guests, had the opportunity to witness Jesus' first public miracle— turning water into wine. Jesus hadn't announced ahead of time what he planned to do that day. He hadn't given the disciples a heads-up to let them know that this day would be the beginning of their ministry.

Some of the most important events in my life took place on very ordinary days. The day I became aware of my need for Jesus started out as a very ordinary day. Likewise, the day I met Pam, the woman who would become my wife, was an ordinary day. So was the day I met my best friend and the day I met the man who would become my most influential mentor.

Does life seem very ordinary to you right now? Then look up! God may be about to do something extraordinary for you very soon.

Jesus, teach me to expect you to do extraordinary things on my most ordinary days.

TO READ
John 2:13-17

Jesus made a whip from some ropes and chased [the merchants and money changers] out of the Temple. He drove out the sheep and oxen, scattered the money changers' coins over the floor, and turned over their tables. JOHN 2:15

A Real Man

Jesus was a *real* man. Yes, he was kind and forgiving, but this "meek and mild" Jesus wasn't afraid to confront. We all know and embrace the Jesus who forgives and loves, but we tend to shy away from the Jesus who chased people out of the temple with a whip, don't we?

Jesus came to forgive and to redeem, but he also calls men to confront obstacles in life in the same way that he confronted the merchants who were misusing the house of God. For example, when Jesus walked on water, he called Peter out to join him. When the five thousand men and their families needed to be fed, Jesus told the disciples to feed them. And when Peter questioned him about paying taxes, Jesus told him to go to the lake and look in the mouth of the first fish he pulled out.

Jesus calls men to be strong and to walk by faith. This means confronting obstacles and taking risks. This means stepping out and doing and saying the things he would have us do and say.

We men like the "strong" things in life. We like the rush of closing a big negotiation. We like fast, powerful machines. We like building things with our hands. We like the drama of athletic competition. In other words, we like to solve problems.

We men feel strong when we get the opportunity to confront and conquer an obstacle. Jesus teaches us to do that while at the same time being humble, meek, and gentle, as he was. In following his example, we discover part of what it means to be a real man.

Jesus, help me find the balance between being meek and being one who confronts obstacles.

TO READ
John 2:18-22

"What!" they exclaimed. "It took forty-six years to build this Temple, and you can do it in three days?" But by "this temple," Jesus meant his body.

JOHN 2:20-21

Holding to the Truth

From the perspective of the religious leaders in Jesus' day, the Temple of God was a building made of stone and mortar. They didn't understand that Jesus was God, and therefore his body was the temple of God.

These men's perspective was so limited that they couldn't see the forest for the trees. All Jesus could do was speak the truth to try to shock them into awareness.

I have a number of friends who won't accept the fact that Jesus is the only way to a relationship with God and the only way to eternal life. They desperately want to believe that all roads lead to the same place.

One of these friends said, "I can't accept that God would send some people to hell. I believe that anyone who sincerely seeks spirituality ought to be allowed into heaven."

"Emotionally, I want to agree with you," I told him. "But that doesn't make it true. I don't like knowing that people who do not know Jesus will suffer for eternity, but I am still convinced that it is true. Jesus is the only person on earth who lived, died, then came back to life. He knows exactly what is going on, and he always reports accurately."

My friend's response still echoes in my mind: "I admire you for holding to your beliefs, but I just can't accept that."

During the course of our walk with Jesus, we are sure to encounter those who, for one reason or another, are not willing to accept the truth of who Jesus is. But that doesn't make it any less true. We should be willing to hold to that truth and continue speaking it, regardless of what others do with it.

Lord, help me cling to and speak the truth of who you are, regardless of how others respond to it.

TO READ
John 2:22-25

But Jesus didn't trust them, because he knew what people were really like. No one needed to tell him about human nature. JOHN 2:24-25

The Dark Side

It is an enormous challenge to come to grips with the dark parts of our souls. Within every man's heart is a sinister place where he hides the evils that could destroy him. Sexual sin, the hunger for power, the desire for control, violence, and intimidation all lurk in this dark place. A man's decisions regarding what he does with these dark companions determine the strength and quality of his life.

It can be disheartening to see this dark side in action. Most of us have had good friends who chose to become either strangers or enemies. Many of us have friends who shocked us by revealing hidden sins and habits they'd engaged in for decades. All of us have been amazed at how angry some men can get over the most meaningless things.

People were saying great things about Jesus. They publicly noticed his accomplishments and offered him their allegiance. But Jesus knew the dark side of their hearts. He knew that in an instant they could go from supporting him to subverting his work. Yet he loved them. He was on earth to provide eternal life for people just like these, and in order to accomplish this mission, he had to walk a fine line of loving them without fully trusting them.

All of us must walk the same line Jesus walked as we learn to love others. We must love those around us yet still be aware of that dark side within them. And we must realize that we, too, have that very same darkness within our own hearts.

Lord, give me the strength to overcome the dark side of my soul. Help me respond to the dark side in others.

TO READ
John 3:23-36

At this time John the Baptist was baptizing at Aenon, near Salim, because there was plenty of water there and people kept coming to him for baptism.

JOHN 3:23

✳ *Necessary Resources*

You cannot fulfill the purpose for which God has called you without the necessary resources. For that reason, God will often use the resources around you to lead you where he wants you to go.

John the Baptist was a good example of this. God had called him to baptize people. But John could not baptize anyone without water, so to fulfill his calling, he chose places where there was plenty of water.

I attended a pastor's conference where Dr. Howard Hendricks from Dallas Theological Seminary was the speaker. It was refreshing to listen to him because of his vast experience.

One person asked him, "How do you do it all? You teach at the seminary, write books, and speak at conferences. And you have a family."

His answer? "I recover quickly. If I get one good night's sleep, I am ready to go for another week. If God hadn't given me that ability, I could not have had this ministry."

Dr. Hendricks's answer forced us all to ask, *God, what ability have you provided or what resources have you made available to me so that I can do your will?*

God may have given you an unusually high energy level or the ability to work with your hands. He may have blessed you with the ability to speak publicly or organize behind the scenes. Maybe you've been given an abundance of money or technical expertise. The list of possible resources goes on and on. You have been given something that enables you to take part in God's plan to redeem humankind. What will you do with your resources?

Lord, what have you provided in my life to fulfill your purpose in me?

I sent you to harvest where you didn't plant; others had already done the work, and you will gather the harvest. JOHN 4:38

Remembering Those Who Gave

I have an eighty-year-old friend who remembers when his father bought his first pickup truck and drove it for the first time. To get it to stop, he pulled back on the wheel and shouted, "Whoa!"—just like he did with his horses. Of course, the truck didn't stop, and he drove it right into a ditch. He walked back to his farm, hitched up his horses, and towed the truck back to the barn, where it stayed until it became my friend's first vehicle.

Throughout history, some people have had a difficult time adjusting to "new" technology. But previous generations also worked tirelessly to develop a society in which we could flourish. Their relentless pursuit of technological advances has given us privileges that no previous generation has enjoyed. We can wash our dishes and clothes in machines. We can transmit information around the globe in a matter of moments.

Just as we today benefit from the work of others in past generations, those who served Jesus during his earthly ministry benefited from the work of those people of God who lived in centuries past.

Jesus' disciples were simply added to the long list of men and women God had incorporated into his plan for bringing salvation to humankind. Some succeeded magnificently, and some even lost their lives in the struggle. Most faced insurmountable obstacles.

Who are the people who established a spiritual heritage for you? What obstacles did they face? How did they encourage you in your faith? What spiritual legacy will you pass on as a result?

Jesus, thank you for those people who have helped bring me the privilege of knowing you.

TO READ
John 5:16-47

You search the Scriptures because you believe they give you eternal life. But the Scriptures point to me! Yet you refuse to come to me so that I can give you this eternal life. JOHN 5:39-40

Getting the Point

It is possible for someone to spend years diligently studying God's Word and still miss the point. It's true now, and it was true two thousand years ago.

In today's Scripture passage, we read about Jesus addressing the spiritual leaders of the nation of Israel, who had spent most of their adult lives looking deeply into the truths of what we now call the Old Testament. They could describe the events in Scripture in vivid detail, but they had missed the point—Jesus himself.

I once took a group of college students to our local college campus to talk with a number of followers of Hare Krishna who were holding a festival. We engaged in a fascinating conversation with them in which it became obvious they were dedicated to their religion and had studied a number of religious books, including the Bible. I read John 14:6 to them—"No one can come to the Father except through me"—and asked them if they could interpret it for me.

One of them responded, "If you are a Christian, that is true for you."

"So it isn't true for everyone? It is only true for Christians?" I asked in astonishment.

"That is correct," he confidently said.

Like the Jewish leaders of Jesus' day, this devoutly religious young man knew the details of Jesus' teaching, but he had missed the point.

When God gave us the Bible, he gave us everything we need in order to know him intimately and to live the kind of life he wants us to live. We need to make sure we never miss the point of his written Word.

Jesus, help me to always get the point of your Word.

TO READ
John 6:1-14

Then Andrew, Simon Peter's brother, spoke up. "There's a young boy here with five barley loaves and two fish. But what good is that with this huge crowd?" JOHN 6:8-9

More Than Enough

Sometimes our greatest moments of growth occur in the midst of stress. In today's Scripture reading, Jesus intentionally put the disciples in a stressful situation so that they could grow in their faith.

Jesus challenged the disciples to figure out a plan for feeding thousands of hungry people. Jesus knew exactly how he was going to meet that need, but rather than tell the disciples his plan, he asked them to solve it themselves. There was, after all, a lesson to be learned that day.

Philip immediately did the math and concluded that it would have required eight months' wages to pull off the task. Of course, the disciples didn't have eight months' wages at their disposal, so the conclusion was obvious—this was an impossible situation. You can just hear Philip announcing to the other eleven disciples, "There is no hope of us getting this done."

Then Andrew told Jesus what they did have at their disposal. It wasn't much—only five small loaves of bread and two small fish that a small boy had been carrying—but it was something. Compared with the need, it might as well have been nothing. But it was the best anyone had to offer. As it turns out, it was enough.

Jesus took the bread and fish, blessed them, and began giving. By the time he was finished giving, everyone in the crowd of thousands had more than enough to eat. Not only that, there were twelve baskets of leftovers!

There are two reasons the five loaves of bread and two fish were enough. First, it was the best any of the disciples had to offer. Second, and more importantly, it was in the hands of Jesus.

Lord, as I give you the best I have to give, please multiply it with your power.

TO READ
John 6:22-32

They replied, "What does God want us to do?"

JOHN 6:28

Seeking His Plan

I had been the pastor of our church for ten years before I realized the importance of seeking *God's* plan for my ministry, not my own.

I was taking a certain approach to figuring out how to maximize our church's impact on the community. First I would determine what the people of the church were willing to do, then I would lead them with that in mind. The congregation was a creative, hardworking group of people, so we accomplished some amazing things. Our drama presentations were second to none. We had a thriving women's ministry. We had a large, active youth ministry.

But in the midst of all this success, something was missing. We were not experiencing the kind of joy I had expected. In fact, we were getting tired and burned-out.

I knew we needed a different approach. One day I decided I would ask God what he wanted us to do rather than asking the people what they were willing to do. *Lord,* I prayed, *what do you want to do in this ministry?*

It was an awesome experience. New thoughts and ideas immediately began to flood my mind. A plan bigger than I ever could have dreamed up on my own instantly began to form. It was a plan big enough to include anyone who wanted to get involved. It would achieve worldwide as well as local and personal impact. It was too big a plan for us to accomplish on our own, but I knew it was exactly what God wanted us to do.

Do you want to accomplish great things for the kingdom of God? If so, don't ask yourself what *you* want to do; instead, ask God what *he* wants you to do.

Jesus, remind me to ask you for your vision for my life rather than following my own.

TO READ
John 6:33-40

It is my Father's will that all who see his Son and believe in him should have eternal life—that I should raise them at the last day.   JOHN 6:40

✿ *A Journey to Manhood*

In my late twenties, I was wrestling with the realities of my journey into manhood. I was hungry to learn and be successful. Today's verse sharpened the focus of that hunger for me. I realized that I had been forgiven for every wrong decision I would make along the way. I had been given eternal life. The God of the universe would be looking after me. I was left wondering, *If Jesus has already provided for my needs, what should I put my efforts toward?*

I was reminded of a very simple illustration I had heard in college. A fellow student encouraged me to picture my life as an endless line with a dot as its starting point. That beginning dot represents my life here on earth. It is just a small dot on the line, but it gets everything started. Once I visualized my life that way, I was asked this searching question: "Are you going to invest in the entire line or just in the dot?"

It was if the doors of my mind were blown open! In the dot I would develop a career, have an active ministry, and influence people's lives. In the dot I would get married, have children, and impact future generations. In the dot I would buy and sell houses, drive cars, and utilize a wide range of technology. I was captivated by the thought, *If all this happens in the dot, imagine the possibilities along the line.*

I became hungry to live a life that would be significant forever. Spiritual disciplines became strategic activities. Personal relationships became valuable investments.

What are you hungry for? What can you do today that will invest in both the dot and the line?

Jesus, grant me an eternal perspective as I choose ways to invest in my life on earth.

TO READ
John 6:35-58

Jesus replied, "Don't complain about what I said."

JOHN 6:43

Our Limited Understanding

The crowd was confused. Jesus had just announced that he was the bread of life who came down out of heaven. But they thought they knew Jesus and understood his history. They knew his parents, and they knew his brothers and his sisters. They could talk about his birth and his childhood. They watched him grow up, get his education, and develop his career. But they just could not grasp what he meant when he said he had come down from heaven. And if they couldn't understand his words of truth, they weren't going to accept them. In their confusion, they began to grumble among themselves.

Jesus' response to the crowd's complaints was startling. Rather than take the time to explain what he meant when he said he was the bread of life, he simply told them, "Don't complain about what I said." It was as if he was saying, "Sit down and be quiet. You don't have all the answers, and you never will. Your job is just to listen and learn."

Part of the call to follow Jesus is learning to live with ambiguity. It's realizing that God is bigger and smarter than we are. He is beyond us. As a result, there is much about him we know to be true even though it is beyond our ability to fully understand.

And well it should be. If we could fully understand God, he would be no greater than we are. We will never be able to fully understand the person of God, nor should we try. We must settle for knowing what he has revealed about himself in his written Word, the Bible.

Lord, rescue me from needing to fully understand you. Teach me to allow you to be bigger than I am.

TO READ
John 6:60-66

Even his disciples said, "This is very hard to under-stand. How can anyone accept it?" JOHN 6:60

Hard Words

Jesus is the most caring, compassionate individual you will ever meet, but he has a lot of hard things to say to those who seek him.

Jesus had just finished telling the people around him that they could have eternal life only through him. In doing so, he challenged their entire belief system.

I remember one sermon I preached that demonstrated to me how hard Jesus' words are to take for those who seek to follow him.

That Sunday I was nervous because it was the first time my father heard me preach. Dad is a kind, respectful man who has never sensed a need to depend on God. Because of that, he has never understood the intensity with which I follow Jesus.

In my sermon, I pointed out that each man and woman has a sin nature and that the remedy for sin is a personal, heart-transforming relationship with Jesus Christ.

Afterward, I asked my dad what he thought of my sermon. I was hoping for encouragement.

But his response was, "I thought you were kind of hard on everyone."

In a way, I was grateful for Dad's observation. To those who don't know Jesus, his words are hard to take. Following him means changing in our hearts, our thinking, and our behavior. It means living a life contrary to what the world around us teaches.

It's a hard truth to take and sometimes an even harder truth to speak. But it's a truth we must never shy away from telling others.

Lord, prepare me and motivate me to boldly proclaim even your hardest teaching.

May

TO READ
John 7:1-11

"You can't become a public figure if you hide like this! If you can do such wonderful things, prove it to the world!" For even his brothers didn't believe in him. JOHN 7:4-5

The Right Agenda

Jesus' brothers were in a unique situation because they had grown up with him. The Bible gives few details about Jesus' childhood, but it appears that he grew up in a "normal" home. Jesus' brothers probably wrestled with one another and argued with one another. They regularly saw the best and worst in each other.

Now they were trying to figure out what Jesus was doing.

Jesus' brothers could see that he was influential and talented, and they assumed he wanted to be known far and wide. After all, conventional wisdom says that you should aggressively market yourself.

But Jesus was much too relaxed for his brothers' liking.

The real issue for Jesus' brothers is that they didn't believe he was who he said he was. They had concluded that the real Messiah would go public and take the world by storm. They had assumed the real Messiah would be more assertive in challenging the status quo.

Jesus' brothers tested him with a challenge to go public and prove who he was. But what they didn't realize was that they were the ones being tested. Jesus stuck to his agenda to see if they would make adjustments for one who was greater than they were.

What is your agenda for Jesus? Some people expect Jesus to make them happy. Others expect him to make them wealthy. Still others anticipate that he will make their lives easier. But Jesus' agenda is not always your agenda for him. When that happens, you need to decide whose agenda you will follow.

Jesus, help me to make your agenda my own.

TO READ
John 7:12-24

No one had the courage to speak favorably about him in public, for they were afraid of getting in trouble with the Jewish leaders. JOHN 7:13

Courage to Speak Up

Opinions about Jesus were mixed. Some said he was a great man, while others said he was a deceiver who could not be trusted. Everyone who met Jesus had a different opinion about him, but they all had one thing in common: They talked about him in private because they were afraid to say anything in public.

There was a cost to speaking out about Jesus then, and there still is today. It amazes me that we believers feel such fear when we tell our stories about Jesus. I've been there myself. There was a time early on in my Christian experience when I found myself surprisingly nervous when I shared my faith.

I once approached a peer on my college campus and asked him if I could read some literature to him that talked about the most important decision I had ever made. He said I could, so I sat down and started reading. But by the time I got to page two, I was running out of breath because of the tightness in my chest. I had to pause, catch my breath, and then continue.

Fortunately, the young man was patient with me. He even said he would think about what I had read to him.

I walked away from that scene feeling embarrassed but determined to not let fear run my ministry. Jesus was the most important person in my life, and I knew he was more powerful than any opposition I would face. It was time for my heart to catch up with my head.

In what situations are you most susceptible to fear or embarrassment? What could you do differently in those situations that would add more boldness to your story?

Jesus, give me a bold faith to fearlessly tell others my story.

TO READ
John 7:25-36

But how could he be? For we know where this man comes from. When the Messiah comes, he will simply appear; no one will know where he comes from. JOHN 7:27

Lord of the Ordinary

People often long for the spectacular in their spiritual lives. When spiritual truth is found in the mundane and the routine, it is not nearly as attractive or exciting. For that reason, many of Jesus' contemporaries wouldn't accept him as the Messiah.

The Jews of Jesus' day wanted a savior with an aura, a savior who came out of nowhere. But Jesus came in the flesh. He was born of a woman, and he appeared in most ways to be an ordinary man. And, early on anyway, he lived a very ordinary life.

It is tempting to look for Jesus in the spectacular, but we need him most—and we most often find him—in the everyday.

Loving your wife daily takes strength of character, the kind Jesus demonstrated in his everyday life. Investing in your kids through all their life transitions takes courage and wisdom, the kind Jesus showed in his every word and action. Being faithful in the daily demands of your career requires perseverance, the kind Jesus had as he lived a life of purpose. And forgiving others daily demands love, the kind Jesus demonstrated on the cross when he said, "Father, forgive these people, because they don't know what they are doing" (Luke 23:34).

We can certainly find Jesus in the mysterious and the amazing. He hears us when we pray, invisibly protects us from evil, and consistently prays on our behalf. And sometimes he does those things in spectacular fashion.

But where we find Jesus most is in our ordinary, daily routines.

Jesus, thank you that you are there in the ordinary, daily grind of life.

TO READ
John 7:37-44

On the last day, the climax of the festival, Jesus stood and shouted to the crowds, "If you are thirsty, come to me! If you believe in me, come and drink! For the Scriptures declare that rivers of living water will flow out from within." JOHN 7:37-38

Warning Signs

Three young men had taken summer jobs at Yellowstone National Park so they could put their responsibilities behind them for a time and enjoy the wonders of that magnificent place. One August day they were looking for some fun and decided to go swimming when they got off work.

Thinking they were diving into one of the many cool Yellowstone pools, the trio jumped in unison into a 178-degree hot spring. Some friends who happened to be nearby heard their screams and ran to help them out of the scalding water. For one of the men, it was too late. He was dead at the scene. The other two had severe burns all over their bodies.

This incident is especially tragic because it could have been avoided had the young men simply seen the warning signs. The thermal pools at Yellowstone National Park are surrounded by thin, fragile crusts that identify them as hot springs. In addition, numerous warning signs are posted around the pools. Either those swimmers missed the signs, or they ignored them.

Life is full of warning signs, isn't it?

Today's Scripture tells the story of Jesus posting a warning sign for people who had no idea that they were in trouble. Life for them was comfortable enough that they didn't recognize their desperate need for Jesus. But he knew their need. He knew that disaster was imminent if they did not heed his warnings, so he shouted out for all to hear.

Jesus wanted as many people as possible to hear him. Sadly, however, many people refused to heed his warning.

Are you heeding the warnings God has given you through his written Word?

Jesus, give me the will to heed the warnings you give me.

TO READ
John 7:45-49

"We have never heard anyone talk like this!" the guards responded. JOHN 7:46

Ultimate Authority

In April 2001, in the midst of a flare-up in the Israeli/Arab conflict, a motorcade carrying the Security Service chief of Gaza came under fire from Israeli troops. From his car, the frightened security official called Palestinian Liberation Organization leader Yasser Arafat for help. Arafat in turn called a United States ambassador, who then called U.S. secretary of state Colin Powell. Powell phoned Israeli prime minister Ariel Sharon, who ordered the shooting to stop immediately. And it did.

It is impressive to watch someone of authority in action. They are decisive and have the kind of influence that most people only dream of having. They make things happen—and right away.

Though Jesus bore no earthly title, he still had that kind of authority.

The chief priests and Pharisees had sent temple guards to arrest Jesus and bring him before them. This was an attempt to intimidate Jesus because he was taking away their influence. But the guards couldn't carry out this order. Why? Because they had never met anyone like him. Jesus spoke with authority like none they had ever heard. But his was not a harsh authority. Jesus never shied away from speaking the truth, but he also showed people that he genuinely cared for them.

These temple guards were thrown into turmoil that day because they had been ordered to arrest the best person they had ever met.

Jesus has ultimate authority over every person that will ever exist and every event that will ever take place. And that authority is a great blessing because he is genuinely and personally interested in you.

Will you choose today to live under that authority?

Jesus, show me how to willfully and gladly live under your authority, knowing how much you love me and care for me.

TO READ
John 7:50-53

Nicodemus, the leader who had met with Jesus earlier, then spoke up. JOHN 7:50

The Whole Nine Yards

The phrase *the whole nine yards* may have originated among fighter pilots serving in the South Pacific during World War II. The pilots' warplanes were armed with .50-caliber machine guns that reportedly used ammunition belts measuring exactly twenty-seven feet in length. Thus, when the pilots fired all their ammo at a target, the target was said to have gotten the whole nine yards.

Nicodemus, a prominent Jewish leader, was in the midst of a debate with his colleagues about the identity of Jesus. He had personally concluded that Jesus was the Jewish Messiah. He was, however, surrounded by leaders who were opposed to Jesus. In an attempt to keep his fellow Jewish leaders from coming to the wrong conclusion about Jesus, Nicodemus gave them the whole nine yards about who Jesus was.

But Nicodemus had to be careful. He knew that a full frontal attack would have removed him from the debate. To say nothing would be an act of cowardice he could not live with, so he strategically and wisely challenged them with the law in hopes that an analysis of their own teachings would bring them to understand who Jesus really was.

Everyone who pursues the truth about Jesus enters a battle, a battle he or she must fight wisely. There are two sides contending in this battle—the side who wants to believe the truth and the side who wants to believe a lie. We are to give this battle our whole nine yards, but there will come a time when both sides need to go home for the day.

The vital question for you is this: Will you give today's battle the best you have?

Oh Lord, teach me to give my whole nine yards for you.

TO READ
John 8:1-20

Jesus made these statements while he was teaching in the section of the Temple known as the Treasury. But he was not arrested, because his time had not yet come. JOHN 8:20

He's Always in Control

Jesus was debating the religious leaders of his day and making them angry. Much to their embarrassment, he was effectively and successfully arguing his points over and over again. He fielded their every challenge with skill and answered their every question with far-reaching insight.

These men violently disagreed with Jesus, but they couldn't arrest him "because his time had not yet come." That time would be of his Father's choosing.

It is difficult for some to believe that nothing ever happened to Jesus that he did not allow. But Jesus has never been a victim and has never been taken advantage of or outwitted. Everything he suffered, he suffered voluntarily. He allowed men to arrest him, try him, beat him, then hang him on a cross. He had to give up his life because, as the Son of God, no one could take it from him. And he did all of this so that even his opponents would have the opportunity to come to their senses and repent.

Jesus calls us to do the very same thing today.

You may be facing opposition. If so, remember that none of it surprises your Savior or escapes his notice. And also remember that the challenges you now face may be for the benefit of others.

Jesus suffered so we could have life, and he allows us to suffer so others can see his faithfulness demonstrated in our lives. The hope is that they too will come to their senses and repent.

Are you willing to allow him to use you that way as part of his plan?

Jesus, remind me that you are always in control, that you chose to suffer for my benefit, and that you allow me to suffer for the benefit of others.

TO READ
John 8:21-24

Then [Jesus] said to them, "You are from below;
I am from above. You are of this world; I am not."

JOHN 8:23

God's Mind and Our Limited Understanding

In his written Word, the Bible, God consistently explains to us the realities
of life, but our limited capacity of mind puts us at a serious disadvantage as
we try to understand. For that reason, we often find it impossible to fully
understand just what God is doing in our lives.

In his book *Detours: Sometimes Rough Roads Lead to Right Places*, author
Clark Cothern illustrates how God's thoughts are above our own. He tells
of a Christmas when his family encountered a squirrel that had fallen down
their chimney into the wood-burning stove:

> I thought if it knew we were there to help, I could just reach in and gently lift it
> out. Nothing doing. As I reached in . . . it began scratching about like a squirrel
> on espresso. We finally managed to construct a cardboard box "cage" complete
> with a large hole cut into one side, into which the squirrel waltzed when we
> placed the box against the wood burner's door. We let it out into the safety of
> our backyard.
>
> Later, I thought, isn't it funny how, before its redemption, our little visitor
> had frantically tried to bash its way out of its dark prison? It seemed that the
> harder it struggled in its own strength to get free, the more pain it caused itself.
> In the end, he simply had to wait patiently until one who was much bigger—
> one who could peer into his world—could carry him safely into that larger
> world where he really belonged.[1]

We may be like that squirrel in that we don't understand what God is
trying to do for us—during the good times and during the difficult times.
Our responsibility is to trust him, even when we don't have all of the
answers.

Jesus, help me trust you even when I don't fully understand your plan.

TO READ
John 8:25-29

"Tell us who you are," they demanded. Jesus replied, "I am the one I have always claimed to be."

JOHN 8:25

A Matter of Faith

Though the truth of Jesus Christ is an old message, it has always been true and it always will be. Jesus has always been the only Son of God and the only Savior of the world.

Though Jesus had explained this truth numerous times, the Jewish leaders of his day were unwilling to accept it. He had illustrated it for them and backed it up with mountains of evidence. He had never changed his story, but they could not adjust their hearts to embrace it.

These religious men were not the only ones who wouldn't see the truth of Jesus.

In *World* magazine, famed interviewer Larry King was quoted as saying, "I can't make that leap that a lot of people around me have made into belief that there's some judge somewhere. . . . I have a lot of respect for true people of faith. . . . I've done so many interviews on it. I've always searched. But as someone said, 'Did you ever sit down and read the Bible cover to cover?' The answer's no, because I don't know who wrote it. I'm too into my head to be into faith. Faith is a wonderful thing. I envy people who have it. I just can't make the leap."[2]

Mr. King was correct in saying that believing God's message of salvation for humankind is a matter of faith. It's not a matter of head knowledge or of simply giving mental assent to the facts. Rather, it's a matter of allowing the truths of God's Word to touch your very heart.

Today, open your heart and listen. Jesus has clearly revealed himself in many different ways. He has not kept his identity hidden, but you must allow your heart to see the truth of who he is.

Lord, adjust my heart so that my ears can hear you and my eyes can see you.

TO READ
John 8:30-38

Then many who heard him say these things believed in him. Jesus said to the people who believed in him, "You are truly my disciples if you keep obeying my teachings." JOHN 8:30-31

Finish Well

Many of the people who heard Jesus speak were inspired enough by his words to put their faith in him. They believed he was the Messiah and anticipated that he would lead them. But Jesus knew obedience and focus were going to be vital to their spiritual survival. He understood that the starting line was their faith but the course of the race would require them to "keep obeying my teachings."

Then the people brought up the name of Abraham. Abraham started the race well by simply obeying God's words; he picked up and moved. Along the way he faced a remarkable struggle. He was promised a son, even though Sarah was past the years of childbearing. Abraham had no idea how this would happen, but he trusted God. After a while, his faith waned, and he took things into his own hands. As a result, Ishmael was born to one of Sarah's servants. After talking with God, Abraham regretted his actions and got back on track.

Not long after, Sarah became pregnant and gave birth to Isaac. Abraham was thrilled. He had a son, and the promise had come true.

But one day God asked Abraham to sacrifice his son of promise. Father and son made preparations, then traveled for days. Abraham tied his son up, laid him on the altar, and prepared to put him to death, when God dramatically stopped him and provided a ram to sacrifice instead. Abraham had finished well. In response, God called Abraham his friend.

God is looking to be your friend too. As your friend, he knows your reward is waiting at the finish line. What has God called you to that will require perseverance to finish? Take a step toward that finish line today.

Lord, help me run the race of my life with the finish line in sight.

TO READ
John 8:39-53

The people said, ". . . . Are you greater than our father Abraham, who died? Are you greater than the prophets, who died? Who do you think you are?"

JOHN 8:52-53

❋ *Confident Living*

Scott Adams, creator of the popular *Dilbert* cartoon, tells this story about his beginnings as a cartoonist:

> You don't have to be a "person of influence" to be influential. In fact, the most influential people in my life probably are not even aware of the things they've taught me. When I was trying to become a syndicated cartoonist, I sent my portfolio to one cartoon editor after another—and received one rejection after another. One editor even called and suggested that I take art classes. Then Sarah Gillespie, an editor at United Media and one of the real experts in the field, called to offer me a contract. At first, I didn't believe her. I asked if I'd have to change my style, get a partner—or learn how to draw. But she believed I was already good enough to be a nationally syndicated cartoonist. Her confidence in me completely changed my frame of reference and altered how I thought about my own abilities.[3]

Scott Adams didn't allow rejection or the doubt of others to keep him from doing what he knew he wanted to do.

Living with a purpose requires confidence, doesn't it?

Jesus was the most confident man who ever lived. He knew who he was, where he came from, and what he was doing on earth. But the religious leaders attempted to discourage Jesus from living out his Father's purpose in his life.

People today will try to discourage you from living out yours. But as you live out the purpose for which you know God has called you, you never need to allow the words or actions of others to discourage you.

Jesus, give me confidence to live out your purpose for my life—no matter how others may try to discourage me.

TO READ
John 8:54-59

Jesus answered, "If I am merely boasting about myself, it doesn't count. But it is my Father who says these glorious things about me." JOHN 8:54

Power and Responsibility

In the movie *Spider-Man*, before Peter Parker goes public with his newfound superpowers, he has a heart-to-heart conversation with his uncle. Sitting in the car, Ben admonishes him, "These are the years when a man becomes the man he's going to be for the rest of his life. Just be careful who you change into. You're feeling this great power, and with great power comes great responsibility."

The Jewish leaders challenged Jesus concerning his assertion that God had sent him into the world. Jesus conceded to these men that if he had been engaging in simple self-promotion, his ministry would have been worthless. But he went on to tell them that he could make these claims because he had the endorsement of God his Father.

In making this stunning statement, Jesus not only testified to the power of God in him, he also took on the responsibility of backing up his words. And he did—as he lived, suffered and died, then rose from the dead so that the world would know he was indeed who he had claimed to be.

Jesus had the responsibility of bringing salvation to the world. The disciples had the responsibility of bringing the New Testament to the world. And we as men have the responsibility of bringing the Good News of salvation to the world we live in.

Just as the Father empowered Jesus to do the work he came to the world to do, and just as the Holy Spirit empowered the disciples to carry out their mission, we have been empowered to take Jesus to the world around us.

Knowing that God has empowered us, each of us must ask ourselves this all-important question: *What am I going to do with that power?*

Lord, remind me daily that the power you give me comes with the great responsibility of using it to reach others for you.

TO READ	Lazarus came out, bound in graveclothes, his face
John 11:44-48	wrapped in a headcloth. Jesus told them, "Unwrap him and let him go!" JOHN 11:44

✱ A Spirit of Partnership

News stories called it "The Miracle at Quecreek." Nine Pennsylvania miners trapped for three days in a water-filled mine shaft 240 feet underground survived, largely because they decided early on that they were going to live as a group or die as a group.

The fifty-five-degree water threatened the men with slow death by hypothermia. But because they had chosen partnership, they held on. "When one would get cold, the other eight would huddle around the person and warm that person, and when another person got cold, the favor was returned," one of the survivors later said.

"Everybody had strong moments," miner Harry B. Mayhugh told reporters after being released from the local hospital. "But any certain time maybe one guy got down, and then the rest pulled together. And then that guy would get back up, and maybe someone else would feel a little weaker, but it was a team effort. That's the only way it could have been."[4]

Today's Scripture is an example of team effort. Jesus approached the tomb of Lazarus and called him out of the grave. Lazarus had been certifiably dead, but now he was alive. But when he came out of the tomb, he was still wrapped up like a mummy. In order to get Lazarus's family involved in what was happening, Jesus asked them to unwrap Lazarus.

God calls all of us men to partnership with him. That starts when he transforms our hearts through the work of Jesus Christ and continues as we choose to walk daily with him in obedience.

What does God want to accomplish today through your partnership with him?

Lord, thank you for calling me to walk in partnership with you. Show me daily my part in that partnership.

TO READ
Ezra 3:8-13

All the people gave a great shout, praising the Lord because the foundation of the Lord's Temple had been laid. EZRA 3:11

Celebrate the Small Stuff

Praise is a decision you make because you believe God is good. We praise him because he is powerful. We praise him because he is faithful. We praise him because he is always working his plan.

The nation of Israel was in the process of rebuilding the temple. They had raised the funds and collected the building materials. They had organized the workers and set construction schedules. They had a vision of what it would look like when it was finished. They dreamed of the days they would once again offer sacrifices in the presence of God.

But the work was just getting started. At the point in the story described in Ezra 3, the Israelites had only completed the foundation. Months of hard work lay ahead of them. But they celebrated anyway. The priests put on their robes, the musicians warmed up their voices and their instruments, and the people gathered together to worship.

Each of us should diligently look for opportunities to praise God. If you finish a project at work, praise God. If you make it home safely, praise God. If you complete anything on your "to do" list this weekend, praise God. If you get along with the most important people in your life today, praise God. If you resolve a conflict with anyone this week, praise God.

Think about the things happening in your life right now that can give you an opportunity to celebrate. Choose one that you would ordinarily take for granted, and celebrate the victory.

Jesus, thank you for the little things I can celebrate this week. Please give me the insight to recognize them.

TO READ
John 9:6-12

[Jesus] spit on the ground, made mud with the saliva, and smoothed the mud over the blind man's eyes. JOHN 9:6

Ordinary Items, Extraordinary Results

I recently received an e-mail containing a list of ordinary items that become extraordinary in the hands of the right people:

- A basketball in my hands is worth about $19. A basketball in Michael Jordan's hands is worth about $33 million. It depends whose hands it's in.
- A baseball in my hands is worth about $6. A baseball in Mark McGwire's hands is worth $19 million. It depends whose hands it's in.
- A tennis racket is useless in my hands. A tennis racket in Pete Sampras's hands is a Wimbledon Championship. It depends whose hands it's in.
- A rod in my hands will keep away a wild animal. A rod in Moses' hands will part the mighty sea. It depends whose hands it's in.
- A slingshot in my hands is a kid's toy. A slingshot in David's hands is a mighty weapon. It depends whose hands it's in.
- Two fish and five loaves of bread in my hands are a couple of fish sandwiches. Two fish and five loaves of bread in God's hands will feed thousands. It depends whose hands it's in.
- Nails in my hands might produce a birdhouse. Nails in Jesus Christ's hands will produce salvation for the entire world. It depends whose hands it's in.

Jesus is the master of transforming the ordinary. One day he met a man who was born blind. No one knew what to do to help him. Jesus spit on the ground, put the mud on the man's eyes, and told him to go wash it off. As the mud was washed off, the man's sight returned.

Is there any ordinary thing in your hands today that you can give to God? When you give it to him, watch out! There's no telling what God will do with it.

Lord, help me to realize that even the most ordinary thing I have to offer you can become extraordinary in your hands.

TO READ
2 Corinthians 4:1-6

The god of this age has blinded the minds of unbelievers, so that they cannot see the light of the gospel of the glory of Christ, who is the image of God. 2 CORINTHIANS 4:4, NIV

Ultimate Misconceptions

A missionary in Africa was trying to explain the Christian way of life to a very old tribal chief. After many hours, the aged warrior said, "I don't understand. You tell me I must not take my neighbor's wife, his ivory, nor his oxen. You also say that I must not dance the war dance, nor ambush my enemy on the trail and kill him."

"That's right!" came the missionary's enthusiastic response.

"But I can't do any of those things anyway," said the chief. "I'm too old for that. Being too old and being a Christian must be the same thing."

Similarly, people in every generation and every culture have made serious decisions in life based on their misconceptions. The most common ones I have heard in my life are

- "God wants me to be happy."
- "Everyone's doing it."
- "All faiths lead to the same place, so it doesn't matter what I believe."

I have watched people break up their families, risk their fortunes, and put their eternal destinies on the line because they believe that these misconceptions are true. The human heart loves to think it is right even when the facts don't line up.

What misconceptions are you tempted to trust? How do those beliefs stack up against God's Word? Do you rely on the Bible or on your misconceptions?

God, let me never build my life on my misconceptions.

TO READ
John 9:24-36

When Jesus heard what had happened, he found the man and said, "Do you believe in the Son of Man?" The man answered, "Who is he, sir, because I would like to." JOHN 9:35-36

❋ The Whole Story

The late Spencer Penrose, brother of Philadelphia political leader Boies Penrose, was regarded as an outcast by his family for choosing to live in the western part of the United States rather than the East. Spencer, fresh out of Harvard University, moved to Colorado Springs in 1897.

Spencer soon wired his brother and asked for a loan of $1,500 to get into a mining deal. His brother telegraphed him $150 for train fare home, warning against the deal. Spencer stayed right where he was.

Years later, Spencer returned to Philadelphia and handed Boies $75,000 in gold coins. Boies looked amazed, then reminded Spencer that he had sent him only $150. "That," replied Spencer, "is why I'm giving you only $75,000. If you'd sent me the $1,500, I would be giving you three-quarters of a million."

Sometimes not knowing the whole story can cost us!

The blind man Jesus healed had only half the story. He knew Jesus was powerful and compassionate because he had healed him. But he didn't yet know who Jesus was.

Some time after he was healed, Jesus asked him, "Do you believe in the Son of Man?" His best response was, "Who is he?"

Then Jesus filled him in on the rest of the story of his healing: The Son of God was the one who had so profoundly touched his body and his life.

We should never settle for knowing half the story. When Jesus makes an investment in our lives, we should ask him to reveal even more about himself. When we do that, we will not just believe in the Son of God, we'll get to know him in a deeper and more personal way.

Jesus, give me the wisdom to know the whole story of your investment in my life.

TO READ
John 9:37-38

"Yes, Lord," the man said, "I believe!" And he worshiped Jesus. JOHN 9:38

The Effects of Adversity

Adversity always changes us at our very core. Here is an illustration of that truth.

A daughter complained to her father about how hard things were for her. "As soon as I solve one problem," she said, "another one comes up. I'm tired of struggling."

Her father took her to the kitchen and filled three pots with water. In one pot he placed carrots, in another, eggs, and in the last, ground coffee beans. He let them sit and boil.

After a while, he put the carrots, eggs, and coffee in separate bowls. Turning to her, he asked, "Darling, what do you see?"

"Carrots, eggs, and coffee," she replied.

He explained that each of the items had faced the same adversity—boiling water—but each had reacted differently. The carrot went in strong, hard, and unrelenting, but after being subjected to the boiling water, it became soft and weak. The egg went into the water fragile—its thin outer shell protecting the liquid interior. But after sitting in the boiling water, its insides hardened. The ground coffee beans were different from the other two, however. Instead of being changed by the boiling water, they changed the water.

The man then asked his daughter, "When adversity knocks on your door, which are you?"

How does adversity affect you? Does it cause you to become soft and weak? Does it make you hard and immovable? Or does it drive you closer to Jesus?

Lord, use the adversity of life to make me strong enough to change the world around me.

TO READ
John 9:39-41

Then Jesus told him, "I have come to judge the world. I have come to give sight to the blind and to show those who think they see that they are blind."

JOHN 9:39

Faith: A Matter of the Heart

Vesper Bauer of Audobon, Iowa, recounts, "My aunt and uncle had a missionary family visiting. When the missionary children were called in for dinner, their mother said, 'Be sure to wash your hands.' The little boy scowled and said, 'Germs and Jesus. Germs and Jesus. That's all I hear, and I've never seen either one of them.' "[5]

There is something about the human spirit that longs to see. We believe that if only we could see something, then we would believe. We have a much harder time believing simply because we recognize something as truth.

People don't believe in Jesus just because they have all the facts or because they "see" him; they believe because God touches them on the inside in a way that softens their heart.

Jesus conducted his ministry out in the open for all to see. He did everything the Old Testament said the Messiah would do when he came. He displayed his compassion in healing, showed his power in miracles, and demonstrated his authority in teaching. But everyone who encountered Jesus still had to come to a point of making a decision. Those whose hearts were open recognized him as their Savior and followed him. Those whose hearts were closed became blind to who he was, sealing their judgment.

Jesus is impossible to fully understand or to fully explain. He is smarter than we can comprehend, bigger than we will ever be comfortable with, and merciful beyond our imagination. And at the same time, he is the one who explains everything.

Lord, give me a heart that believes, even when my eyes can't see you.

TO READ
John 9:40–10:5

After he has gathered his own flock, he walks ahead of them, and they follow him because they recognize his voice. JOHN 10:4

A Friend We Can Count On

John C. Maxwell and Dan Reiland include the following story in their book, *The Treasure of a Friend*:

> Though Jim was just a little older than Phillip and often assumed the role of leader, they did everything together. . . .
>
> After college, they decided to join the marines. By a unique series of circumstances, they were actually sent to Germany together where they fought side by side in one of history's ugliest wars.
>
> One sweltering day during a fierce battle, amid heavy gunfire, bombing, and close-quarters combat, they were given the command to retreat. As the men were running back, Jim noticed that Phillip had not returned with the others. . . .
>
> Jim begged his commanding officer to let him go after his friend, but in an outrage, the officer denied the request, saying it would be suicide.
>
> Risking his own life, Jim disobeyed and went after Phillip. His heart pounding, praying, and out of breath, he ran into the gunfire, calling out for Phillip. A short time later, his platoon saw him hobbling across the field carrying a limp body in his arms.
>
> Jim's commanding officer upbraided him, shouting that it was a foolish waste of time and an outrageous risk.
>
> "Your friend is dead," he added, "and there was nothing you could do."
>
> "No sir, you're wrong," Jim replied. "You see, I got there just in time. Before he died, his last words were, 'I knew you would come.' "[6]

Who are the friends you count on? Is Jesus one of them?

Jesus, thank you that you are a friend who will always be there for me.

TO READ
John 10:6-10

The thief's purpose is to steal and kill and destroy.
My purpose is to give life in all its fullness.

JOHN 10:10

Bigger Hands

Brian Harris of New Zealand tells the story of a young boy who went with his mother to the local store. The storeowner, a kindly man, passed him a large jar of suckers and invited him to help himself to a handful.

Uncharacteristically, the boy held back. So the storeowner pulled out a big handful of suckers and handed them to him.

Once they were outside, the boy's mother asked him why he had suddenly been so shy that he wouldn't put his hand in the jar and pull out a handful of suckers.

The lad looked up at his mother and replied, "Because his hand is much bigger than mine!"[7]

Indeed, there is a lot to be said for allowing someone with bigger hands to provide for us.

When Jesus compared his followers to sheep, he vividly portrayed what their lives in him were to look like. As his sheep, his followers were to fully depend on him and rest in the fact that he was watching over them and leading them.

As Jesus' sheep, we are confronted with a question: Will we follow the Shepherd and allow him to care for us and provide for us, or will we try to make our own way?

We need to remember always that our Shepherd came to give life in abundance. And we also need to remember that his hands are bigger and able to give much more than we could ever provide for ourselves.

Lord, help me never to settle for what my hands can produce when yours are so much bigger.

I am the good shepherd. The good shepherd lays down his life for the sheep. JOHN 10:11

Unselfish Sacrifice

Because you are a sheep of the Good Shepherd, he is committed to protecting you. In Jesus' day, sheep were often the victims of thieves and wild animals. They were totally unable to defend themselves, so it was up to the shepherd to keep them from harm.

In the same way, we are not able to provide salvation for ourselves. When it comes to the eternal, we are totally unable to defend ourselves from judgment. Our survival required our Good Shepherd to lay down his life so we could be safe. This kind of sacrifice proves the love of the shepherd for his sheep.

Jesus made the ultimate sacrifice. Every time people sacrifice for others, we are reminded of the true nature of love. We put aside our selfishness and commit ourselves to the nobler pursuits of life.

A Montana sheepherder wrote a strange request to a Chicago radio station. He lived a lonely life with his dog, four thousand sheep, a battery-operated radio, and an old violin. He loved to listen to the symphony orchestra and wished he could play along with it in the parts that he knew. Unfortunately, his violin was out of tune. He asked the radio station, "Some time before you start the next program, would you have the orchestra play an *A* for me?"

Just before the next Chicago Symphony broadcast, thousands of listeners heard these words: "The orchestra will now play an *A* for a sheepherder in Montana."

In what areas of your life is God asking you to give of yourself for the benefit of others? What areas of your life need God's protection? Ask Jesus to provide his protection today.

Jesus, give me the courage to live my life for the benefit of others.

TO READ
John 10:22-26

It was now winter, and Jesus was in Jerusalem at the time of Hanukkah. JOHN 10:22

Remembering Our Victories

The Jewish holiday of Hanukkah, or Feast of Dedication, commemorates the reconstruction of the Temple in 165 BC by Jewish leader Judas Maccabeus after its desecration by Syrian king Antiochus IV in 168 BC. The festival took place in the winter, the harshest time of the year. The reason for the festival as well as the time of year it took place made it a reminder of the Jewish people's scars of life.

Sometimes scars aren't such a bad thing.

A fascinating television commercial aired a few years ago showing a series of athletes who have one thing in common—a nasty injury or scar. There's a cowboy with a huge scar around his eye and something wrong with the eye itself, a wrestler with a bulbous cauliflower ear, and a track athlete with horribly callused feet. There's no explanation or narrative, just Joe Cocker crooning "You are so beautiful . . . to me" in the background and Nike's swoosh and slogan, "Just Do It," ending the ad.

The message in the commercial was this: To these athletes, injuries and scars are marks of victory; and to their fans, the athletes are beautiful not in spite of their injuries, but because of them.

God's grace is a lot like the love those athletes' fans feel for their heroes. But our beauty is found in him, not in us. He looks down at us—injured, blind, and scarred as we are—and sings, "You are so beautiful to me."[8]

If life has left you with scars, they are more than reminders of past injuries or hurts; they are reminders of the healing God has done. As such, they are marks of victory.

Jesus, help me to wear my scars of life proudly and see them as reminders of victory.

TO READ
John 10:27-41

Once again the Jewish leaders picked up stones to kill him. Jesus said, "At my Father's direction I have done many things to help the people. For which one of these good deeds are you killing me?"

JOHN 10:31-32

What's Your Excuse?

The presence of Jesus overwhelmed the Jewish religious leaders of the time. He did not fit their previously held conceptions of what the Savior would be like. Since Jesus didn't fit their mold, in their defiant confusion these men picked up rocks to stone him.

Obviously, these religious leaders believed they had good excuses for not believing Jesus. But what about us? What is our excuse for not following Jesus with abandon? Is it because his speaking the truth bothers us? Is it because we take his free offer of eternal life for granted? Is it because he doesn't correct us immediately when we stray, so we think we can get away with sin? Zig Ziglar once wrote:

> My brother, the late Judge Ziglar, loved to tell the story of the fellow who went next door to borrow his neighbor's lawnmower. The neighbor explained that he could not let him use the mower because all the flights had been canceled from New York to Los Angeles.
>
> The borrower asked him what canceled flights from New York to Los Angeles had to do with borrowing his lawnmower. "It doesn't have anything to do with it, but if I don't want to let you use my lawnmower, one excuse is as good as another."[9]

When it comes to our excuses for not closely following Jesus, one truly is as good as another. But when we take our eyes off our own rationalizations and look at Jesus himself, we find that for every excuse we have for not following him, there are many more and better reasons to follow with abandon.

Oh God, may I never focus on my excuses, but only on you.

TO READ
John 11:1-8

But his disciples objected. "Teacher," they said, "only a few days ago the Jewish leaders in Judea were trying to kill you. Are you going there again?"

JOHN 11:8

Facing Challenges with Confidence

Jesus loved a good challenge, and his plan to go to Judea was one of the biggest challenges he would face during his earthly ministry.

The last time Jesus had been in Judea, the Jewish leaders tried to take him by force, intimidate his followers, and stop his ministry. But Jesus went anyway.

A few years ago at the Promise Keepers "Go the Distance" Conference, Kevin Miller gave an interesting insight into how to handle those who try to intimidate you. He had competed with his relay team in the 1,600-meter championship race of the Pennsylvania Relays, a famous Eastern track meet. Kevin was the lead-off man and in the second lane, right next to the man who held the record for prep school runners in the 100-meter dash. As Kevin approached the starting line, this record-holder said, "May the best man win. I'll be waiting for you at the finish line."

"We went into the blocks," Kevin recalled. "The gun sounded. He took off, and the other seven of us settled in behind him. We went around the first turn and down the backstretch. About 180 meters into the race, I suddenly saw the record holder in front of me, holding his side, bent over, and groaning as he jogged along. We all passed him like he was standing still."

At the end of the race, Kevin's coach took him aside and said, "I hope you've learned a lesson today. It makes little difference whether you hold the record for the 100-meter dash if the race is 400 meters long."[10]

Jesus promises us that we will face opposition as we attempt to live for him and do great things for the kingdom of God. Knowing that our ultimate victory is assured, we can face any challenge with absolute confidence.

Jesus, give me passion, wisdom, and perseverance as I face the challenges before me.

TO READ
John 11:9-12

Jesus replied, "There are twelve hours of daylight every day. As long as it is light, people can walk safely. They can see because they have the light of this world." JOHN 11:9

The Good News about Bad News

Jesus' life appeared to be full of bad news. Ordinary people were irritated with him, the Jewish leaders were out to kill him, and now his friend Lazarus was dead. But rather than shy away from the bad news, Jesus faced it and walked courageously forward. He understood something we need to learn: that the greatest opportunities sometimes appear amidst what looks like bad news.

Jesus knew that bad news would turn into good the moment he raised Lazarus from the dead.

All of us will face bad news at some point. In his book *Business @ the Speed of Thought*, Bill Gates had this to say about bad news:

> A good e-mail system ensures that bad news can travel fast, but people have to be willing to send you the news. You have to be constantly receptive to bad news, and then you have to act on it. Sometimes I think my most important job as CEO is to listen for bad news. If you don't act on it, your people will eventually stop bringing bad news to your attention. And that's the beginning of the end.
>
> The willingness to hear hard truth is vital not only for CEOs of big corporations but also for anyone who loves the truth. Sometimes the truth sounds like bad news, but it is just what we need.[11]

There is good news about bad news: If we keep our eyes on who we are in Christ and on what he wants to do in and through us, God will use the bad news to accomplish good things.

Lord, help me to see the opportunities for good that come with bad news.

TO READ
John 11:14-16

Thomas, nicknamed the Twin, said to his fellow disciples, "Let's go, too—and die with Jesus."
JOHN 11:16

The Need for a Challenge

The disciples had tried to talk Jesus out of going to Judea because there was imminent danger waiting there for him. But when Thomas realized that Jesus was determined to go against their advice and head to Judea, he rushed to the front line.

Men have always run to stressful situations and to danger. It may be that we have an actual need to do so.

Researchers at the University of California at Berkeley did an experiment some time ago demonstrating the apparent need for some level of danger or stress in life. The experiment involved introducing an amoeba into a perfectly stress-free environment in which it had to make no adjustments whatsoever: ideal temperature, optimal concentration of moisture, and a constant food supply.

You would think that would have been one happy little amoeba. Whatever stress that gives amoebas ulcers and high blood pressure was gone from its environment.

Yet oddly enough, it died.[12]

Apparently all living creatures require challenges in the same way we require food and air. Too much comfort will keep us from thriving and could even kill us.

Few men live in a completely stress-free and safe environment. Yet when we are in an environment that challenges us, God moves in and through us in a way he couldn't in a "safe" situation.

Lord, give me enough danger to challenge me but not so much that I shrink back out of fear.

TO READ
John 11:17-27

Jesus told her, "I am the resurrection and the life. Those who believe in me, even though they die like everyone else, will live again." JOHN 11:25

✿ *Our Source of Life*

During several summers in the 1950s, the Methodist pastor Howard Mumma served as a guest minister at the American Church in Paris. At that time, the existentialist writer Albert Camus had been coming to church, first to hear Marcel Dupré play the organ, and later to hear Mumma's sermons.

Mumma became friends with Camus, who by then was famous for his novels *The Plague* and *The Stranger* and for essays such as "The Myth of Sisyphus." The two men met on several occasions to discuss Camus's questions concerning religious beliefs.

In one conversation, Camus told Mumma: "The reason I have been coming to church is because I am seeking. I'm almost on a pilgrimage—seeking something to fill the void that I am experiencing—and no one else knows. Certainly the public and the readers of my novels, while they see that void, are not finding the answers in what they are reading. But deep down you are right—I am searching for something that the world is not giving me."[13]

Albert Camus wasn't looking for *something*; he was looking for *someone*—Jesus Christ, who had created him and provided for him.

Likewise, Lazarus and his family were about to find something the world was not giving them. In the intensity of their experience with death, they were about to discover that Jesus was the source of everything they would ever need or want in life.

Jesus didn't just tell Lazarus's sisters that he could raise their brother from the dead. He simply said, "I am the resurrection."

Is he your source of life?

Jesus, help me love you more than the things you provide.

TO READ
John 11:33-35

Then Jesus wept. JOHN 11:35

Compassion in Action

Mary and Martha had watched their brother die and were deeply saddened. They knew in their hearts that Jesus could have kept him from dying, because they saw him heal the sick many times. They had hoped Jesus would show up and heal Lazarus, but he didn't.

Jesus was fully invested in the lives of those he loved, and Mary and Martha's pain moved his spirit deeply. Their pain touched his heart. So before he performed a miracle for them, he wept. Before he replaced their sorrow with intense joy, he cried. Before he changed their perspective so they could realize that all power and all authority belong to him, he shed tears. The strength of his power could only be compared to the depth of his compassion.

Michael Tait of the Christian music group DC Talk saw this kind of compassion in action in his father and proudly said this about him:

> Let me tell you the two most important things I learned from my dad. Number one, love people. He cried with people, he laughed with people. Everybody was his friend. He could care less about your race, your nationality, your socio-economic status, whatever. All he cared about was you, your soul. Number two, live for God and don't get caught up in the things of this world, because they're just fleeting. The world will get the best of you if you let it, so we need to truly live for God. Those two things have shaped who I am today. I love people; I realize that life is short, God is real and that I need to live for Him.[14]

Jesus is a Savior of compassion deeper than even the most loving father can imagine, a Savior who puts action behind his words of compassion. He calls each and every man who follows him to have just that kind of compassion.

Dear Lord, may your compassion be a big part of my manhood.

TO READ
John 11:36-42

The people who were standing nearby said, "See how much he loved him." But some said, "This man healed a blind man. Why couldn't he keep Lazarus from dying?" JOHN 11:36-37

A Matter of Choice

When we are in difficult, painful situations, we have a choice to make. Will we allow Jesus to comfort us, or will we accuse him of being either inept or uninterested because he did not intervene to keep what caused our pain from happening?

Jesus' friends had just lost their brother Lazarus. He was deeply moved by his friends' grief and deeply saddened at their loss. And he heard the one question on everybody's mind that day: "Why couldn't he keep Lazarus from dying?"

I believe that all of us during painful and difficult times have asked a question like that one. With pain in our hearts, we ask, if God really loves us and is control, why doesn't he just rescue us?

I don't believe there is an adequate answer to that question. The reality is that sometimes life hurts. Each of us has been in situations that caused us personal pain, and we will experience such situations again. When Jesus takes us into his presence for eternity, he will rescue us from all pain and grief; but as long as we are on this earth, we will suffer along with the rest of mankind.

We need to remember that Jesus is intimately acquainted with the brokenness of the world we all live in and deeply concerned with the way it affects each of us. And we need to understand that while Jesus won't always rescue us from the situations that cause us pain, he will always be at our side during those times, giving us comfort.

When we suffer, we lose once. But when we turn bitter or blame God, we lose again. Knowing that, the question we each need to ask ourselves is, "How many times will I lose?"

Lord, teach me to never lose twice in a painful situation.

TO READ
John 11:45-54

From that time on the Jewish leaders began to plot Jesus' death. JOHN 11:53

The Power of Decisions

The Jewish leaders of Jesus' time had seen the miracles he performed and heard him teach the truth with an authority like none they had ever seen. They had argued with him and found him to be a man of integrity.

Then they heard that Jesus raised Lazarus from the dead. This should have been good news to them, but they didn't respond as if it was. Instead of humbly giving their allegiance to Jesus, they became jealous.

These men had a decision to make. They could choose to acknowledge who Jesus was and worship him, or they could choose to allow their hearts to become corrupted with thoughts of murder. They chose corruption.

It has often been said that we make our decisions, and our decisions make us. We either become stronger and more focused, or we become corrupt.

Consider the following survey of 198 Olympic sprinters, swimmers, powerlifters, and other athletes reported in an issue of *Sports Illustrated*:

A scenario . . . : You are offered a banned performance-enhancing substance, with two guarantees: 1) You will not be caught. 2) You will win. Would you take the substance?

One hundred and ninety-five athletes said yes; three said no.

Scenario II: You are offered a banned performance-enhancing substance that comes with two guarantees: 1) You will not be caught. 2) You will win every competition you enter for the next five years, and then you will die from the side effects of the substance. Would you take it?

More than half the athletes said yes.[15]

What will you do to make your choices godly ones?

Lord, may I never underestimate the power my decisions will have on my life.

June

TO READ
John 12:1-8

Judas Iscariot, one of his disciples—the one who would betray him—said, "That perfume was worth a small fortune. It should have been sold and the money given to the poor." JOHN 12:4-5

Misunderstood Patience

Judas Iscariot was a member of the most privileged group of men who ever lived. He was chosen to be one of Jesus' disciples. He listened as Jesus instructed the multitudes. He saw miracles firsthand. And yet it was not enough to soften Judas's heart.

Amazingly, Jesus was willing to entrust Judas with the treasury of his ministry even though Jesus knew Judas was not trustworthy. But Judas took money out for his own purposes.

Judas had been taking money from the treasury for so long that he had grown used to it. He mistakenly thought that he would never get caught, and his appetite grew. When Mary anointed Jesus with some expensive perfume, it was too much for Judas. To the casual observer, he appeared to be sincere. It sounded as if he had a great concern for the poor and for doing what was best for them. His conviction about not wasting precious resources appears to be well intentioned. But it wasn't.

Jesus is patient with each of us because he wants our hearts to soften. He knows we struggle with selfishness, intense desires, and self-deception. He often withholds immediate punishment to give us an opportunity to confess and repent. When we own up to the reality of our lives, our hearts soften and our relationship with Jesus grows. When we mistakenly think we can get away with things, our hearts harden.

What is the reality of your life? Be honest with Jesus today about the areas in which you are most vulnerable. He has seen the same struggles in other men and is not surprised by them.

Jesus, rescue me from thinking I can be right apart from you.

TO READ
John 12:9-11

Then the leading priests decided to kill Lazarus, too.

JOHN 12:10

❋ Smart Actions

I have come to the conclusion that sin actually impairs a person's ability to think clearly. The chief priests were educated men. They were leaders in their community. They had committed their lives to serving the public. They knew full well that Lazarus had been dead and was brought back to life by Jesus. That was an accomplishment way beyond anything they had ever seen. But their souls had become so corrupt that they decided to kill Lazarus as well as Jesus. I wonder if it ever occurred to them that Jesus could just as easily raise Lazarus from the dead again? It seems, though, that once bad thinking settles in, it runs an unbelievable course.

Doctors at Metropolitan Hospital in New York City operated on a thirty-eight-year-old man whom they believed had an abdominal tumor. What they found surprised them, to say the least. During the operation the surgical team removed more than three hundred coins, including quarters, dimes, nickels, pennies and subway tokens, from the man's stomach. They said they found broken thermometers, can openers, knives, forks, spoons, nuts, bolts, chains and car keys. The surgeons were told the patient had an enormous appetite and often ate double portions at meals. Amazingly, the surgeons found no damage to the patient's esophagus or intestinal tract.

The coin eater's actions led him to spend a lot of time eating things that were unnecessary. The priests' actions led them to a conclusion that didn't make sense. It doesn't have to be this way in your life. When you choose to obey God, your thinking will get clearer. As you maintain your moral standards, your insight will sharpen. When you seek to do God's will, your mind will line up with the mind of Christ.

Lord, teach me the value of consistent obedience.

TO READ
John 12:12-15

A huge crowd of Passover visitors took palm branches and went down the road to meet him. They shouted, "Praise God! Bless the one who comes in the name of the Lord! Hail to the King of Israel!" JOHN 12:12-13

Fame or Faithfulness?

A very interesting and telling contrast occurred during what is commonly called the Triumphal Entry—when Jesus made his final entry into Jerusalem.

Jesus was faithfully fulfilling the prophecy that said the King of Israel would come, riding on a donkey (see Zechariah 9:9). At the same time, crowds of people were trying to lavish him with fame.

These people wanted a hero to applaud. They longed for a leader to rescue them from the tyranny of the Roman regime. They desired someone to transport them, even if only temporarily, from the mundane routine of their everyday lives. In short, they wanted a star.

But what they got was a faithful servant of God. That's the kind of servant God still looks for.

There is a tendency in every man to desire fame over faithfulness. We need to realize, however, that when we are faithful, God himself rewards us. But when we focus on gaining fame or recognition, any reward we receive comes from the hands of other people.

In summarizing his accomplishments, Walt Disney said, "As far as I can remember, being a celebrity has never helped me make a good picture . . . or command the obedience of my daughter or impress my wife. It doesn't even seem to help keep fleas off our dog, and if being a celebrity won't give one an advantage over a couple fleas, then I guess there can't be that much in being a celebrity after all."[1]

In the eternal picture, we really don't stand to gain much by being a celebrity. But when we faithfully serve God without concerning ourselves with the recognition of people, we stand to gain everything.

Lord, may I faithfully follow and serve you without concerning myself with public recognition.

TO READ
John 12:16-18

His disciples didn't realize at the time that this was a fulfillment of prophecy. But after Jesus entered into his glory, they remembered that these Scriptures had come true before their eyes. JOHN 12:16

Understanding Jesus

The disciples thought constantly about the things Jesus said and did, but many of those things still didn't make sense to them. They heard people praise Jesus, but he would not "build" his ministry, at least not in the way they thought he should. They saw him heal the sick, then retreat by himself. They observed Jesus' very deliberate methods, but they didn't understand many of the details.

But then Jesus was glorified, and things became clear for them.

After Jesus' resurrection, the things he had done and said suddenly made perfect sense. The disciples didn't understand why Jesus shunned publicity—until after his resurrection. They didn't understand why he put himself in danger of death—until after his resurrection. They didn't grasp the power of salvation—until after his resurrection.

In the same way, many things about Jesus don't make sense to us until we experience him for ourselves. The Bible does not make much sense to us until Jesus has been glorified in our lives. Spending time in church seems like a waste of good time—until we meet Jesus in a personal way. We find it easy to be critical of "organized religion"—until Jesus invades our lives. And other people's enthusiasm for the things of God can be an irritation—until we discover a vital relationship with Jesus.

Do you want a relationship with Jesus that thrills your heart? Do you want that burning desire to know what Jesus' words and deeds really mean? Then ask him to glorify himself in your life daily. Your personal buy-in will make all the difference.

Lord, give me a deeper understanding of you and your words and deeds as you glorify yourself in my life.

TO READ
John 12:17-19

Those in the crowd who had seen Jesus call Lazarus back to life were telling others all about it.

JOHN 12:17

❁ A Courageous Faith

In his *BreakPoint* commentary on April 14, 1999, Chuck Colson told the story of an evangelist named John Harper, one of the unfortunate souls to perish in the *Titanic* disaster of 1912.

Harper boarded the *Titanic* with his six-year-old daughter. When the ship struck the iceberg and began to sink, Harper made sure his daughter was placed into one of the lifeboats, then he swam from one person to another, pleading with each to accept Christ.

Only six of the people who struggled in the freezing North Atlantic water that night were rescued, including a man who later identified himself as Harper's last convert. This young man had climbed up on a piece of debris. Harper, struggling in the water near him, shouted out, "Are you saved?"

"No," the man replied.

Harper then shouted these words from Scripture: "Believe on the Lord Jesus Christ and thou shalt be saved."

The man did not answer. A few minutes later, Harper asked, "Are you saved?" Once again, the answer was no. With his dying breath, Harper shouted, "Believe on the Lord Jesus Christ and thou shalt be saved." Then he slipped under the waves for the last time.

Then and there, the young man turned his life over to Christ.

We should all pray that no matter what situation we find ourselves in, we will have the kind of courage to share our faith that Harper had.

Jesus, give me the courage to share my faith with others.

TO READ
John 12:20-27

Those who love their life in this world will lose it. Those who despise their life in this world will keep it for eternal life. JOHN 12:25

Focusing on the Permanent

David Lawrence, the founder of the magazine *U.S. News &World Report,* was the only non-senator who regularly attended the Senate Prayer Breakfast. He was often asked to speak at the event.

On May 5, 1956, Lawrence wrote the following as part of an editorial:

It is a temporary answer to the threat of world disturbance that we face. The North Atlantic Treaty is temporary. The United Nations is temporary. All our alliances are temporary. Basically there is only one permanence we can all accept. It is the permanence of a God-governed world, for the power of God alone is permanent. Obedience to his laws is the only road to lasting solutions to man's problems.

One of the hardest lessons for us men to learn is that there are certain things we can never accomplish on our own. We're taught to be strong, aggressive, and self-sufficient. We spend our lives competing for a place in the world. This started on the playground as we wrestled with other boys to test our strength, and it continues into our professional pursuits as we seek to maximize our potential.

But at some point, we are all confronted with the fact that no matter how talented and gifted we are, we are limited in what we can do. We must still face death—and God.

When the time comes for us to face God, our strength and our conquests will mean nothing. The only thing that will matter is what we believed about Jesus.

Lord, give me a greater love for what is permanent and a looser grip on what is temporary.

TO READ
John 12:27-30

[Jesus said,] "Father, glorify your name!" Then a voice came from heaven, "I have glorified it, and will glorify it again." JOHN 12:28, NIV

✳ *Glorify Your Name, Lord!*

From our imperfect, human perspective, it often appears that God is inactive or uninterested in the world around us. From where we stand, it appears that men get away with all kinds of evil and manipulation. When we look around us and see suffering and injustice, we are tempted to cry out, "God, why don't you do something?"

In response to these accusations, he simply says, "I have glorified my name and will glorify it again."

Retired United States Marine Corps general Charles Krulak recounted a critical event in the Gulf War of 1991 in his message at the October 2000 Leadership Prayer Breakfast in Wheaton, Illinois:

"The prevailing winds in the Gulf area blow from northeast to southwest. If you attack from the southwest, your enemy can release biological weapons into the air, and the chemicals will blow right into your face. It was a tremendous concern for the military in the southwestern desert and a grave prayer concern for many, both overseas and back home.

"On February 21, 1991, American forces began an attack from the southwest at four in the morning. Only three hours before, the prevailing winds had shifted from southwest to northeast, exactly 180 degrees from the direction the prevailing winds normally blow.

"The winds blew in that direction for four days, the four days of the duration of the war. Within thirty minutes of the surrender, the winds shifted back. That is the unbelievable power of prayer."

If you ask God to glorify his name in your life today, rest assured that he will do it.

Jesus, glorify your name in my life, however you see fit.

TO READ
John 12:31-41

But despite all the miraculous signs he had done, most of the people did not believe in him.

JOHN 12:37

Our Human Stubbornness

Jesus healed the sick, raised the dead, confounded the wise, overcame the impossible, and showed men and women unprecedented compassion. Yet the very people who witnessed these things stubbornly concluded that they still would not believe in him. Their reason? He did things according to his own agenda, not theirs. And the truth is, we aren't very different from those people who saw Jesus up close and personal two thousand years ago.

There is an old story of one particularly stubborn young boy who wrote God a letter about the Christmas presents he badly wanted: "I've been good for six months now," he wrote. After a moment's reflection, the boy crossed out *six months* and wrote *three months*. After a pause, he crossed that out and replaced it with *two weeks*. After still another pause, he erased that too.

The boy then got up from the table and went over to the little nativity scene that included figures of Mary and Joseph. He picked up the figure of Mary and went back to his writing. He started again: "Dear God, if ever you want to see your mother again . . . "

We have a tendency to make deals with God, don't we? We have the attitude that we will believe in him if he comes through for us. But if he dares to be sovereign and do things according to his own plan, we turn away from him in disappointment.

When we base our faith on how God responds to our selfish requests, we are sure to be disappointed. But when we believe in him as the sovereign God who knows what is best for us and for his kingdom, we will live a powerful, life-changing faith.

Oh Lord, give me a pure faith, one that isn't based on selfish, stubborn desires.

TO READ
John 12:42-50

Many people, including some of the Jewish leaders, believed in him. But they wouldn't admit it to anyone because of their fear that the Pharisees would expel them from the synagogue. For they loved human praise more than the praise of God.

JOHN 12:42-43

❋ Who's Your Audience?

We all live for an audience. People are watching, and so is God. The all-important question we must ask ourselves is, Which audience is most important?

In his book *A Father for All Seasons*, Bob Welch wrote:

Last summer, my son Jason was a seventh-grader playing in a seventh/eighth-grade league. The third pitch, unintentionally I'm sure, came right at Jason. He turned to avoid being hit and fell to the ground. His bat went flying. His helmet bounced off. The ball seemed to have skimmed his shoulder.

"Take your base," said the umpire.

"It didn't hit me," Jason said to the ump.

"Take your base, son," said the ump.

"But honest, it didn't hit me," Jason pleaded.

The umpire looked at Jason and out to the infield ump, who just shrugged. "Okay," said the ump, "the count is one-and-two."

The towering pitcher rocked and fired. Jason ripped the ball into left-center for a stand-up double. Our crowd roared. The manager of the team in the field was standing a few feet behind me. He had no idea that the kid on second base was my son. He spit out his sunflower seeds and slowly shook his head.

"Man," he said, "you gotta love that."[2]

Jason got a big hit in a baseball game because he chose to do what was right rather than settle for what the umpire thought he had seen. In much the same way, we should always live as if God is our only audience.

Jesus, remind me daily to make you my audience for everything I do and say.

TO READ
John 13:1-5

[Jesus] got up from the table, took off his robe, wrapped a towel around his waist, and poured water into a basin. Then he began to wash the disciples' feet and to wipe them with the towel he had around him. JOHN 13:4-5

A Sacrifice of Love

On November 19, 2000, the *Detroit Free Press* reported the poignant story of a man who lost his life while saving that of his daughter.

Scott Saunders waited in the driveway of his Hanover, Michigan, home for his four-year-old daughter, Danielle, to get off her school bus. A pickup truck was stopped behind the bus, so Saunders knew it was safe to cross the street to meet Danielle and walk her back to their home.

Saunders and his daughter had crossed the street and entered their driveway when he noticed that a car behind the bus was traveling too fast to stop safely before entering the crossing zone. The car swerved to avoid the pickup and ran headlong into the Saunders's driveway—directly at father and daughter.

Saunders grabbed Danielle by the arm and flung her away from him and into their front yard. Unfortunately, he was not able to get out of the car's path. He was struck and killed. Danielle was treated for minor injuries at a nearby hospital and was released.

Later, sheriff's captain Tony Philipps said, "It was a heroic act by a father to save his child. He did everything he could, and in the process, he lost his own life."

That's the kind of sacrificial love Jesus had for those he loved. In today's Scripture, we read how he was willing to wash the disciples' feet, the job reserved for the most humble of servants. But that was just the beginning of his service on their behalf. Later he would give his very life on the cross so that they could live with him for all eternity.

What sacrifices are you willing to make for others?

Lord, may I never be afraid of the cost of love.

TO READ
John 13:18-30

Now Jesus was in great anguish of spirit, and he exclaimed, "The truth is, one of you will betray me!" The disciples looked at each other, wondering whom he could mean. JOHN 13:21-22

✳ *Moments of Decision*

Throughout history Jesus' love has been rewarded with demands. His sacrifice has been minimized. His graciousness has been taken for granted. In place of the obedience he deserves, we manipulate to get our way, and then we are confused when our lives get complicated.

Jesus was spending an important night with his disciples. It was the last meal he would share with them. He had just finished washing the disciples' feet and encouraging them to follow his example. They were comfortably reclining, experiencing the Passover meal. Everybody was relaxed. The atmosphere was casual. Then Jesus spoke words that rocked their world: "One of you will betray me!"

There were twelve disciples in the room, and only one knew what Jesus was talking about. The public announcement hit home in the heart of that individual. Judas had to decide if he was going to follow through with the plans that he laid out or turn back from his betrayal.

Moments such as these create points of decision in our lives. The truth tends to hit us at unexpected times. You attend church thinking it will be just another Sunday, and you come away feeling like the message was just for you. You listen to the radio as part of your driving routine, only to hear something that transforms your life. You attend a social gathering where people are sharing their experiences with one another, and somebody's story touches the deepest part of your soul.

You can't predict these moments, but you must be prepared for them. They are points of decision that clarify your purpose and direct your heart. How will you respond to the next one that Jesus sets up for you?

Lord, prepare me for the next life-changing moment in your plan for me.

Your love for one another will prove to the world that you are my disciples. JOHN 13:35

✳ *Demonstrations of Love*

One day not long before the Thanksgiving holiday, an elderly man in Phoenix, Arizona, calls his son, who lives in New York City, and tells him, "I hate to ruin your day, but I have to tell you that your mother and I are divorcing—forty-five years of misery is enough."

"Pop, what are you talking about?" the son asks, his voice rising in alarm.

"We can't stand the sight of each other any longer," the father says. "We're sick of each other. And I'm sick of talking about this, so you call your sister and tell her."

Now frantic, the son calls his sister, who lives in Chicago, to tell her of their father's announcement.

"Yeah right they're getting divorced!" she explodes. "I'll take care of this."

After hanging up the phone, the sister calls Phoenix immediately and screams at her father, "You are not getting divorced! Don't do a single thing till I get there. I'm calling my brother back, and we'll both be there tomorrow. Until then, don't do a thing."

The old man hangs up the phone and turns to his wife. "Okay," he says with a wry smile, "they're coming for Thanksgiving and paying their own fares. Now what do we do for Christmas?"

We never have to worry about God using deception to get us to spend time with him. Instead, he demonstrates his love through his Son.

Knowing what our Father has done for us, can we do any less for others?

Dear God, make my love for others so obvious that they will never doubt it.

TO READ
John 13:36-38

"But why can't I come now, Lord?" [Peter] asked. "I am ready to die for you." Jesus answered, "Die for me? No, before the rooster crows tomorrow morning, you will deny three times that you even know me." JOHN 13:37-38

Getting Back Up

Author John Hersey once said, "Learning starts with failure; the first failure is the beginning of education."[3] Peter learned this lesson in a very painful way. He boldly proclaimed in front of the other disciples that he would follow Jesus anywhere and would be willing to die for him. But Jesus corrected Peter, telling him—again, in front of the other disciples—that before the next morning he would publicly disavow any knowledge of him not once but three times.

As Jesus predicted, Peter thrice denied his Lord. Humiliated and ashamed, Peter spent what must have seemed like an eternity grieving over his failure. He felt the deep heartache of having failed his Savior. He spent long days and nights wondering if he would get another opportunity to serve Jesus or if he had permanently disqualified himself.

But Jesus, in his grace, reached out and restored the fallen apostle and "recommissioned" him to feed his lambs.

Peter, who would play a key role in the beginnings of the Christian church, saw up close and personal a truth we all need to know about our Savior: Jesus truly is the God of the second chance for those who humbly come to him.

Each of us at some point in our walks with Christ will fail him in some way or another. Whether we move on from there and rediscover God's plan for us depends on this question: Will we get back up again?

Jesus, turn the pain of my failures into reminders of your grace.

TO READ
John 14:6-11

Jesus told him, "I am the way, the truth, and the life. No one can come to the Father except through me."

JOHN 14:6

✳ *Great Lengths*

Because Jesus is God, he knows without a doubt that all other ways to God are deceptive attempts to lead people astray. In love, he has sounded the alarm. He went to great lengths to ensure that a safe way was provided for each of us to discover salvation.

I have watched two stadiums taken down by demolition crews: the Kingdome in Seattle and Three Rivers Stadium in Pittsburgh. They were slated for destruction to make room for new, modern stadiums. The demolition was absolutely fascinating to watch.

With both stadiums, the companies in charge of the demolition went to great lengths to ensure both the success and the safety of the operation. The placement of the explosives was first carefully designed on paper. During the placement and arming of the explosives, engineers checked, rechecked, and checked again to establish confidence in the implementation of the plan. People from the surrounding blocks were evacuated. Public announcements were made for weeks. Every worker was accounted for before the order was given to trigger the explosion. Large public address systems were used to alert any spontaneous visitor to the site. Prior to the beginning of the chain reaction of explosions, a shrill alarm was sounded so there would be no mystery about what was about to happen. Because people heeded the instructions, both structures came down successfully and without harm to anyone.

Similarly, God has gone to great lengths to provide salvation for us. He knows our self-sufficient nature needs to be torn down to make room for his provision. He has given his Word to guide us, his Spirit to empower us, and leaders to encourage us. All we need to do is respond to the instructions.

Teach me, Jesus, not to question you when you sound the alarm.

TO READ
John 14:7-29

[Jesus said,] "If you really knew me, you would know my Father as well. From now on, you do know him and have seen him." JOHN 14:7, NIV

"If You Really Knew Me . . ."

My friend Dan is a responsible husband and father. He loves his family and is learning to love life. And he's also learning to know Jesus better.

In a recent conversation, Dan told me, "I have found myself during the past year. I always thought that Jesus' goal for my life was to turn me into a soft, really nice guy. It sounded right to me, but it also sounded boring. I wanted more. I wanted adventure. I wanted something that would capture my heart and beckon me out of bed every day. During this past year, I came to realize that Jesus actually modeled a more robust and compelling vision of masculinity. He was the entire package. He was compassionate and kind, but he was also assertive and aggressive. He turned people's hearts, and he turned over tables. He brought peace to people's lives as he did battle with the devil. I have come to love these words: 'If you really knew me . . .'."

Dan has discovered that God is everything he needs. And he has discovered something we all need to know: that the pathway to abundant life is a greater and deeper knowledge of our Savior.

"I have learned to pray with greater interest," Dan said. "I can do battle in prayer as I resist the devil, and I can seek peace in prayer as I pray for those who are most important to me. I have gained a new interest in the Bible. Sometimes I read it as a warrior. Sometimes I read it as a scholar. Sometimes I read it as a son who just got a letter from his dad."

"If you really knew me . . ."

Lord, lead me to desire the things that help me see you as you really are.

TO READ
John 14:12-15

The truth is, anyone who believes in me will do the same works I have done, and even greater works, because I am going to be with the Father.

JOHN 14:12

Opportunities to Help

I recently read the account of Dennis Castellano, a project manager at Standard and Poors, who wanted to be of some help at the site of the World Trade Center disaster of September 11, 2001. Dennis recounts:

"My wife and I work near the World Trade Center. I was in one of the towers when the first plane hit and I evacuated the building and went to my wife's building across the street at Three World Financial Center. We were standing one block away from the World Trade Center when it collapsed. There was debris everywhere and we went running north. As we ran, I was helping people who couldn't make it on their own. Finally, we reached safety at Chelsea Piers. Then I made a decision. I told my wife, 'I'm going back.' "

Having gone back to help, he noticed there were no food provisions for the myriad rescue workers. He went to the local supermarket, bought sandwich supplies, and set up a makeshift center. When the Salvation Army arrived, they saw his efforts and stocked him up with food, cots, and bedding.

When Dennis was asked why he had gotten involved, he replied, "When I was a kid, my heroes were firemen. When I saw that I had the opportunity to help these guys here, I saw it as the greatest honor I could have. It is an honor to be here. It's like finding a dream in the midst of a nightmare."[4]

Jesus said we would have opportunities to do greater works than he did. We never know when those opportunities will appear or how much they will require of us. We do know, however, that God blesses those who reach out like he did. Are your eyes open to the possibilities that today might bring?

Lord, I want to be open to the opportunities you provide for ministry.

TO READ
John 14:16-21

I will ask the Father, and he will give you another Counselor, who will never leave you. He is the Holy Spirit, who leads into all truth. JOHN 14:16-17

Jet Skis and the Power of the Spirit

Being with Jesus was an experience like none the disciples could have imagined before they met him. But they didn't realize that Jesus had to leave in order to put his power within them. Jesus understood that his disciples would benefit more from the presence of the Holy Spirit within them than from his physical presence.

Last summer, I encountered a perfect illustration of what it means to walk in the power of the Holy Spirit—Jet Skis! My son and I were on the Colorado River, camping and fishing with some of our friends. To add to the adventure and fun of the trip, we took Jet Skis with us. It was amazing to watch my son and his friends skim over the water at speeds up to sixty miles per hour.

As I reflected on the trip, I starting thinking, *What if they had tried to do these things on their own power?*

On their own, those young men could not swim in circles at twenty-five miles per hour or jump a wake. But with a Jet Ski they could. The difference was the source of power. When they relied on the power of the Jet Ski, they could do remarkable things.

Without the power of the Holy Spirit, there are a lot of things we can't do—like effectively sharing our faith with others; like living the kind of life God calls us to live; like loving him. With the power of the Holy Spirit within us, we can do those things every day of our lives.

The difference, of course, is the source of our power.

Lord, teach me to rely only on the power of your Holy Spirit in my life.

TO READ
John 14:22-31

I have told you these things before they happen
so that you will believe when they do happen.

JOHN 14:29

Prior Knowledge

At noon on a spring day around the year 1910, an old motortruck broke
down in the center of the Place de l'Opera in Paris, requiring the driver to
spend a half hour under the vehicle making repairs. After apologizing to
several policemen for the traffic problems he had caused, the man drove
away, laughing to himself. That night he collected several thousand dollars
from friends who had bet him he could not lie on his back for thirty minutes
at the busiest hour in the busiest traffic center in Paris. This man was the
late Horace DeVere Cole, England's great practical joker and hoax artist,
who died in 1936.

It is entertaining when you hear something, like this story about Cole,
after it has already happened. But it is amazing when you see something
happen that someone told you about ahead of time.

That is exactly what Jesus did for the disciples—and for us.

Yet we sometimes have trouble processing what we are told because we
are so tied to what we can see. We think something can only be true if we
see it and understand it.

As a result, Jesus often tells us what is going to happen before it happens.
When he was with his disciples, he told them about his death and resurrection before it happened. Since then, he has given us prophecies that will
increase our faith as we see them come to pass.

While Jesus went out of his way to build up the disciples' faith—and
ours—by telling them what would happen ahead of time, he still wants us
to believe even in what we don't see. Is that the kind of faith you have?

Lord, give me the courage to believe what you have said.

TO READ
John 15:1-8

Yes, I am the vine; you are the branches. Those who remain in me, and I in them, will produce much fruit. For apart from me you can do nothing.

JOHN 15:5

❋ *Flourish or Fail*

Jesus was intent on teaching his disciples to depend on him. He likened that relationship to that of a grapevine and its branches. If you've ever observed how grapes grow, you know that when the branch clings to the vine, it flourishes and produces abundant fruit. But when the branch disconnects from the vine, it stops producing, withers away, and dies.

In other words, there is no middle ground for the Christian. You either flourish or fail; you either move forward or fall.

Making this same point, Presbyterian minister C. E. Macartney once likened the Christian life to the flight of an airplane:

> Between an airplane and every other form of locomotion and transportation there is one great contrast. The horse and wagon, the automobile, the bicycle, the locomotive, the speedboat, and the great battleship—all can come to a standstill without danger, and they can all reverse their engines, or their power, and go back.
>
> But there is no reverse about the engine of an airplane. It cannot back up. It dare not stand still. If it loses its momentum and forward-drives, then it crashes. The only safety for the airplane is in its forward and upward motion. The only safe direction for the Christian to take is forward and upward. If he stops, or if he begins to slip and go backward, that moment he is in danger.[5]

Do you want to produce fruit for your Lord? Remember, that will only happen if you decide daily to move forward with him and depend on him for everything. Without his empowerment, you can accomplish nothing.

Lord, teach me to depend on you and to always move upward and forward in my life.

TO READ
Philippians 2:14-18

Even if my life is to be poured out like a drink offering to complete the sacrifice of your faithful service (that is, if I am to die for you), I will rejoice, and I want to share my joy with all of you.

PHILIPPIANS 2:17

❋ *A Matter of Honor*

About an hour into United Flight 93 from Newark to San Francisco on September 11, 2001, terrorists commandeered the cockpit, herded the passengers to the back of the plane, and turned it back toward a target in Washington DC.

Among those passengers were four remarkable men who didn't much like being herded around.

One was thirty-one-year-old publicist Mark Bingham, who had helped the University of California win the 1991 and 1993 national collegiate rugby championships. He was six feet five, rowdy, and fearless.

One was thirty-eight-year-old medical research company executive Tom Burnett, who told his wife over the phone, "I know we're going to die. Some of us are going to do something about it."

One was thirty-one-year-old businessman Jeremy Glick. He called his wife, Lyz, at her parents' home in Windham, New York, to say good-bye to her and their twelve-week-old daughter, Emmy.

One was thirty-two-year-old sales account manager Todd Beamer, who had played third base and shortstop over three seasons for Wheaton College in Wheaton, Illinois.

These four brave men apparently came up with a plan to storm the cockpit and attempt to wrest control of the aircraft from the terrorists. Flight 93 never made it to Washington. Instead, it crashed into a field eighty miles southeast of Pittsburgh. All passengers and crew perished. Nobody on the ground was killed.[6]

What will you do when it is your turn to be poured out for the sake of others?

Dear God, may I value honor more than survival.

TO READ
Philippians 2:5-13

Therefore, my dear friends, as you have always obeyed—not only in my presence, but now much more in my absence—continue to work out your salvation with fear and trembling.

PHILIPPIANS 2:12, NIV

The Workout

Spiritual health is a lot like physical health. A good diet and regular exercise lend themselves to a healthy body. In the same way, a steady diet of God's Word and exercise in the spiritual disciplines of prayer, study, fellowship, and witnessing lend themselves to a growing relationship with God. To stay healthy, we must work at it. At the beginning, growth seems attractive and exciting. But when we come to realize the work involved, we are tempted to slow down and create shortcuts, much like the young man in the following story.

Though skeptical of his teenage son's newfound determination to build bulging muscles, a father followed his teenager to the store's weight-lifting department, where they admired a set of weights.

"Please, Dad," pleaded the teen, "I promise I'll use 'em every day."

"I don't know, Son. It's really a commitment on your part," the father said.

"Please, Dad?"

"They're not cheap either," the father said.

"I'll use 'em, Dad, I promise. You'll see."

Finally won over, the father paid for the equipment and headed for the door. After a few steps, he heard his son behind him say, "What! You mean I have to carry them to the car?"[7]

We laugh at stories like this because they reveal the stubbornness in our hearts. We want it our way, and we want life to be played out for our benefit. But if we want vibrant, fruitful lives, we must be willing to work out regularly and enthusiastically. What can you do today to energize your spiritual health?

Jesus, give me the motivation to stay in shape spiritually.

TO READ
Joshua 6:1-10

"Do not shout; do not even talk," Joshua commanded. "Not a single word from any of you until I tell you to shout. Then shout!" JOSHUA 6:10

A Time to Wait and a Time for Action

At a 1999 conference in Houston, Texas, speaker Marti Ensign, a missionary to Africa, told of bringing some African pastors to the United States for a big meeting. During their free time, the visitors wanted to go shopping. Even though they were in a small town, Marti knew there was a chance that one or more of the pastors might have difficulty finding his way around or might even get lost. She gave them her phone number for just such an emergency.

Less than an hour after the African pastors left, Marti's phone rang. It was one of the pastors. "I am lost," he said.

Marti said, "Lay the phone down, go to the street corner, find out the names of the two streets, come back and tell me, and I will come get you."

In a few minutes the pastor returned to the phone and reported, "I am at the corner of Walk and Don't Walk."

Sometimes when God leads us, we feel like we are looking at a "Walk/ Don't Walk" sign.

God led the nation of Israel to the city of Jericho and gave their leader, Joshua, clear directions. The people were simply to wait for his command. When he called them to action, they were to take action.

God is charting the course of your life so that you will fulfill his purpose. Part of his plan involves waiting while he orchestrates the circumstances; part of it involves being alert and ready to move into action when he tells you to.

Jesus, teach me the balance between being willing to wait and being ready to move out.

TO READ
John 16:1-15

Oh, there is so much more I want to tell you, but you can't bear it now. JOHN 16:12

Our Need to Know

In 1741, George Frideric Handel wrote *Messiah*, one of the finest and most inspiring pieces of music ever composed. In the time leading up to his greatest accomplishment, Handel's health and fortunes had reached a low ebb. His right side had become paralyzed due to a stroke, and all his money was gone. He was heavily in debt and threatened with imprisonment. He was tempted to give up the fight.

I wonder if Handel would have chosen another path had he known what was ahead of him. I can't help but think that if he had known ahead of time the suffering he would endure, he would have chosen another journey. Had that happened, the world would have missed out on the blessing of one of the most renowned and beautiful compositions of praise.

It may not seem fair to us, but each of us is on a "need to know" basis with God. That includes the events in our very own lives.

Jesus knows your future, and he knows your purpose in life. He knows exactly what everyone around you is doing and will do, and he knows how those actions will affect you. He knows everything you will ever learn—and infinitely more. He has seen everything you will ever see—and infinitely more. He knows how much of that information you can handle and when you can handle it. For that reason, he "filters" information about you and parcels it out to you in strategic bursts—when you need it.

While you can't always know ahead of time the things that will take place in your life, you can be confident that God is using every event to prepare you for and move you toward his purposes. You can also be grateful that he tells you only what you can handle right now.

Jesus, thank you for telling me what I need to know, when I need to know it.

TO READ
John 16:16-22

Truly, you will weep and mourn over what is going to happen to me, but the world will rejoice.

JOHN 16:20

Redeeming Our Losses

God did not design us to endure loss. Adam and Eve—as well as their children—were supposed to live forever. But all that changed when Adam and Eve sinned. Everything became difficult, and loss became a "normal" part of life—loss of innocence, loss of perfect fellowship with God, loss of life. Since Adam and Eve were not designed for loss, grief became part of the human experience.

But in his amazing love, Jesus gave himself on the cross to redeem us and redeem the loss we all suffer. But there's more: Somehow, he brings good things out of even the worst of circumstances. Here is one example:

> Henry P. Crowell, affectionately called "The autocrat of the Breakfast Table," contracted tuberculosis when a boy and couldn't go to school. After hearing a sermon by Dwight L. Moody, young Crowell prayed, "I can't be a preacher, but I can be a good businessman. God, if You will let me make money, I will use it in Your service."
>
> Under the doctor's advice Crowell worked outdoors for seven years and regained his health. He then bought the little run-down Quaker Mill at Ravanna, Ohio. Within ten years Quaker Oats was a household word to millions. Crowell also operated the huge Perfection Stove Company.
>
> For over forty years Henry P. Crowell faithfully gave 60 to 70 percent of his income to God's causes, having advanced from an initial 10 percent.[8]

Sooner or later we will all suffer a loss of some kind. But in the midst of those difficulties, you can be confident that God is willing and able to redeem even your worst losses and pain.

Lord, thank you that you redeem the pain in my life.

TO READ
John 16:25-33

I have told you all this so that you may have peace in me. Here on earth you will have many trials and sorrows. But take heart, because I have overcome the world. JOHN 16:33

❋ A Better Plan

As Jesus was preparing to be crucified and resurrected, he told his disciples that they would face turmoil and trouble. If they turned to him in the midst of their struggles, he would give them peace. If they fought the battles on their own, the struggle would only intensify.

The disciples had no choice except to yield to the one who had overcome the world. Here is another example of that truth:

> Mort Meyerson, who ran Perot Systems from 1992 to 1997, created a stir when he canceled the company's annual Christmas party. He saw that the event (for 13,000 employees) was costing $360,000 and decided the money could be put to better use.
>
> He said, "We'll take the $360,000 and buy food and clothes and toys and we will get our employees to take those things personally and deliver them to the inner city, to people who don't have anything."
>
> The first reaction to his decision was outrage, followed by depression, then recognition that they were doing something different, and finally elation on the part of the people who made the deliveries.
>
> What did the event do for their employees?
>
> Meyerson stated: "It made them more human. It made them more effective as employees. It made them better family members."
>
> One employee told Meyerson, "This has changed my life."[9]

Mort Meyerson had a better plan, a plan that gave the employees of Perot Systems more lasting joy than a Christmas party.

Jesus has a better plan too. When we stick close to him, he empowers us to carry it out, no matter what kind of opposition we may face.

Lord, remind me daily that your plan is always better.

TO READ
John 17:1-12

My prayer is not for the world, but for those you have given me, because they belong to you.

JOHN 17:9

❁ The Prayer of Jesus

There's nothing more comforting than knowing that someone cares for you and would do anything to help you out when you are in a jam. The following story is a demonstration of just that kind of devotion:

> For the firefighters of Newark, New Jersey's Company Engine 11, there was no place to be but at the disaster site at the World Trade Center. Coming out of Ground Zero on Tuesday afternoon, the men looked tired and drained but were full of resolve to help their fellow firefighters.
>
> "It's a brotherhood," said Firefighter John Perdisatt of Engine 11. "We're thinking and knowing that there are over 300 firemen in that rubble."
>
> "You always feel that there's hope and you're hoping there's hope," he said.
>
> Asked how the rescue workers are coping now that the search is in its second week, he said, "It's what always happens in a tragedy, we pull together and everyone tries to do their best."[10]

Just as those firefighters trapped in the ruins of the World Trade Center had people looking out for them, we have someone who looks out for us daily. His name is Jesus, and he not only looks out for us, he prays for us!

Jesus told his followers that he was leaving them but that he would send the Holy Spirit to teach them and guide them. In the meantime, however, the news that Jesus was going away left the disciples feeling confused, frustrated, and aimless. So Jesus prayed for them.

Jesus' prayer for the disciples was also a prayer for all who would follow him—and that includes you! As you face the challenges or successes of life, Jesus prays for you.

Jesus, remind me every day that you are an advocate who prays for me.

TO READ
John 17:13-16

I'm not asking you to take them out of the world, but to keep them safe from the evil one.

JOHN 17:15

❋ *Safe from Evil*

When we walk with Jesus, we walk into a battle with evil. The battlefield is covered with land mines of temptation, and the enemy wages guerrilla warfare, using manipulation and deceit. His slick-talking recruiters seek to persuade us to leave Jesus and join the evil pursuit.

All men are susceptible to the treachery and deceitfulness of our enemy, the devil. For that reason, Jesus asked his Father to "keep [us] safe from the evil one."

William Wimmer, pastor of Grace Chapel Church of God in Benton, Arkansas, once told a story that illustrates the evil and deceptiveness of this world.

William was traveling one summer night with his wife and their three-year-old son, Micah. After many miles of driving in the darkness, they came to a stop in a remote area. As they sat in the car, the light of the oncoming traffic revealed all of the dirt, dead bugs, and insects on their car's windshield. Micah said, "Look! How dirty!"

Neither William nor his wife thought much of their son's observation until a moment later when they started the car and began to drive on-away from the light of the traffic. Upon reentering the darkness, they could no longer see the mess on the windshield. Micah quickly piped up and said, "Now the glass is clean!"[11]

Don't let yourself be fooled. Though we can't always see it, evil is everywhere on the battlefield we call life. But also take heart; you can live courageously and victoriously in this world because our Father in heaven keeps us safe from the evil one.

Jesus, let me be aware of the evil in the world around me and let me be confident that you keep me safe from that evil.

TO READ
John 17:17-26

Make them pure and holy by teaching them your words of truth. JOHN 17:17

Words of Truth

There is a cleansing quality to truth. Those who are willing let it cleanse their souls, and they find freedom and consistency in their lives.

People look everywhere for truth. They set out on what they consider the pursuit for truth, thinking that it is somehow randomly available throughout the universe. In contrast, Jesus says to God the Father, "Your word is truth" (John 17:17, NIV).

In his *New York Times* best seller *The Gifts of the Jews*, Thomas Cahill wrote:

[The Ten Commandments] require no justification, nor can they be argued away. They are not dependent upon circumstances, nor may they be set aside because of special considerations. They are not propositions for debate. They are not suggestions. They are not even (as a recent book would have us imagine in the jargon of our day) "ten challenges."

They are exactly what they seem to be—and there is no getting around them or (to be more spatially precise) out from under them. But the only thing new about them is their articulation at this moment amid the terrifying fires of Sinai. They have been received by billions as reasonable, necessary, even unalterable because they are written on human hearts and always have been. They were always there in the inner core of the human person—in the deep silence that each of us carries within. They needed only to be spoken aloud.[12]

Indeed, God's truth is not open for debate, and it is not something we can rationalize or negotiate. There is only one place you will find ultimate truth, and that's in the pages of God's written Word, the Bible.

Jesus, cleanse my life with your truth.

TO READ
John 18:1-27

One of the household servants of the high priest, a relative of the man whose ear Peter had cut off, asked, "Didn't I see you out there in the olive grove with Jesus?" Again Peter denied it. And immediately a rooster crowed. JOHN 18:26-27

Heeding God's Warnings

Peter had very sincerely stated that he would never deny Jesus. He earnestly believed he would be willing to give up his life for his Messiah and best friend. Yet Peter failed. At the moment of truth, Peter denied that he even knew Jesus. His failure was even more devastating to him because he had been warned.

Peter's denial of Christ demonstrates something about the hearts of human beings: We are drawn to the very things we are warned against.

In the magazine *Marketing News*, Herb Rotfeld reported that at a 1997 marketing and public policy conference in Boston, psychology professor Brad J. Bushman of Iowa State University presented the results of a series of experiments exploring the potential of warning labels to attract audiences to violent television programs. The results showed that warning labels actually increased interest in the violent shows, especially when the source of the warning was the United States Surgeon General, and particularly when the target of the warnings was "all viewers" and not just "young viewers."

The research also showed that labels providing information and a warning ("This film contains violence. Viewer discretion is advised.") increased interest in the violent programs even more than the ones that just provided information ("This film contains violence.") In other words, telling people what to do with the information actually drew them to the violent programs more than just giving the information.

In the same way, each of us has within us a desire to pursue the very things God has warned us against. Knowing that, we should be careful not to just read his warnings, but to heed them as well.

Lord, give me a healthy respect for my potential to be drawn astray. Help me to actively heed your warnings.

TO READ
John 18:28-32

Jesus' trial before Caiaphas ended in the early hours of the morning. Then he was taken to the headquarters of the Roman governor. His accusers didn't go in themselves because it would defile them, and they wouldn't be allowed to celebrate the Passover feast. JOHN 18:28

The Problem with Focus

The Jewish leaders of Jesus' day were a focused lot as they took part in the process of condemning the Messiah. Although Jesus performed miracles too numerous to list and had compassion on the poor, they were more focused on not missing the Passover feast than on carefully considering the evidence that confirmed his identity as the Messiah. Therefore, they were single-minded and determined to push him through their system of "justice" and be finished with him.

Focus can be a great thing in the life of a believer, as long as your focus is on what God is really doing in your life and not on man-made distractions.

Architect Frank Lloyd Wright once told of an incident that seemed insignificant at the time it took place but had a profound influence on the rest of his life. The winter he was nine, he went walking across a snow-covered field with his reserved, no-nonsense uncle. As the two of them reached the far end of the field, his uncle stopped him. He pointed out his own tracks in the snow, straight and true as an arrow's flight, and then young Frank's tracks, which meandered all over the field.

"Notice how your tracks wander aimlessly from the cattle to the woods and back again," his uncle said. "And see how my tracks aim directly to my goal. There is an important lesson in that."

Years later the world-famous architect told how this experience contributed to his philosophy in life. "I determined right then," he'd say with a twinkle in his eye, "not to miss most things in life, as my uncle had."[13]

Where is your focus today? Is it on something that keeps you from seeing Jesus, or is it on him and him alone?

Jesus, may my focus be on you so that I see you every day.

July

TO READ
John 18:33-40

[The people] shouted back, "No! Not this man, but Barabbas!" (Barabbas was a criminal.) JOHN 18:40

❁ *Less Than a Savior*

People will settle for almost anything but a savior. We prefer human leaders because they are a lot like us. They look like us and have flaws like us.

A savior, on the other hand, is a much different story. While influential men are flawed, a savior is perfect in every way. A savior is able to give what is completely beyond our reach. A savior demands humility because he can do what we can't do ourselves.

And so we see the people at Jesus' trial choosing the very human, very limited criminal, Barabbas, rather than the Savior, Jesus.

John R. Rice, one of this country's most successful evangelists and a friend of Billy Sunday, captures this as he contrasts the limitations of being a father with the awesome nature of the Savior:

> My six daughters sometimes gather around me, telling me how they need shoes, money for music lessons, and for many other things. Sometimes I have been compelled to say, "Go easy! I am not made out of money. We will just have to get what we can afford and go without the rest."
>
> But I never read in God's Word where He ever told anybody, "Go easy! I don't have very much. I have already strained Myself giving to others. I cannot give as much as you ask." No, no! One of our greatest sins about praying is that we do not ask for enough. We do not take what God is willing to give. . . . God forgive us our little, stingy, unbelieving prayers![1]

All people have much to give us, but their abilities have limitations. On the other hand, Jesus Christ, our Savior, has no limits in what he can give. All we need to do is ask.

Lord, let me never settle for less than a Savior.

TO READ
John 19:1-15

[Pilate] took Jesus back into the headquarters again and asked him, "Where are you from?" But Jesus gave no answer. JOHN 19:9

❈ Actions That Speak

Some years ago, twelve thousand people marched in a demonstration in New York City. In the procession were three vans packed full of men, women, and children. In one van was a court of appeals judge and in another was a ragged street boy. On the sides of another car, these words were written: "These people have been saved from burning buildings by the New York Firemen." Behind the automobiles marched the firemen who had saved them, all wearing their medals of honor. [2]

As they marched, the firemen smiled and waved at the crowd. But they didn't say a word. After all, they didn't have to. Their actions had already said it all.

When your work speaks for itself, there really isn't a need to speak, is there?

Pilate knew that Jesus had proved himself over and over. He had never met anyone like Jesus, and he had found no evidence of wrongdoing on his part. But he wanted to know some things about him.

Pilate thought he was in charge and that he had the power to determine whether Jesus would live or die. He thought he had the authority to demand a response from Jesus. Because of his limited human perspective, he interrogated Jesus. And he was astonished when Jesus would not answer him.

Some may see Jesus' refusal to answer Pilate as an acknowledgment of defeat. But Jesus was in control. His silence was yet another demonstration that he knew who he was and why he had come to earth.

Jesus didn't have to defend himself before Pilate, and he doesn't have to defend himself today. His actions on our behalf have already spoken for him.

Lord, thank you for all the things you have done and continue to do on my behalf.

TO READ
John 19:16-27

[Jesus] said to this disciple, "She is your mother." And from then on this disciple took her into his home. JOHN 19:27

Mom's Special Role

In the midst of his agony on the cross, Jesus asks John to watch out for his mom. It is hard to imagine Jesus making a greater request than to have John take care of his mother after his crucifixion.

In a couple of simple statements, Jesus demonstrates for all of us the special place Mom carries in our hearts. She was chosen by God to give us life. She was there when we were the most helpless. She was concerned about every detail of our lives when others did not have the patience.

It is strange to think about Jesus, the Son of God, having a mother, but we see her at all the most important moments of his life. When the shepherds gave a report of their encounter with the angels, she treasured the words in her heart. She took Jesus to the Temple to be dedicated as an infant. She found him in the Temple when he was twelve and mildly corrected him. She was an integral part of his first public miracle at a wedding in Cana. She interacted with him throughout his public ministry. She was present at the crucifixion, weeping as she watched him give up his life.

In one of the most touching scenes in all of the Bible, we see Jesus make provisions for his mom, even while he is suffering excruciating pain. He assigns his closest friend, John, a position in the family as a son of Mary. He assigns his mom a mother-son relationship with John. In a powerful sense he is saying, "Mom, thanks for being there. Thanks for tackling the challenge of bringing me into the world. Thanks for taking on the journey of raising the Son of God. You will never be forgotten!"

Does your mom know you appreciate her? What have you done lately to honor her for her role in your life, which God chose her for?

Lord, give me a creative idea for showing honor to my mom this week.

TO READ
John 19:28-42

When Pilate gave him permission, [Joseph] came and took the body away. Nicodemus, the man who had come to Jesus at night, also came, bringing about seventy-five pounds of embalming ointment made from myrrh and aloes. JOHN 19:38-39

Extravagant Giving

Joseph and Nicodemus both believed in Jesus. They had talked with him enough to know that he was the Messiah. But they stood by silently while he was tried, convicted, and crucified.

Now that it was time to bury Jesus, they stepped up. At the risk of losing their standing in society, they asked for the body of their Lord.

Nicodemus wanted to give Jesus an extravagant burial, so he spent an enormous amount of money to acquire seventy-five pounds of ointment for the embalming process. But there was no way he could have known the eternal significance of what he and Joseph were about to do.

The body of Jesus would be wrapped in cloth and packed with the fragrant spices. These elaborate preparations were transformed into evidence of Jesus' resurrection. When Jesus' glorified body left the tomb, the seventy-five pounds of ointment would have caused the wrappings to collapse in the middle, making it obvious that Jesus had not simply revived from the torture of the crucifixion and unwrapped himself. It was also obvious that no one had found a way into the tomb to steal the body.

Joseph and Nicodemus thought they were sparing no expense in honoring Jesus with a proper burial. But they had no way of knowing they were investing in the everlasting evidence that Jesus had risen from the dead.

Likewise, you may think you are only investing in today when you give to your church. But in reality, you are giving to the God who transforms everything he touches. Your generosity today may well make the difference in the lives of those you may never meet this side of heaven.

Jesus, make me extravagantly generous when it comes to giving to you.

TO READ
John 20:1-10

Then [Peter and John] went home. JOHN 20:10

✤ The Comforts of Home

When you aren't sure where to go, you head home. Home is a place to regroup and reconnect to the roots of your life.

The disciples had followed Jesus for three intense years. They had seen the unimaginable on a daily basis. They had grown accustomed to interacting with Jesus. But then it suddenly ended. Jesus was tried, falsely convicted, and crucified. The disciples showed up at the tomb on Sunday morning to find Jesus' body missing. No doubt they were filled with questions.

Since they weren't sure what to do, they went back to their homes.

I watched my oldest son go through a similar experience this year. He was in his sophomore year of college, playing quarterback at a community college in southern California. His freshman year had been outstanding. He was surrounded by experienced offensive players.

After that year, most of Brock's offensive teammates graduated, so his sophomore year was characterized by an inexperienced offense. He struggled to find his rhythm. About halfway through the season, the frustration caught up with him, and he called me.

"Dad, can I come home and talk with you?"

The act of coming home gave Brock an opportunity to regroup and gain a new perspective.

The next time you get disillusioned or your perspective on life is distracted, spend some time at home in the presence of Jesus.

Lord, help me know when I need to go home to you.

TO READ
John 20:11-29

[Jesus] said to Thomas, "Put your finger here and see my hands. Put your hand into the wound in my side. Don't be faithless any longer. Believe!" "My Lord and my God!" Thomas exclaimed. JOHN 20:27-28

Jesus, the Master Motivator

George Washington was a master of the art of motivation. In 1777 his soldiers faced a cold, bleak winter of inactivity on a mountain near Morristown, New Jersey. As winter set in, Washington began to notice restlessness and grumbling among the men.

Washington had a plan. Grim-faced but determined to motivate his men, he told his engineering officers that a fort must be built quickly. Then he had the sentry guard increased.

Work on the fortifications started immediately. The soldiers snapped out of their lethargic attitudes and began guessing when the attack might take place. When the spring thaw came, the fort was not quite finished, but the general ordered a move.

"But will we move before the fort is finished?" the chief of engineers asked.

"It has served its purpose," Washington replied with a twinkle in his eye. "The fort was just nonsense, to keep the men busy at something they thought important."

The structure came to be known as Fort Nonsense—though it symbolized the good sense one leader used to maintain the morale of his men.

That winter, George Washington knew what his troops needed, and he did it for them. The same is true of Jesus.

Some of Jesus' disciples were content with hearing eyewitness reports about his resurrection. But that wasn't enough for "Doubting Thomas," who needed to see Jesus' scars and touch his wounds. He needed evidence he could see and touch, and Jesus, being the Master Motivator, obliged.

Does your faith need a shot in the arm today? Do you need to be motivated? Seek God for answers. He knows exactly what you need!

Lord, do whatever you need to do in order to keep me motivated.

TO READ
John 21:1-9

[Jesus] said, "Throw out your net on the right-hand side of the boat, and you'll get plenty of fish!" So they did, and they couldn't draw in the net because there were so many fish in it.   JOHN 21:6

❀ *Believing What You Hear*

FBI agents raided San Diego's Southwood Psychiatric Hospital, which had been under investigation for medical insurance fraud. After hours of reviewing medical records, the agents decided to order pizza. Imagine their conversation.

Agent: I'd like to order nineteen large pizzas and sixty-seven cans of soda.

Pizza Man: And where would you like them delivered?

Agent: We're over at the psychiatric hospital. I'm an FBI agent.

Pizza Man: You're an FBI agent?

Agent: That's correct. Just about everybody here is.

Pizza Man: And you're at the psychiatric hospital?

Agent: That's correct. And make sure you don't go through the front doors. We have them locked. You will have to go around to the back. How soon can you get here?

Pizza Man: You say everyone at the psychiatric hospital is an FBI agent?

Agent: That's right. We've been here all day and we're starving.

Pizza Man: How are you going to pay for all of this?

Agent: I have my checkbook right here.

Pizza Man: And you're all FBI agents?

Agent: That's right. Everyone here is an FBI agent. Can you remember to bring the pizzas and sodas to the service entrance in the rear? We have the front doors locked.

Pizza Man: I don't think so. *Click!*[3]

As with this urban legend, it really is hard to believe what we are hearing. But Jesus wants his disciples to believe his words. Do you?

Jesus, may I never doubt your word or your promise to back it up.

TO READ
John 21:10-23

"Now come and have some breakfast!" Jesus said. And no one dared ask him if he really was the Lord because they were sure of it. JOHN 21:12

An Everyday Kind of Savior

Sometimes we expect Jesus to be a Savior who constantly does the spectacular for us. In fact, we are often stunned when he enters our everyday life and invites us to do everyday things with him.

Only Jesus would invite his disciples to have a simple breakfast with him so soon after the spectacular event of his resurrection. We might expect him to tell a story, give a lecture, or do some miracles for his followers. Instead, he simply invited his disciples to sit down and eat with him.

David Peterson, former pastor at the First Presbyterian Church in Spokane, Washington, tells about a wonderful "everyday" encounter he had as he was in his office preparing a sermon.

David's little daughter walked into his office and said, "Daddy, can we play?"

He answered, "I'm awfully sorry, sweetheart, but I'm right in the middle of preparing this sermon. In about an hour I can play."

She said, "Okay, when you're finished, Daddy, I am going to give you a great big hug."

"Thank you very much," he said, then watched her go to the door, do a U-turn, and come back to give him a bone-breaking hug.

David said to her, "Darling, you said you were going to give me a hug after I finished."

She answered, "Daddy, I just wanted you to know what you have to look forward to!"[4]

David Peterson saw Jesus in an everyday encounter with his daughter. We too can see him in our everyday lives. We just need to have our eyes open.

Jesus, may I recognize you in the everyday activities and incidents of my life.

TO READ
John 21:24-25

I suppose that if all the other things Jesus did were written down, the whole world could not contain the books. JOHN 21:25

✹ An Unfinished Story

Apparently Jesus performed so many miracles while he was on earth that it was impossible to write them all down. He must have healed many more lives, taught many more sermons, and encouraged many more hurting people than could possibly have been recorded in the Gospels.

That work continues to this day and beyond.

Consider J. Oswald Sanders. Before he was fifty, he was so badly afflicted with arthritis that he could barely get out of bed. He could have taken a nice retirement, but instead he was about to enter the most productive and creative years of his life. At age fifty Sanders left a prosperous career as an attorney in New Zealand to lead the China Inland Mission (now called Overseas Missionary Fellowship).

After several years of leading the mission, Sanders "retired" again, only to take on the directorship of a Christian college. Then, once again, he took retirement. The twice-widowed Sanders certainly deserved rest. But rather than taking it easy, he spent his last twenty years traveling around the world to more than three hundred speaking engagements per year.

Respect for him grew even though he never sought the limelight or tried to maintain his position. And remarkably, as he entered his second and third careers, he was totally freed from arthritis.

By the time most men approach ninety years of age, they are long finished accomplishing great things. But not J. Oswald Sanders. He was working on his last book when he passed into eternity at eighty-nine years of age.[5]

Sanders was an example of the remarkable work Jesus still does in men's lives—of the work he wants to do in you.

Jesus, make my life a wonderful, productive part of your story.

TO READ
Joshua 5:1-9

At that time the Lord told Joshua, "Use knives of flint to make the Israelites a circumcised people again." JOSHUA 5:2

The Mark of Commitment

The nation of Israel was coming out of forty years of survival in the wilderness. The traditions of their culture seemed irrelevant in the desert, so they failed to circumcise those who had been born in the wilderness.

All of this was about to change. Before the men of Israel went into battle, God called them to pledge their allegiance to him and to their nation. The obvious mark of that allegiance was circumcision.

Circumcision was an unconventional but strategic outward expression of the covenant between God and the nation of Israel. It was performed on the most private part of a man's body. This was for a number of reasons.

First of all, God was intimately involved in the lives of his people. He was working through the nation of Israel in such a way that the rest of the world could see his love, grace, and power. As a result, he wanted a total commitment, the kind of commitment demonstrated through circumcision.

Second, circumcision represented a commitment on the part of Israel's people to maintain their national purity. God wanted to keep the nation of Israel alive and identifiable. This was a part of God's plan for the nation of Israel to give birth to the Savior of the world.

Finally, circumcision was a painful commitment that required a period of recovery. As such, it represented a courageous rededication to the purposes for which God was preparing his people.

Following God meant self-sacrifice on the part of his people. It still does. The level of investment you make in your relationship with Jesus determines the effectiveness with which you live for him.

Lord, make me willing to sacrifice myself for you daily.

TO READ
Joshua 5:10-15

"I am commander of the Lord's army." At this, Joshua fell with his face to the ground in reverence. "I am at your command," Joshua said. "What do you want your servant to do?" JOSHUA 5:14

A Passion to Hear Him

Joshua carried the responsibility for the entire nation of Israel. It was a humbling responsibility, and it left him hungry to hear from God. He came to the Lord with an intense focus because he needed to know what message he had for him.

We need a passion for hearing from God, the kind of passion Pulitzer Prize–winning author Annie Dillard writes about in her book *For the Time Being*:

> In Highland New Guinea, now Papua New Guinea; a British district officer named James Taylor contacted a mountain village, above three thousand feet, whose tribe had never seen any trace of the outside world. It was the 1930s. He described the courage of one villager. One day, on the airstrip hacked from the mountains near his village, this man cut vines and lashed himself to the fuselage of Taylor's airplane shortly before it took off. He explained calmly to his loved ones that, no matter what happened to him, he had to see where it came from.[6]

God brings to our lives power, wisdom, and perspective that is beyond our ability to comprehend. Yet that power, wisdom, and perspective is intended for us. This is what he meant when, speaking through the apostle Peter, he told us he has given us "everything we need for living a godly life" (2 Peter 1:3).

When you realize just what Jesus came to bring, you will strap yourself to his gifts until you see where they come from.

Jesus, make me desperately hungry to hear from you.

TO READ
Galatians 5:1-10

It is for freedom that Christ has set us free. Stand firm, then, and do not let yourselves be burdened again by a yoke of slavery. GALATIANS 5:1, NIV

❈ *God of the Unconventional*

At the heart of the Civil War was the issue of slavery. Slaves had none of the rights that free people experienced, none of the privileges of being free, and none of the opportunities free people were able to pursue. A large portion of free people concluded that such things ought not to be.

In the movie *Gettysburg*, Union colonel Joshua L. Chamberlain learns that his regiment is going to receive 120 Union soldiers who had mutinied. Chamberlain is given permission to shoot any of the mutineers who didn't cooperate. Here is what he tells this rather unconventional band of fighters:

> Here's the situation. The whole Reb army is up that road a ways, waiting for us. This is no time for an argument. I tell you, we could surely use you fellows. . . . This regiment was formed last summer in Maine. There were a thousand of us then. There are less than three hundred of us now. All of us volunteered to fight for the Union, just as you did. Some came mainly because we were bored at home. Some came because we were ashamed not to. Many of us came because it was the right thing to do. And all of us have seen men die.
>
> This is a different kind of army. If you look back through history, you'll see men fighting for pay, for women, for some other kind of loot. They fight for land, power, because a king leads them, or just because they like killing. But we are here for something new. This has not happened much in the history of the world. We are an army out to set other men free.

Throughout history, God has been calling men and women to give of themselves so others can be free. When God asks you to sacrifice so others can be free, what will you do?

Lord, help me do whatever you want in my life to set others free.

TO READ
Joshua 6:6-12

Joshua got up early the next morning, and the priests again carried the Ark of the Lord.

JOSHUA 6:12

Motivation and Risk-Taking

Joshua was finally in action. He had spent forty years wandering around in the wilderness with a generation of people under God's discipline. Through it all, he had protected his integrity and developed his abilities. Now it was time to carry out his dream. So Joshua got up early in the morning.

When life is boring or out of focus, sleeping in is easy. But when life calls you to action and you know what you were made for, you are motivated to do what it takes to live up to that purpose. That includes taking some risks.

In a July 23, 1999, article, the *Chicago Tribune* tells the story of a group of men in Naperville, Illinois, who gather twice a week to compete in old-timer pickup softball games. Writer Ted Gregory explains that these men risk more than just pulled muscles and sprained ankles in these games; sometimes they even risk heart attacks from exerting themselves in the hot sun.

Despite the risks, sixty-three-year-old Bill Body explains why he plays: "If I'm going to die, I'm going to die doing what I love doing, whether it's playing softball, fishing, hunting, or something else."

After reading about Body's remarks, writer and editor Mark Galli commented, "We're often tempted in the church to slow down, cut back, take it easy because we get tired of taking risks—and in Christ's work, there are a lot of emotional or spiritual risks. But Bill Body is exactly right: life itself is a risk—we're all going to die. So we might as well get involved, take the risks, and do the things in Christ we really love."[7]

Indeed, we need to understand that life itself is a risk and that there are some things worth stepping out and taking risks for. After all, if old men are willing to risk their lives for softball, surely we can risk ourselves for the cause of Christ.

Jesus, give me the motivation to fearlessly risk myself for you.

Everything made from silver, gold, bronze, or iron is sacred to the Lord and must be brought into his treasury. JOSHUA 6:19

What Is Ours and What Is His

Israel was moving into the Promised Land. God had given it to his people, so it was their privilege to own it and use it. But God made it clear that the gold, silver, and bronze from the city of Jericho belonged to him.

When God gives us something, it belongs to us, and we have the freedom to make decisions regarding how we use it. But it is different with the things that God declares belong to him alone. One of life's tests is what kind of respect we have for his things.

In C. S. Lewis's classic novel *The Screwtape Letters*, a demon makes these observations about man:

Prosperity knits a man to the world. He feels that he is finding his place in it, while really it is finding its place in him. His increasing reputation, his widening circle of acquaintances, his sense of importance, the growing pressure of absorbing and agreeable work, build up in him a sense of being really at home on earth, which is just what we want. You will notice that the young are generally less unwilling to die than the middle-aged and the old. The truth is that the enemy, having oddly destined these mere animals to life in his own eternal world, has guarded them pretty effectively from the danger of feeling at home anywhere else.[8]

God gives us great blessings here on earth, but he reserves some things for himself alone. Our ultimate eternal home is with him in heaven, where he will lavish on us without reservation all the things he has made for us. In heaven, everything truly will be ours.

Which of these "inheritances" will you focus on today?

Lord, don't let the good things of this world make me feel too at home here.

TO READ
1 Samuel 14:1-23

"Let's go across to see those pagans," Jonathan said to his armor bearer. "Perhaps the Lord will help us, for nothing can hinder the Lord. He can win a battle whether he has many warriors or only a few!"

1 SAMUEL 14:6

Made for Victory

Jonathan was the son of the king and an effective soldier. He had a good reputation and a good track record in battle. And he had a strong sense of adventure when it came to what God could do. The Philistines were the primary enemy of Israel. They were proud, perverted, and powerful.

Because Jonathan believed God had given them the land and that God can defeat any enemy, he took a risky step. Since he was a soldier, he was shadowed by an armor bearer who carried his shield and extra weapons. The armor bearer rushed into war with his warrior. They fought side by side and in concert with one another. Jonathan approached his armor bearer one day and said, "Let's go across to see those pagans. . . . Perhaps the Lord will help us, for nothing can hinder the Lord."

The plan was impossible without God's intervention. But evil was afoot, and God was willing to intervene. Jonathan and his armor bearer experienced a resounding victory. They caught the Philistines off guard. Their initial assault was highly effective, then God threw the entire Philistine army into confusion. As word of the victory spread, the rest of the army of Israel began to rejoice and join the battle.

It was one of the great victories for the nation of Israel, but it started with the actions of just one man. Sometimes all it takes for evil to be defeated is for one good man to do something!

Will you be ready for the day you need to act? God may call you to begin a campaign that helps defeat evil. Or he may call someone else to get it started, then ask you to join in the victory. Either way, you get to rejoice as you make your vital contribution.

Lead me in victory, Lord.

TO READ
Luke 1:11-20

Your wife, Elizabeth, will bear you a son! And you are to name him John. You will have great joy and gladness, and many will rejoice with you at his birth, for he will be great in the eyes of the Lord.

LUKE 1:13-15

The Definition of Success

In every generation there are individuals who are highly visible and unusually influential. People of influence face unique challenges. Actors and politicians grow weary of having their personal lives broadcast for public consumption. Community and business leaders get tired of living and serving in a fish bowl. People in ministry grow weary of the constant compassion that men and women require. Despite all this, the world needs people who accept public recognition because they provide leadership and inspiration for everyone else. Companies needs CEOs, nations need statesmen, kids need role models, and sheep need a shepherd.

And every one of these influential people has parents! Parenting a successful child is as much a challenge as raising difficult kids. It is also a remarkable privilege. Zechariah and Elizabeth were godly people who were entrusted with the awesome task of raising John the Baptist. They took care of his most basic needs and helped shape in him the character that would be required to announce the coming of the Messiah.

It is interesting to note that highly influential people tend to have quality parents. *The Voice* magazine reported a study that famed statistician Roger Babson did of the leaders of one hundred top industries. He found that 5 percent of these outstanding men were the sons of bankers, 10 percent were the sons of merchants and manufacturers, 25 percent were the sons of doctors and lawyers, and better than 35 percent were the sons of preachers.[9]

Choose a highly influential person to pray for this week. We all need to pray for these public figures and their families, because we depend on them and their character.

Jesus, give me the character to handle the success you want me to have.

TO READ
Ephesians 4:1-13

Always keep yourselves united in the Holy Spirit,
and bind yourselves together with peace.

EPHESIANS 4:3

✾ *Lose the Selfishness*

Adversity is no problem for the united, but the slightest bit of selfishness can have disastrous results. For that reason, we men must stand united with our brothers in Christ.

General Colin Powell underscored this important fact of life when he wrote the following:

> ABC correspondent Sam Donaldson was interviewing a young African-American soldier in a tank platoon on the eve of the battle in Desert Storm. Donaldson asked, "How do you think the battle will go? Are you afraid?"
>
> "We'll do okay. We're well trained. And I'm not afraid," the GI answered, gesturing toward his buddies around him. "I'm not afraid because I'm with my family."
>
> The other soldiers shouted, "Tell him again. He didn't hear you." The soldier repeated, "This is my family, and we'll take care of each other."
>
> That story never fails to touch me or the audience. It is a metaphor for what we have to do as a nation. We have to start thinking of America as a family. We have to stop screeching at each other, stop hurting each other, and instead start caring for, sacrificing for, and sharing with each other. We have to stop constantly criticizing, which is the way of the malcontent, and instead get back to the can-do attitude that made America. We have to keep trying, and risk failing, in order to solve this country's problems. We cannot move forward if cynics and critics swoop down and pick apart anything that goes wrong to a point where we lose.[10]

Each of us is called to take part in a collective life mission far bigger than ourselves. We need to ask ourselves if we are willing to submit our own wills to that mission and to its leader. Are you?

Jesus, remind me daily that I am part of a team with a noble purpose.

TO READ
Joshua 7:1-5

Approximately three thousand warriors were sent, but they were soundly defeated. JOSHUA 7:4

What's under the Surface?

Greg Asimakoupoulos is a regular contributor to *Leadership Journal*. He relates the following observation from his trip to Nome, Alaska:

> Nome, Alaska, a city sitting at the edge of the Bering Sea, is like many villages of the Arctic. The ground on which the community sits is spongelike tundra that is frozen and covered with snow most of the year. Burying the dead is a real challenge. Sanitation landfills are unheard of. Garbage trucks do not haul off the kind of refuse we in the "Lower Forty-eight" leave at the curbside twice a week. For that reason, a typical Nome, Alaska, front yard is home to broken washing machines, junked cars, old toilets, scrap wood, and piles of nondegradable refuse.
>
> Tourists who visit Nome in the summer are amazed at the amount of debris just sitting around the residents' yards. How could anyone live like that, they wonder. But what these visitors do not realize is that for nine months of the year, Nome is covered under a blanket of snow that covers the garbage. During those months, the little Iditarod town is a quaint winter wonderland of pure white landscapes.[11]

It is possible for something to look pristine on the outside while there is a mess developing on the inside. Today's Scripture gives us an example.

The city of Ai was undermanned and vulnerable to attack. The battle should have been a rout, but there was a fatal problem. Achan's sin put the nation in a precarious position.

In the same way, it is important for you to make sure that the good on the surface matches what is really underneath.

Jesus, may I never appear to be on the outside what I am not on the inside.

TO READ
Joshua 7:6-26

Lord, what am I to say, now that Israel has fled from its enemies? JOSHUA 7:8

❋ Time for an Adjustment

The men of Israel took their self-sufficiency into battle with Ai. But after their defeat, Joshua's only prayer was, "Lord, what am I to say?"

Failure is never easy; however, if we humble ourselves and make strategic changes, our failures can be some of our most valuable experiences. Here is an illustration of that truth.

For much of the nineteenth century, fish merchants' attempts to ship fresh North Atlantic cod from Boston to San Francisco failed miserably. At that time, the only way to ship the fish to the West Coast was to dress them out, pack them in ice, load them on a ship, and sail them around the South American continent—a trip that took months. As you can imagine, by the time the cod reached California, they weren't fit for human consumption.

In an attempt to overcome that problem, the merchants tried placing live cod in holding tanks full of water and shipping them to California. Most of the fish survived the trip, but because they didn't get much exercise in the tanks, their flesh was pasty and relatively tasteless. Another failure.

Finally, someone suggested that they place live catfish in the tanks with the cod, then ship them. Why? Because catfish are a cod's natural enemy, and having a few catfish in their tanks with them would keep them alert and swimming around. The idea worked. By the time the cod reached San Francisco, they were in perfect condition.[12]

Do you see your failures as ultimate defeat, or do you see them as God's way of forcing you to make adjustments, thus making you a man more suitable for serving him?

Lord, use my failures to help me make adjustments in my life that strengthen my faith.

TO READ
1 Peter 4:1-19

The time has come for judgment, and it must begin first among God's own children. And if even we Christians must be judged, what terrible fate awaits those who have never believed God's Good News?

1 PETER 4:17

Wrong Conclusions

Some people just have a knack for not getting things right. They may make some good observations, but they regularly come up with the wrong conclusions and guarantee themselves a complicated, difficult life.

Here are two stories that illustrate this point.

The Russian cosmonaut Gherman Titoy said after his return from space, "Some people say there is a God out there . . . but in my travels around the earth all day long, I looked around and didn't see Him. . . . I saw no God nor angels. The rocket was made by our own people. I don't believe in God. I believe in man, his strength, his possibilities, his reason."[13]

A drunken man got on the bus late one night, staggered up the aisle, and sat next to a woman who was clutching a Bible. She looked the wayward drunk up and down and said, "I've got news for you, mister. You're going straight to hell!" The man jumped up out of his seat and shouted, "Oh, man, I'm on the wrong bus again!"[14]

Both of these men reached wrong conclusions about their observations, conclusions that carried eternal consequences.

At the end of our lives, we will all give an answer for what kind of conclusions we came to. Will you base your conclusions on your own faulty thinking or on the truth of the Word of God?

Lord, help me to trust the truth of your Word more than that of my own faulty conclusions.

TO READ
James 4:1-16

How do you know what will happen tomorrow? For your life is like the morning fog—it's here a little while, then it's gone. JAMES 4:14

❋ The Value of Today

RiShawn Biddle of *Forbes* magazine shares this recollection of a man who paid the ultimate price on September 11, 2001:

> Meeting the late Thomas Burnett Jr. last Friday, I would not have marked him down as a hero. Thoratec's chief operating officer was just another of the many executives who insist on stopping by *Forbes*' Los Angeles bureau to rhapsodize about their products in hopes of getting some ink. . . .
>
> As it turns out, Burnett, 38, has emerged as one of the early heroes in Tuesday's catastrophic terrorist attacks on the World Trade Center and the Pentagon. Before the hijacked United Airlines Flight 93 made its deadly plunge into an empty field near Pittsburgh, he reportedly called his wife four times. During the last call he made before perishing with 45 other passengers and crew members, Burnett said that he and several others would try to overpower the hijackers and avert more carnage. They succeeded, but at the cost of their lives. But that early Friday morning, sitting in a conference room with Thoratec Chief Executive Officer D. Keith Grossman and a company spokeswoman, Burnett didn't appear to be a man of action.
>
> When I told the little contingent that they had only 20 minutes to make their case, Burnett joked that "we'll start with ten minutes and you can kick us out after that if you want." They were gone 30 minutes later. Burnett, jovial and athletic looking, left little of a lasting impression otherwise.
>
> Afterward, I went back to my office to help close another edition of *Forbes* magazine. Burnett would later board several planes on a scheduled business trip. He then caught an early flight out of Newark, N.J., so he could go home to his wife and three young children.[15]

What you do today can have an effect on eternity.

Give me strength, Lord, to live for you today.

Then he said to me, "This is what the Lord says to Zerubbabel: It is not by force nor by strength, but by my Spirit, says the Lord Almighty."

ZECHARIAH 4:6

The Key to Lasting Work

I am a typical man in that I focus on results. I like to make my plans and trust that they will be my key to success. In fact, I find it much easier to believe in the effectiveness of my methods than on the power of God.

My methods are predictable and easy to evaluate, and since they are my methods, I can adjust them as necessary. But God is not so easy to hem in. His ways are often unpredictable. He is not impressed with numbers or the impact of *now*. His view is history-wide and eternity-wide, so he recognizes how important and influential the "little" things in life truly are.

Dr. J. B. Hawthorne was a noted orator sought by scores of churches and heard by tens of thousands of listeners. One time he went to help a southern church in a two-week evangelistic campaign. By the end of the meetings, only one person—a little, unpromising lad—was saved. Understandably, Dr. Hawthorne was a bit chagrined. But what he didn't know at the time was that the boy, A. T. Robertson, would later become the greatest Greek scholar of the twentieth century.

I would never suggest that we should be content with small results or that we should settle for mediocre methodology. While we know that God can bless our smallest efforts—as long as we make them with sincere hearts—it is simpler for him to bless excellence. But whether our efforts are large or small, we need to recognize that the only work that lasts is that which God does in the midst of our efforts.

Lord, allow me to see what you are doing by getting my eyes off what I am doing.

TO READ
Romans 1:1-23

From the time the world was created, people have seen the earth and sky and all that God made. They can clearly see his invisible qualities—his eternal power and divine nature. So they have no excuse whatsoever for not knowing God. ROMANS 1:20

The Wonders of Creation

No matter where you look in creation, you encounter the wonder of God's creativity. He has put his signature on everything he has made. We are impressed with our own creativity because we can make one thing out of another. But God has created everything out of nothing.

God's creation displays his eternal power and divine nature. It also displays how much he likes variety. Take, for example, two birds that are as different as can be: the ostrich and the bee hummingbird.

Ostriches are the largest living birds. The typical male ostrich grows to about eight feet tall and weighs three hundred pounds. The female ostrich, which lacks the familiar black and white coloration, is smaller.

Ostriches may live up to fifty years, both in and out of the wild. They have extremely strong legs and two-toed feet that serve them well both for speed and for self-defense. If cornered, their legs can deliver a blow powerful enough to kill an adult lion. They can run at speeds of up to forty-four miles per hour, making them the fastest animals on two legs. However, ostriches cannot fly.

The Cuban bee hummingbird, so named because it can be mistaken at a glance for a bee, is the smallest living bird. At two inches long and with a two-inch wingspan, it is smaller than the eye of an ostrich.

Bee hummingbirds are much more colorful than ostriches. They not only fly at high speeds, but they can hover, much like a helicopter. Their legs and feet are useful for perching and balance in flight, but nothing more.

The ostrich and the bee hummingbird are but two examples of the wonderful creativity of God. If you want to see more examples, just open your eyes and look around you. What do you see?

Lord, may I never lose my sense of wonder at your creativity.

TO READ
2 Timothy 2:10-16

Work hard so God can approve you. Be a good worker, one who does not need to be ashamed and who correctly explains the word of truth.

2 TIMOTHY 2:15

Studying for Yourself

Diligent Bible study is important for many reasons, one of which is the bridging of the culture gap. Like other books, the Bible was written in a cultural context. The writers used events of their times to record and illustrate truth. But we do not live in those cultures. Therefore, we need to study the Bible so we can understand it in the context in which the truth was written so we can apply it to our lives here and now.

Failure to understand the culture of the Bible yields some ridiculous results. Here's one example.

One Christmas season, author and educator Janet S. Teitsort and her first-grade public school class were studying Christmas customs from around the world. Seeing that she had an ideal opportunity to share the Christmas story with these children, she explained that Mary and Joseph had gone to Bethlehem to pay their taxes. Just then, it was time for the baby Jesus to be born, and they needed a place to spend the night. Janet told her students that when Mary and Joseph went to the inn, there were no empty rooms. She compared the inn to a modern-day hotel or motel. She was leading up to telling them about the stable when she asked, "What do you suppose they had behind the inn?" One little guy who had been listening intently began frantically waving his hand to answer. When Janet pointed to him, his face was alight with knowledge: "A swimming pool," he answered.

God wants you to fully understand the truth he has given you in the pages of his written Word. But in order to understand, you have to put in a little personal effort. That means consistently and diligently studying the Bible for yourself.

Jesus, motivate me to study the Bible for myself so that I don't pull up short in my understanding of your Word.

TO READ
Jeremiah 3:1-20

I will give you leaders after my own heart, who will guide you with knowledge and understanding.

JEREMIAH 3:15

✳ *Purpose in the Mundane*

As a pastor, I have to attend numerous meetings every week. They are necessary but seldom exciting. When my kids ask, "What did you do today?" it is hard to enthusiastically say, "I went to a bunch of meetings." When I have told them that, they have never responded with, "When I get older I want to go to meetings just like my dad!" In fact, I have heard just the opposite. When my oldest son was sixteen, I asked him if he had ever thought about entering the ministry. His answer was, "No, I don't want to go to that many meetings."

When my youngest son, Caleb, was eight years old, he figured out something important about meetings. He was riding in our car with my wife, Pam, when he asked, "Where's dad?"

"He is in a meeting," Pam answered matter-of-factly.

"He's always in a meeting," Caleb observed. "When will he not be in a meeting?"

Pam replied, "I don't know."

Caleb thought for a moment and then said, "I know. When all the people in the world are dead, there will be no more meetings."

Indeed, as long as there are people to lead there will be planning to do, and as long as there is planning to do, there will be meetings. Knowing that has helped me see meetings not as a burden but as another part of my ministry for Jesus.

Is there some part of your life in Christ that you find mundane, even boring? Ask God to show you the importance not just of the exciting, high-profile parts of life, but of those things you'd just as soon miss.

Jesus, help me to see your purpose in every little thing I have to do, even in attending meetings.

TO READ
Deuteronomy 31:1-8

Do not be afraid or discouraged, for the Lord is
the one who goes before you. He will be with you;
he will neither fail you nor forsake you.

DEUTERONOMY 31:8

Overcoming the Devil's Obstacles

I once heard a story about the devil holding a public auction to sell the tools
of his trade. When the prospective buyers assembled, they saw an array of
implements: hatred, jealousy, deceit, lying, pride—all at expensive prices.
But there was one odd-looking tool at the auction site labeled "Not for sale."

When one of the buyers asked the devil why this tool wasn't for sale, he
explained, "I can spare my other tools, but I cannot spare this one. It is the
most useful implement I have. It is called Discouragement, and I can use it
to work my way into hearts that are otherwise inaccessible. When I get this
tool into a man's heart, the way is open for me to plant anything there."

Life is a challenge that requires us to give of ourselves wholeheartedly.
If we hold back, we can miss out on opportunities. If we focus on the negative, we can feel overwhelmed. If we think too long without taking action,
we can lose heart and conclude that the task is too large.

But in this world filled with obstacles, God offers his presence. And if we
remind ourselves daily that God is with us and that he filters everything that
comes our way, we can overcome any tool the devil uses on us and move
forward with courage.

On the path of life there are pitfalls that will discourage you if you focus
on them and there are weary travelers who will discourage you if you listen
to them. But Jesus is also on that path, and he will be with you, encouraging
you every step of the way.

God, thank you that you will always be bigger than the challenges in
my life.

TO READ
Philippians 1:3-11

I am sure that God, who began the good work within you, will continue his work until it is finally finished on that day when Christ Jesus comes back again. PHILIPPIANS 1:6

❋ *Called as Ambassadors*

Jesus is the perfect Savior. He has no flaws, no shortcomings, and no needs. No accusation against him has ever stuck because he has never done anything wrong. He has never failed to do exactly what he set out to do. When he died on the cross, he accomplished everything necessary for our salvation.

The gospel is the perfect message because God himself is the author. It is available to everyone and completely effective for anyone who will embrace it. It absolutely meets the greatest need in man. It delivers comprehensive forgiveness, exhilarating purpose, and eternal hope.

The only shortcoming concerning the gospel is its messengers—us! God has chosen imperfect men to be the ambassadors for his perfect message. For that reason we need to be improving constantly. But God, in his amazing grace, has promised to finish what he started in us and make us worthy ambassadors for him.

A certain soap maker had run out of superlatives to define the perfection of his product. One day he came up with a novel and compelling way to communicate that perfection: "As we couldn't improve our product, we improved the box."

Indeed, there is nothing we or anyone can do to improve the "product" of the gospel message. But Jesus is committed to finishing his work in our lives and making us the perfect package for that product.

Jesus, thank you that your grace is bigger than my shortcomings.

TO READ
Matthew 5:17-37

Just say a simple, "Yes, I will," or "No, I won't." Your word is enough. To strengthen your promise with a vow shows that something is wrong.

MATTHEW 5:37

Yes or No?

We men have a knack of saying too much, which complicates our communication—and our lives. We try to be more profound than we are capable of being. We set up systems that are more complex than we are able to manage. We create protocol so unnatural that it turns us into actors.

We can see this played out to perfection in our nation's courtrooms.

Get a load of these actual courtroom conversations, as found in the books *Humor in the Court* and *More Humor in the Court*:

Lawyer: "Doctor, did you say he was shot in the woods?"
Doctor: "No, I said he was shot in the lumbar region."

Lawyer: "Doctor, how many autopsies have you performed on dead people?"
Doctor: "All my autopsies have been performed on dead people."

Lawyer: "And lastly, Gary, all your responses must be oral. OK? What school do you go to?"
Gary: "Oral."
Lawyer: "How old are you?"
Gary: "Oral."[16]

Life can be much simpler and more effective for us if we would only learn to honestly and concisely answer every question that comes our way. Start simplifying your life today by making it your ambition to simply say yes or no when you are asked a question or requested to do something.

Lord, give me the grace to simply say what I have to say.

TO READ
2 Thessalonians 2:1-17

May our Lord Jesus Christ and God our Father, who loved us and in his special favor gave us everlasting comfort and good hope, comfort your hearts and give you strength in every good thing you do and say. 2 THESSALONIANS 2:16-17

❋ Eternal Encouragement

Everything that happens to us happens in the shadow of eternity. Jesus' death and resurrection secured for us "eternal encouragement." This means that our existence in the presence of God will last so long and be so good that the setbacks of this world will pale in comparison.

If we fail on earth, we have eternity to recover. If we get behind on earth, we have eternity to catch up. If we suffer tragedy on earth, we have eternity to enjoy better things. And if things go well here on earth, we have eternity to share the story.

But the promise of victory in Jesus isn't just for when we enter into eternity with him. We can be encouraged here on earth.

Author Stan Toler told an amusing story that illustrates the encouragement we can have in Christ, even when we feel anything but victorious: "A man stopped at the park to watch a Little League baseball game. He asked one of the youngsters what the score was.

" 'We're losing 18-0,' was the answer.

" 'Well,' said the man. 'I must say you don't look discouraged.'

" 'Discouraged?' the boy said, puzzled. 'Why should we be discouraged? We haven't come to bat yet.' "[17]

You may feel like you're losing in the game of life. It may seem that the enemy of your soul is winning. But your turn at bat comes when you decide to follow Jesus. That's when you begin to live and walk in that eternal encouragement.

Jesus, thank you for encouraging me with the promise of eternity with you.

TO READ
Psalm 139:1-12

I can never escape from your spirit! I can never get away from your presence! PSALM 139:7

Since You're Here Anyway . . .

You are going to spend today in the presence of God. He will be everywhere you go. He will hear everything you say and know everything you think. When you are hidden from others, you are still in plain sight to him.

The Reverend A. Skevington Wood wrote of the *omnipresence* of God: "We can never talk about God behind his back. We cannot speak of God in his absence. . . . The God who is being discussed is also there. The attitude people take to Him can never be merely theoretical. To deny Him is to spite Him to His face."[18]

It is remarkable that God is so patient with us, even when we act as if there are things he can't see and words he can't hear. It started with Adam and Eve in the Garden of Eden. After they sinned, they tried to hide from God—as if that were a real possibility. We all carry on their legacy when we try to hide from him, when we fail to pray at all times and in all situations.

I have learned that since God is always present and that he already knows about all the junk in my life, I should do everything I can to include him in my every thought and my every conversation.

A few years back, I started beginning my prayers differently. I began saying to God, "You go first." Then I would quietly wait for thoughts to start crossing my mind. I assumed that God would bring to mind the most important things I needed to pray about. If they were positive thoughts, I would pray them back with joy. If they were negative thoughts, I would pray about them with courage and honesty.

When you approach God in prayer, approach him understanding that he already knows what's going on in your life and in your heart. Have an attitude that since he's there anyway, you might as well let him speak to you first.

Lord, since you are here anyway, you go first.

TO READ
Ecclesiastes 4:1-10

Two people can accomplish more than twice as much as one; they get a better return for their labor.

ECCLESIASTES 4:9

The Choice of Teamwork

Teamwork is woven into the entire fabric of creation. Here are some examples:

On top of the Spanish Pyrenees Mountains lives the magnificently beautiful but elusive mountain goat. This animal is often hunted for its incredible coat, but it is extremely difficult to get within shooting range of one. Why? Because it has a companion: a young goat who follows it wherever it goes and sounds the warning of enemies around it.

The rhinoceros is another magnificent animal. It is rugged and can run at remarkable speeds for such a large animal. It is fearless in charging its enemies, despite its very poor eyesight. But the rhinoceros gets natural help in navigating the realities of life. The rhino's hide is infested with burrowing ticks, which are a delicacy to a certain robin-sized bird that rides on its back, feeding on the insects. The birds have keen eyesight, and when they sense danger they sound the alarm, which alerts the rhino.

A badger-like animal called the ratel and a small bird called the honeyguide both love honey. They go out together to feed because they are better as a team than they are on their own. The keen eye of the honeyguide pinpoints a beehive, and the ratel's powerful claws tear up the hive, making the honey available to both.

Animals team up out of instinct. We men need to team up with others too, but for us it's a matter of making ourselves stronger in how we live out our faith. Have you teamed up with men who can help you live your life in Christ to its fullest?

Jesus, give me teammates so that my effectiveness and theirs may be increased.

August

TO READ
James 4:1-8

Humble yourselves before God. Resist the Devil, and he will flee from you. JAMES 4:7

Knowing Your Enemy

The formula for victory in the spiritual realm would be simple if it weren't lived out on such an intense battlefield: (1) submit to God, (2) resist the devil, (3) the devil runs. But Satan often looks bigger than life to us.

It really is a matter of knowing our enemy, isn't it?

During the Second World War, C. J. Auchinleck, British commander-in-chief of the Middle East force, wrote the following order to all commanders and chiefs-of-staff under his authority:

> There exists a real danger that our friend Rommel is becoming a king or magician or bogey-man to our troops, who are talking far too much about him. He is by no means a superman, although he is undoubtedly very energetic and able. Even if he were a superman, it would still be highly undesirable that our men should credit him with supernatural powers.
>
> I wish you to dispel by all possible means the idea that Rommel represents something more than the ordinary. The more important thing now is to see that we do not always talk of Rommel when we mean the enemy in Libya. We must refer to "the Germans" or "the Axis powers" or "the enemy" and not always be harping.
>
> Please ensure that this order is put into immediate effect, and impress upon all commanders that, from a psychological point of view, it is a matter of the highest importance.[1]

Satan is a formidable foe with great—albeit limited—powers. But his power is nothing compared to God's. Knowing that, we should never allow the devil to intimidate us or overwhelm us with his propaganda.

Jesus, remind me daily that Satan's power is nothing compared with yours and that you have empowered me to do battle with his forces.

TO READ
Philippians 4:4-9

Don't worry about anything; instead, pray about everything. Tell God what you need, and thank him for all he has done. If you do this, you will experience God's peace, which is far more wonderful than the human mind can understand.

PHILIPPIANS 4:6-7

Don't Worry!

Most of us tend to think too highly of ourselves. We love having the answers, and we tend to think we are right most of the time. We also fall prey to the notion that we are ultimately responsible for everything in our lives. Consequently, we spend a lot of time worrying because we somehow have come to believe that worry is a productive tool.

A businessman once drew up what he called a "Worry Chart," in which he kept a record of his worries. He discovered that 40 percent of his worries were about things that probably would never happen, 30 percent were about past decisions that he could not now unmake, 12 percent were about other people's criticism of him, and 10 percent were about his health. He concluded that only 8 percent of his worries were really legitimate—in other words, things he could do something about.[2]

Most of us are like that businessman, aren't we? Instead of spending our time concentrating on things we can control or change, we spend most of our time fretting over things that haven't happened, won't happen, or happened in the past and can't be changed now.

The key to ridding our hearts and minds of unnecessary worry is to get our eyes off ourselves and pray aggressively, knowing that God rewards an active prayer life with his peace. When you have that peace, you know that everything God leads you to do will ultimately succeed. Knowing this is your best defense against worry.

Are you facing some problem or decision today? Spend more time talking to God about it than you normally would, and let him bring his peace to the situation.

Lord, help me to give up my worries, knowing that you are in control and have promised me success in the things you have for me to do.

TO READ
1 Thessalonians 5:1-11

Be on your guard, not asleep like the others.
Stay alert and be sober.   1 Thessalonians 5:6

✻ Be Aware

At Dublin's Abbey Theatre, poet-playwright W. B. Yeats was looking for realism in creating the lighting effects for a glorious sunset. Hour after hour, he had the electricians try every conceivable combination of colors and rheostats. At last he saw exactly the effect he wanted. "That's it!" he cried. "Hold it, hold it!"

"We can't hold it, sir," came a stagehand's apologetic voice. "The bloody theater's on fire!"

Sometimes focusing on our own concerns and interests keeps us from seeing impending destruction.

Most of us today are so engrossed in our own lives that we fail to see the spiritual danger around us. This is the only way to explain the developments of modern society during the past forty years. We have advanced more technologically than anyone could have dared to predict.

At the same time that our ability to manipulate our environment is exploding, it seems our moral fiber is unraveling. Violent crimes, as well as drug and alcohol abuse, are on the rise. The family as God designed it is coming apart. We have murdered millions through abortion and have abandoned our children to their own devices. And there appears to be no end to the rise of these problems.

At some point, we as men of God need to be aware of the destruction around us. We not only need to see it, we need to do something about it. We can start by getting on our knees and praying to God for healing and direction.

Jesus, make me aware of what is going on in the spiritual realm despite all the distractions in my life.

TO READ
Matthew 6:24-34

Look at the birds. They don't need to plant or harvest or put food in barns because your heavenly Father feeds them. And you are far more valuable to him than they are. MATTHEW 6:26

His Eye Is on Us!

It is a strange paradox that God has given us remarkable talents but calls us to be completely dependent on him. We were created with some incredible abilities. We can make money, build projects, solve problems, and make decisions. We can also observe life around us and reach conclusions about what we see. In this we must be careful, for it is possible to think our way right into the wrong conclusions.

We have a tendency to come to wrong conclusions about ourselves. Sometimes we think we are stronger than we actually are, and sometimes we think we are weaker. Sometimes we think we are more important than we are, and other times we think we are less important.

Jesus' challenge is for us to realize that no matter how strong or weak we think we are, he always has his eye on us. He has already given us the abilities we need to succeed in life, but he wants us to walk humbly in cooperation with him because that's what we are designed to do.

Throughout the natural world, God has given us illustrations of his provision for us. For instance, God designed a bird's wing muscles so that they are proportionally a hundred times stronger than the arm muscles of the strongest man. A swallow, after one thousand miles of flight, will seek his nest at sundown—not because he is tired but because night has come. And another thing God tells us about birds: he feeds them!

God has provided for birds in a remarkable way. Knowing that you are more valuable to him than all the world's birds combined, do you have any doubt that he'll provide for you too?

Lord, help me to remember that I am very important to you and that you provide for me and have your eye on me always.

TO READ
Colossians 1:9-23

We also pray that you will be strengthened with his glorious power so that you will have all the patience and endurance you need. COLOSSIANS 1:11

The Power of the Holy Spirit

When the apostle Paul speaks of God's glorious power, he uses the Greek word *dunamis*, from which we get the English word *dynamite*. In this context, Paul is talking about the explosive ability of the Holy Spirit to give us the resources we need at the exact time we need them.

When we look at the weaponry of the twentieth and early twenty-first centuries, we get an idea of the kind of power Paul was talking about.

One kiloton is the equivalent of one thousand tons of TNT, and one megaton is the equivalent of one million tons of TNT. The first atomic bomb, exploded in New Mexico, was about nineteen kilotons, and the one dropped on Hiroshima during World War II was a twenty-kiloton bomb.

The largest hydrogen bomb ever exploded was a hundred-megaton weapon tested by the Soviet Union in the 1960s. The force of the bomb was so powerful that pressure pulses from its detonation went around the world two times. Though the hundred-megaton bomb was five thousand times as powerful as the one dropped on Hiroshima, scientists are discussing bombs of ten thousand, twenty thousand, and even one million megatons.

What is the destructive powerful of a hundred-megaton bomb? All the gunpowder, TNT, dynamite, and nitroglycerin made in human history are not equal to one hundred megatons. To equal a hundred-megaton bomb, you would have to drop a twenty-kiloton bomb (like the one dropped on Japan) every day of the year for thirteen years!

Humankind has created some awesomely destructive weapons in its history, but the power contained in those weapons is nothing compared with the power of the Holy Spirit in our lives.

Jesus, give me a powerful life through your Holy Spirit.

TO READ
Revelation 3:1-22

You say, "I am rich. I have everything I want. I don't need a thing!" And you don't realize that you are wretched and miserable and poor and blind and naked. REVELATION 3:17

Lost and Exhausted

Doc Hall could hardly believe his eyes when he flew his plane low to the ground and saw a black bear with a twenty-pound coffee can stuck fast on its head. Unable to see where it was going, the bear was walking around in circles in the area of Devil's Creek, Alaska. Apparently, in rummaging through the local garbage dump for food, the bear had gotten its head stuck inside the can and could not extricate it.

"The bear must have walked more than 500 miles in circles," Hall said. "It had made six worn-smooth circular paths in the thick blanket of leaves and twigs which covered the ground."

Hall didn't know when or if the bear ever stopped walking in circles, but it is very likely that it kept going until it was completely exhausted.[3]

In a way, we men are a lot like that bear. Our tendency when we are lost in the dark is to keep going until we're too exhausted to go on any more. When we're driving and get lost, we keep driving instead of stopping to ask for directions. When we can't figure out our career goals, we just keep working instead of spending time with mentors to seek advice. And when we need direction, we don't turn to God and pray but instead get involved in projects we believe he wants us involved in.

Sometimes we need to stop, admit we need directions, and look for a new way. And God has promised to give us direction and purpose if we just stop and ask him.

Do you feel as if you're running in circles in the dark? Do you feel lost to the point of exhaustion? Then turn to your heavenly Father and ask him for instruction and direction. He'll never fail to give it to you.

Lord, give me the sense to stop and ask you for direction before I reach the point of exhaustion.

TO READ
1 Corinthians 1:18-29

God deliberately chose things the world considers foolish in order to shame those who think they are wise. And he chose those who are powerless to shame those who are powerful.

1 CORINTHIANS 1:27

The Foolish Things

I was at the local Target store doing some shopping recently when I met a young man named Andy. It was obvious from the moment I met him that something had gone wrong for him. I learned that he had suffered a head trauma in a motorcycle accident. As a result, he spoke with a slur and had trouble keeping eye contact. He was loud, even a little obnoxious, and he talked incessantly. His checkout line moved slower than anyone else's as he carried on a conversation with everyone he encountered.

Most people would categorize Andy as one of the foolish people in the world. But I could see that the accident hadn't touched Andy's heart. He had a very sincere and obvious love for Jesus. I only spoke with him for a few minutes, but he said two things I will never forget.

First, he asked me to do a math problem with him. He asked, "What is one cross plus three nails?" A sly grin formed on his face as he watched me struggle to find the answer. When he thought he had waited long enough for me to answer, he smiled and triumphantly said, "Four-given!"

Second, he asked me if I read the Bible. When I told him I did, he said, "That is good, because reading the Bible will scare the hell out of you!" He started laughing. I joined him.

I don't remember what I went to the store to buy that day, but I know I left with a clear reminder that God very often uses the "foolish" things of the world to proclaim his truth.

Lord, let me be more aware of you and how you work. Never allow me to see someone who loves you with all his heart as foolish.

TO READ
1 Peter 2:16-25

You are not slaves; you are free. But your freedom is not an excuse to do evil. You are free to live as God's slaves. 1 PETER 2:16

The Real Meaning of Freedom

One of the most amazing aspects of our relationship with Christ is the freedom he has given us through the gospel. We are free from condemnation, free from the judgment we deserve for our sins, free from having to say yes to the desires of the flesh. We are free to enter the presence of our heavenly Father at any time and talk with him. We are free to live and love in a supernatural way.

There truly is no end to the freedom we have in Christ. Sadly, however, we are prone to being fooled by our freedom. We have a tendency to think that our freedom means we can get away with sin.

Sometimes I think the way many of us view our freedom in Christ can be summed up in the statement: It is easier to ask forgiveness than permission. In other words, rather than pursuing a dynamic relationship with Christ that motivates and enables us to live a life that pleases him, we do what we want, then ask him to forgive us after the fact.

But true freedom—the freedom Christ has given us—leads to excellence. Jesus did not set us free so that we could live by a lower standard or so we could be lazy or mediocre. On the contrary, he set us free so we could be what he calls us to be: reflections of him in our fallen world.

Victor Frankl profoundly captures the balance between freedom and excellence in his book *Man's Search for Meaning*: "Freedom is only part of the story and half the truth. . . . That is why I recommend that the Statue of Liberty on the East Coast be supplemented by a Statue of Responsibility on the West Coast."[4]

Jesus, use the freedom you have given me to develop excellence in every area of my life.

Christ has really set us free. Now make sure that you stay free, and don't get tied up again in slavery to the law. GALATIANS 5:1

❋ Appreciating Our Freedom

Having been set free from slavery to sin, it is far too easy for many Christian men to take their freedom for granted. Michael Blakley of Milwaukee shares the following account that woke him up to the value of freedom:

> While I was attending graduate school in the early 1980s, I stopped for coffee in a Malibu, California, restaurant. Coming from a non-political family, I knew nothing of political activists—but I met one that day in that restaurant.
>
> He told everyone what a mess the United States had become. He ridiculed our government and our educational, industrial, and banking systems. He was on such a roll that he had everyone on his side except for two people: an old man and me. The activist shied away from me, seeing my Pepperdine hat, Ronald Reagan T-shirt, and *Wall Street Journal*. So he went after the old man.
>
> As he approached, the old man continued slurping his soup and turned his back. The activist sat down at the old man's table and offered, "Mister, if you can tell me just one thing the United States has ever done for you, just one measly thing, I will leave you alone."
>
> Finally, the old man looked up. He licked his spoon clean and set it down on the table. His red face indicated years of laboring in the sun. With a heavy Russian accent, he replied, "Ve hold zees truz to be self-evident, dat all men created equal, life, liberty, perzuit of happiness." Then he went back to the soup. The activist, defeated, could not argue against what the old man had experienced on both sides of communism.[5]

Having lived under the oppression of the Soviet government, the old man in this story had an appreciation for freedom that few of us can relate to—at least on that level. How much do you value your freedom?

Lord, teach me to value the freedom you and others have bought for me.

TO READ
Acts 20:18-38

I have been a constant example of how you can help the poor by working hard. You should remember the words of the Lord Jesus: "It is more blessed to give than to receive." ACTS 20:35

The Joy of Giving

The December 15, 1996, edition of the *Los Angeles Times* reported that David Suna and John Tu sold 80 percent of their company, Kingston Technology Corp., the world's largest manufacturer of computer memory products, for $15 billion.

The two men decided to share their windfall with their employees. The average bonus payment their workers received was just over $75,000. Sun summarized their decision: "To share our success with everybody is the most joy we can have."

We truly do find joy in giving to others. However, giving goes against our nature because we are selfish and prone to look out for ourselves to the exclusion of others.

On the surface, our reluctance to give is almost understandable. Most of us will suffer situations in life that make us feel the brokenness and unfairness that is built into this world's system. We will suffer financial loss or have some manipulative maneuver steal opportunities from us. We will be criticized for things we didn't do and watch others get credit for things we did.

But in the midst of this fallen, unfair world, Jesus calls us to give sacrificially and generously. Many times there will be no reward for our giving except the conviction that we have done the right thing. Often people will either fail to recognize our generosity or, worse yet, they will take advantage of it. When that happens, our only benefit from giving comes from the hand of God. In any case, God will put joy in our hearts when we give, because he is pleased.

Lord, make me content with the joy that comes from generous giving.

So now there is no condemnation for those who belong to Christ Jesus. For the power of the life-giving Spirit has freed you through Christ Jesus from the power of sin that leads to death. ROMANS 8:1-2

Rising above Our Sin

Ever feel like you can't overcome a bad habit? Overcoming our sinful nature isn't a matter of willpower or of our own efforts to do better. In fact, overcoming our sinful nature isn't even possible—not without the power of Christ working within us, that is.

That's right! In Christ, we have the ability to rise above our own sinful nature. But it requires help from sources more powerful than ourselves. The possibilities that exist when power is available to you reminds me of airplanes. I fly a number of times each year, and I have never stopped marveling at flight. Without the plane, it is ludicrous to think about traveling several hundred miles per hour, several thousand feet up in the air, while seated with two to three hundred other people. But with the plane, not only can I do what is impossible on my own power, I can invite dozens of other people to join me.

I recently took a flight from Kansas City, Missouri, to Denver. The temperature in Kansas City was twenty degrees and the area had experienced an ice storm during the previous twenty-four hours. Without help, the flight would never have happened. The plane was pushed away from the terminal and then stopped. While we were sitting there, a truck rolled up to the plane and showered the wings with antifreeze. This prevented ice from building up on the wings and made it possible for the pilot to harness the awesome power of the airplane.

Planes transport millions of people around the world because they have power available to them that can overcome gravity. In the same way, we can live godly lives because we have power available to us that can overcome our sinful nature.

Lord, teach me to do through your power what is impossible on my own.

TO READ
Matthew 10:5-42

Look, I am sending you out as sheep among wolves.
Be as wary as snakes and harmless as doves.

MATTHEW 10:16

Giving the Best Answer

Legend has it that a certain college philosophy professor asked just one question on his final exam. He picked up a chair, put it on his desk, and wrote on the blackboard, "Using everything we have learned this semester, prove that this chair does not exist."

Most of the students wrote like crazy for the whole hour, some of them churning out thirty pages of heady philosophical logic. But one student turned in his paper after less than a minute—and he was the only one to get an A. What did he write? "What chair?"

Sometimes the wisest argument is no argument at all.

There is an art to survival in today's world. There are physical and emotional dangers to avoid, using balanced decision-making skills and alert reasoning. And, of course, there are deceptive, ungodly philosophies marketed in our modern world, which require us to give wise answers as we defend our faith in Christ.

As we face the challenges worldly thinking brings against our faith, arguing is not always the best approach. Most people need to be won to Christ through relationships. We are Christ's ambassadors on earth, and we never know when we will be the conduit that connects an apparent enemy of Christ with the Savior.

But sometimes defending our faith requires from us a shrewd, wise answer motivated by a sincere heart. As the apostle Peter wrote, "If you are asked about your Christian hope, always be ready to explain it. But you must do this in a gentle and respectful way" (1 Peter 3:15-16).

How are you preparing yourself to give a wise, gentle answer?

Jesus, give me the discernment to give wise answers.

TO READ
Proverbs 1:20-33

Wisdom shouts in the streets. She cries out in the public square. PROVERBS 1:20

The Gift of Wisdom

In order to make good decisions, we must have both knowledge and wisdom. Knowledge means having information about life, while wisdom is knowing how to apply that knowledge most effectively.

Wisdom gives you confidence because it helps you know what decisions are best for you. Wisdom also builds trust because it helps you provide others with sound counsel. And wisdom can make you laugh because clarity lowers stress in your life.

Former New York Yankee baseball player Yogi Berra is famous not only for his baseball exploits but also for what have affectionately been called "yogi-isms." His unusual ability to coin phrases is like a beacon to the lighter side of wisdom. Consider the following "yogi-isms":

- "It ain't over 'til it's over."
- "Never answer an anonymous letter."
- "I usually take a two hour nap from one to four."
- "When you come to a fork in the road . . . take it."
- "I didn't really say everything I said."
- "You can observe a lot by watching."
- "If the people don't want to come out to the ballpark, nobody's going to stop them."
- "The future ain't what it used to be."[6]

Do you desire the wisdom that will build your confidence and trust? Ask God to give it to you. He will never disappoint you!

Jesus, make confidence, trust, and laughter big parts of my life by giving me your kind of wisdom.

TO READ
James 3:1, 13-18

Dear brothers and sisters, not many of you should become teachers in the church, for we who teach will be judged by God with greater strictness.

JAMES 3:1

A High Calling

Teachers have profoundly affected the life of nearly every man. They have educated us, inspired us, and helped us clarify our direction in life.

My fifth grade teacher, Mr. Folodare, was teaching us how to play softball. He was pitching and I was playing third base. The batter hit a pop fly that traveled just right of the pitcher's mound. I charged hard and cried out, "I've got it!" Mr. Folodare stepped up and caught the ball, but then he said to me, "You think you could've gotten that, don't you? I should have let you try." Whenever I mentor a young man today, that thought guides me.

When I was taking a sermon preparation class in seminary, we asked the teacher, "What has been most helpful to you in ministry?" His answer has been a theme of my life ever since: "Choose well the hills you die on."

Dr. Bing Hunter, who taught a class on the Gospels when I was in seminary, said, "Praying in Jesus' name means living a lifestyle that represents who he is. It is not just a magic phrase we attach to the end of a prayer to make it more valid." That thought helped me integrate prayer into every area of my life.

Erwin McManus, the senior pastor of Mosaic, a church in Los Angeles, made the following statement at a seminar I attended: "People used to ask, 'What is the truth?' Now they ask, 'What works?' " That phrase intensified my desire to make biblical truth as practical as possible for those I teach.

I am sure you have had similar experiences. As men, we have been impacted by those who teach us. We must be willing to step up to the plate and consider teaching others.

Are you willing to be a teacher?

Lord, help me be neither afraid nor overeager to be a teacher of your Word.

TO READ
Philippians 3:15-21

He will take these weak mortal bodies of ours and change them into glorious bodies like his own, using the same mighty power that he will use to conquer everything, everywhere. PHILIPPIANS 3:21

Our Faith: A Matter of Transformation

Christianity isn't just about improvement; it's about transformation. For that reason, we should never be content with just being "better" when our Savior has promised to make everything about us "new."

Bruce Thielemann illustrates the idea of transformation:

> Imagine a colony of grubs living on the bottom of a swamp. And every once in a while, one of these grubs is inclined to climb a leaf stem to the surface. Then he disappears above the surface and never returns. All the grubs wonder why this is so and what it must be like up there, so they counsel among themselves and agree that the next one who goes up will come back and tell the others.
>
> Not long after that, one of the grubs feels that urge and climbs that leaf stem and goes out above the surface onto a lily pad. And there in the warmth of the sun, he falls asleep. While he sleeps, the carapace of the tiny creature breaks open, and out of the inside of the grub comes a magnificent dragonfly with beautiful, wide, rainbow-hued, iridescent wings. And he spreads those wings and flies, soaring out over those waters. But then he remembers the commitment he has made to those behind, yet now he knows he cannot return. They would not recognize him in the first place, and beyond that, he could not live again in such a place. But one thought is his that takes away all the distress: they, too, shall climb the stem, and they, too, shall know the glory.[7]

Just as that grub's transformation into a magnificent dragonfly allowed him to soar, so does God's transformation of us through Jesus Christ allow us to spread our wings and fly. When we meet Jesus, we become someone we weren't before, someone capable of doing great things for him.

Jesus, thank you that you have transformed me and made me something I could never have been on my own.

TO READ
Isaiah 60:1-22

Arise, Jerusalem! Let your light shine for all the nations to see! For the glory of the Lord is shining upon you. ISAIAH 60:1

Turn on the Light!

Once you come to Christ, you become a powerful influence in your world. But for his light to shine, you have to turn it on.

I have become good friends with my sons' high school football coach. He is genuinely committed to helping young men develop character and discipline. The one thing missing in this coach's life is a personal relationship with Jesus. He has interacted with many believers over the years and even attended a Christian college for two years. His conclusion is that Christians are judgmental and unwilling to discuss issues of life intelligently.

Our goal as a family has been to show him a different view. We have worked hard to help the football program. We have developed genuine friendships with his wife and children.

I was very encouraged the day the coach asked me to have lunch with him because he wanted to discuss spiritual matters with me. He told me he was skeptical about Christianity and that he had a very hard time accepting that there is only one way to get to heaven. The idea of a God who would allow anyone to spend time in hell was unacceptable to him.

With all that said, I asked him why he wanted to talk with me since it sounded like his mind was already made up. His response inspired one of my primary goals in life. He said, "You and your family are the most down-to-earth, very religious people I have ever met. I want to know what is different about you."

He didn't ask Christ into his life that day, but we continue to dialogue about the most important issues in life.

People around you desperately need to see the light that God has put within you. Are you ready to flip the switch?

Lord, let me shine the light of Jesus Christ on everyone around me.

TO READ
Colossians 1:15-20

Christ is the visible image of the invisible God. He existed before God made anything at all and is supreme over all creation. COLOSSIANS 1:15

Looking through the Right Lens

I find it amusing that men think it is their responsibility to evaluate Jesus. I have heard people tell me that Jesus is just a good man. I have heard that he is a great teacher. I have heard that he was very sincere. These are all true, of course, but these statements have been spoken by skeptical people who were trying to minimize Jesus. By limiting Jesus to a level we can fully comprehend, men try to dismiss their need to honor him as the creator of the world.

Indeed, we can get things backwards when it comes to our relationship with Jesus.

We tend to view God through the lens of our own experiences when it should be the other way around. We concern ourselves with how God affects our lives, how our circumstances affect us, and why he allowed these situations to happen in the first place.

But in the midst of our everyday lives is Jesus. He is bigger than life and the very image of the invisible God. He knows everything, sees everything, and can do anything at any time. He was in the beginning, but he has no beginning. Before time began, he existed, and when time is no more, he will continue. There is no end to Jesus!

Jesus is the Creator of all that exists and the forerunner of our future. And just as he rose from the dead, we too will one day be resurrected. Then we will go to the eternal dwelling place Jesus has gone before us to prepare.

The path to freedom in life is to get a clear picture of Jesus and to view our life experiences through him. When we do that, we will ask what we can do for him, not what he can do for us.

Lord, help me to focus on what I can do for you, not on what you can do for me, knowing that you already have done everything needed to give me eternal life.

TO READ
Hebrews 13:7-25

Remember your leaders who first taught you the word of God. Think of all the good that has come from their lives, and trust the Lord as they do.

HEBREWS 13:7

Leadership by Example

It is normal and natural for us to follow our leaders. Just as sheep look to their shepherd for guidance, workers look to their managers for direction and children look to their fathers for wisdom on how to live their lives.

It's a simple truth that leadership is necessary to every successful venture, from raising a family to building a business. Good leaders diligently learn how to grow in their leadership ability. Good leaders seek out good advice and pass it on to those under their influence. But most importantly, good leaders lead by example.

It was a very humbling day when I realized that my kids were watching every move I make. My youngest son, Caleb, sits in the front row of our church during every service and listens very intently while I am preaching.

Recently a couple of people from our church approached me and asked if I had noticed what Caleb was doing as he watched me. I immediately jumped to the conclusion that he must have been doing something wrong and these people were coming to me to let me know so I could deal with the situation. I had to admit that I hadn't noticed and was waiting for the bad news when they told me, "He was mimicking every move you made. He mouthed the words you were saying. He wants to be just like you."

A sobering thought ran through my mind: *When I see my sons acting just like me, will I like what I see?*

I decided that day to make sure that my words and actions could inspire others to do greater things for God.

What kind of example are you setting today?

Jesus, may my words and actions inspire those around me to walk closer with you.

TO READ
2 Timothy 4:1-9

A time is coming when people will no longer listen to right teaching. They will follow their own desires and will look for teachers who will tell them whatever they want to hear. 2 TIMOTHY 4:3

Truth and Sincerity

In the classroom setting of one *Peanuts* comic strip, on the first day of the new school year, the students were told to write an essay about returning to class. In her essay, Lucy wrote, "Vacations are nice, but it's good to get back to school. There is nothing more satisfying or challenging than education, and I look forward to a year of expanding knowledge."

Of course, Lucy's teacher was pleased with her and complimented her fine essay. In the final frame, Lucy leans over and whispers to Charlie Brown, "After a while, you learn what sells."

Sincerity and truth should always be vitally connected, yet the history of humankind is littered with messages designed not to be truthful but to sound good.

There should be no hint of that in our lives as Christian men. We need to remember that people's response to the truth determines their eternal destiny, and we must commit ourselves to putting the truth on display in a way that others can trust.

We all encounter individuals who observe our lives to see if what we believe is real. These people evaluate our Savior based on the credibility of our lives and the consistency of our message. For that reason, our lives and our messages should reflect nothing but truth.

Does your life reflect the sincere conviction that what you believe in is the truth? If so, it will stand as an example to everyone around you that Jesus Christ himself is truth personified.

Lord, never let me settle for anything less than the truth.

TO READ
Galatians 5:16-26

When the Holy Spirit controls our lives, he will produce this kind of fruit in us: love, joy, peace, patience, kindness, goodness, faithfulness, gentleness, and self-control. Here there is no conflict with the law. GALATIANS 5:22-23

✳ The Need for Self-Control

In a September 20, 1998, segment of ABC's news magazine show *20/20*, reporter John Stossel interviewed Dr. Roy Baumeister of Case Western Reserve University. Baumeister said, "If you look at the social and personal problems facing people in the United States—we're talking drug and alcohol abuse, teen pregnancy, unsafe sex, school failure, shopping problems, gambling—over and over, the majority of them have self-control failure as central to them. Studies show that self-control does predict success in life over a very long time."

Dr. Baumeister cited an experiment conducted thirty years earlier at Columbia University. In the experiment, children were given a choice: They would get five pieces of candy if they could wait ten minutes until their teacher came back into the room—or just two pieces if they couldn't wait and gave in to the temptation before the ten minutes were up.

Of course, some of the children waited for the bigger reward, while others gave in and took the lesser one.

Over the following decades, the Columbia University researchers checked on the children in the study to see which group tended to do better in life. The results, Stossel said, were astonishingly clear-cut: "Kids who did well on this test years ago tended to do better in life. Better in lots of ways. Their SAT scores were higher. As teenagers, the boys had fewer run-ins with the law. The girls were less likely to get pregnant."

As Dr. Baumeister concluded on *20/20*, "If we're concerned about raising children to be successful and healthy and happy, forget about self-esteem. Concentrate on self-control."

Do your words and deeds reflect self-control in a way others can see?

Jesus, do whatever you must to work self-control into my life.

TO READ
Ecclesiastes 5:1-12

When you make a promise to God, don't delay in following through, for God takes no pleasure in fools. Keep all the promises you make to him. It is better to say nothing than to promise something that you don't follow through on. ECCLESIASTES 5:4-5

The Importance of Promises

Writer and speaker Lewis Smedes wrote:

> Yes, somewhere people still make and keep promises. They choose not to quit when the going gets rough because they promised once to see it through. They stick to lost causes. They hold on to a love grown cold. They stay with people who have become pains in the neck. They still dare to make promises and care enough to keep the promises they make. I want to say to you that if you have a ship you will not desert, if you have people you will not forsake, if you have causes you will not abandon, then you are like God.[8]

I work extensively with married couples, and I hear the best and worst of what goes on in relationships. In the past year I have seen couples overcome affairs, financial catastrophes, and debilitating diseases. At the same time, I have watched people leave their spouses for the following reasons:

- "I am no longer happy."
- "He works too hard and is never home."
- "She is too busy in the neighborhood to care about my needs."
- "We don't have enough sex."

The commitment to keep promises protects families and friendships. Taking promises too casually creates disillusionment and fear.

The people in your life want to know that you will keep your promises. More than money, more than advice, more than gifts, they simply want you to be faithful.

Jesus, show me the value of keeping my promises.

TO READ
Colossians 3:1-15

You must make allowance for each other's faults and forgive the person who offends you. Remember, the Lord forgave you, so you must forgive others.

COLOSSIANS 3:13

The Value of Forgiveness

In his book *On This Day*, Carl Windsor tells a story that underscores the need for forgiveness in any marriage:

> Even the most devoted couple will experience a "stormy" bout once in a while. A grandmother, celebrating her golden wedding anniversary, once told the secret of her long and happy marriage. "On my wedding day, I decided to make a list of ten of my husband's faults which, for the sake of our marriage, I would overlook," she said.
>
> A guest asked the woman what some of the faults she had chosen to overlook were. The grandmother replied, "To tell you the truth, my dear, I never did get around to listing them. But whenever my husband did something that made me hopping mad, I would say to myself, Lucky for him that's one of the ten!"[9]

At some time you will need to forgive every person you know. Intentionally or unintentionally, people will let you down, say things that hurt your feelings, or fail to come through on your behalf. The converse is true too. When you let people down or hurt them with your words or fail them in any way, you will need them to forgive you.

Forgiveness is absolutely essential for the health and growth of any relationship. It's a skill we all need if we are to enjoy good, healthy relationships.

Lord, show me the value of forgiveness. Teach me to forgive and to seek forgiveness when it is needed.

TO READ
Hebrews 13:10-19

With Jesus' help, let us continually offer our sacrifice of praise to God by proclaiming the glory of his name. HEBREWS 13:15

The Praise Jesus Wants

When we give Jesus sacrifices of praise, it is a recognition of his value in our lives. We are, however, prone to seek out acts of "praise" that are in accordance with our own agendas rather than God's.

A man recently asked me, "How much am I supposed to give to my church? Is it really 10 percent?" I told him, "Paul told people to give what they had purposed in their hearts. Jesus told people their hearts would follow their money. So you need to give enough to cause your heart to fall in love with what your church is doing." He left frustrated because he wanted a formula. His sacrifice of praise would be to search his heart before God.

Another man recently told me, "I wish I could preach. I have such a passion for God's Word, but I don't have public speaking gifts." I asked him, "What are you gifted in?" He went on to tell me how God blesses his life every time he organizes leadership training. He arranges for the meeting place, gets the invitations out, and lines up the trainers. The people who attend always leave with a greater sense of purpose and enthusiasm. He is frustrated, though, because he wants to be one of the presenters. His sacrifice of praise would be to find joy in the planning.

A large number of men tell me they don't like singing in church. Some are self-conscious, some are emotionally numb and just like facts, some are just in a hurry to get home. But God has commanded us to praise him in song. For many men, singing despite their objections would be their sacrifice of praise.

Do you want to give Jesus the kind of praise he wants and so richly deserves? Then take the time—through prayer and through study of the written Word of God—to find out what he really desires.

Jesus, teach me how to give you the gifts of praise you deserve.

TO READ
Psalm 139:14-16

Thank you for making me so wonderfully complex!
Your workmanship is marvelous—and how well I
know it. PSALM 139:14

The Wonder of You

Despite the fact that our bodies are subject to the effects of the Fall, they are
awesome creations of God.

Consider the following facts about your body, as reported by Dr. John
Medina, genetic engineer at the University of Washington:

The average human heart pumps more than 1,000 gallons a day, more than
55 million gallons in a lifetime. This is enough to fill 13 super tankers. It never
sleeps, beating 25 billion times in a lifetime.

The lungs contain 1,000 miles of capillaries. The process of exchanging oxygen for carbon dioxide is so complicated that it is more difficult to exchange
oxygen for carbon dioxide than for a man shot out of a cannon to carve the
Lord's Prayer on the head of a pin as he passes by.

DNA contains about 2,000 genes per chromosome—18 meters of DNA are
folded into each cell nucleus. A nucleus is six microns long. This is like putting
30 miles of fishing line into a cherry pit. And it isn't simply stuffed in. It is
folded in. If folded one way, the cell becomes a skin cell. If another way, a liver
cell, and so forth. To write out the information in one cell would take 300 vol-
umes, each volume 500 pages thick. The human body contains enough DNA that
if it were stretched out, it would circle the sun 260 times.

The body uses energy efficiently. If an average adult rides a bike for one hour
at ten miles per hour, it uses the amount of energy contained in three ounces of
carbohydrate. If a car were this efficient with gasoline, it would get 900 miles to
the gallon.[10]

Your body is remarkable. Have you thanked God for it?

Jesus, thank you for the wonders of creation as they are seen in my
own body.

TO READ
Revelation 5:1-14

One of the twenty-four elders said to me, "Stop weeping! Look, the Lion of the tribe of Judah, the heir to David's throne, has conquered. He is worthy to open the scroll and break its seven seals."

REVELATION 5:5

A Balanced View of Jesus

There is great danger in thinking of Jesus as a "soft" Savior. To be sure, he is kind, gentle, and compassionate. He came to earth to give his life because he loves you and me. But Jesus is as tough a man as has ever lived. He conquers every enemy and will execute justice on the wicked.

As today's Scripture tells us, he is the conquering Lion of the tribe of Judah.

Philip Yancey, in the video *The Jesus I Never Knew*, observes:

> As I studied the life of Christ, one impression about Jesus struck me more forcefully than any other. We have tamed him. The Jesus I learned about as a child was sweet and inoffensive, the kind of person whose lap you'd want to climb on. Mister Rogers with a beard. Indeed, Jesus did have qualities of gentleness and compassion that attracted little children. Mister Rogers, however, he assuredly was not. Not even the Romans would have crucified Mister Rogers.

How balanced is your view of Jesus? Have you figured out that his grace is bigger than anything you can imagine but that it never comes at the expense of his strength?

Jesus faces everything in life with a perfect balance of love and toughness. He knows when to gently bring comfort to your heart and he knows when to be tough with you. He knows when to call you to rest and he knows when to push you to your limit.

Jesus is the tenderhearted Lion.

Jesus, give me a balanced, accurate view of you.

TO READ
Psalm 139:13, 17-24

You made all the delicate, inner parts of my body
and knit me together in my mother's womb.

PSALM 139:13

Ordinary Miracles

One of the tests of spiritual vitality is the kind of wonder we have at the ordinary miracles God does every day.

I recently experienced what I consider to be two everyday miracles in one event. Some good friends of mine had been rejoicing for eight months over the pending birth of their first child. They had prayed, prepared the bedroom, and read many books. They had dreamed together about the baby and shared the ultrasound photos with us. In the mother's womb, the miracle of life was taking shape daily.

The second miracle was born out of tragedy. At eight months of development, the baby suddenly died. There was no more heartbeat and no more activity in the womb. We cried together, we asked why together, and we painfully rejoiced over the pictures of their beautiful daughter. In planning the funeral, they decided to do a tribute to the impact their daughter had had on them. That's when the miracle took place.

At the funeral, they both spoke. They thanked God for their daughter because she had forever changed their lives. Everybody in the church that day was amazed at how this grieving couple could show such strength in the midst of tragedy.

God is doing everyday miracles around you, but he is not going to force you to notice them. He has put himself on display and invites you daily to take notice. Will you look around you today and appreciate the "common" miracles of God?

Lord, help me to appreciate your "ordinary" miracles.

TO READ
Genesis 2:4-19

The Lord God formed from the soil every kind of animal and bird. He brought them to Adam to see what he would call them, and Adam chose a name for each one. GENESIS 2:19

❊ *Sharing in God's Creativity*

Amazingly, God has shared with us not just his creation but the very creativity it took to make it happen. This was first evident in the garden of Eden. Once God had finished creating every walking, crawling, swimming, and flying creature, he charged Adam with the responsibility of naming every one of them. In short order, Adam did just that.

We live in a world of fascinating technology because of the creative thinking of men and women. When I was in high school, the personal computer didn't even exist. Now I have a handheld computer that is the same size as my wallet.

Sometimes creativity is entertaining. My middle son, Zachery, thinks creatively and feels bound up when he is too structured. When it is his turn to do the dishes at our house, he puts things away creatively. It is not unusual to open a cabinet after he has been "organizing" the kitchen to find things stacked in unusual ways. One day, I opened the cabinet door to get a glass, and I snapped. It looked to me as if the glasses had been thrown into the cupboard haphazardly.

In exasperation, I called out, "Zachery, get in here!"

He came jogging in and answered, "Yes, Dad. What do you want?"

I pointed at the mess of glasses and asked, "Zachery, what is this?"

Without missing a beat, he said, "It's a volcano!"

His creativity instantly overcame my frustration. As I started to laugh, all I could say to him was, "You're right. It's a volcano. Now get out of here."

Creativity is God's gift for us men today. It's our choice what we do with it.

Jesus, thank you for giving me the gift of creativity. May I always use it for your glory.

TO READ
Matthew 7:7-14

If you sinful people know how to give good gifts to your children, how much more will your heavenly Father give good gifts to those who ask him.

MATTHEW 7:11

Good Gifts

Today's verse may seem rather obvious. Of course God will give good gifts to people who sincerely ask. Of course parents have a desire to give good gifts to their kids, and they go to great lengths to provide for their families. Why would Jesus state such an obvious truth?

I believe Jesus spoke these words because of the times in our lives that are difficult to go through. It is hard to remember in the midst of turmoil that character is forged in struggles.

Recently I had a meeting with Mike, a very good friend of mine. We have been working on some business together, and we had some planning to do. The meeting, however, took a very different turn. Last year some of our mutual friends and I had been faced with an unsettling situation. It meant a lot of change in each of our lives. One of these friends asked Mike to get involved. Mike was having an extremely strenuous year in his business, so he had to decline. But he had been feeling guilty about it ever since. In our meeting, we started talking about the situation, and Mike broke down in tears. We spent the entire two hours talking about the previous year's struggle without getting any of our scheduled work done.

We met again the next week, and Mike said, "Thanks for last week's meeting. I know we didn't get anything done that we planned, but it was important for me. I have been carrying a lot of guilt over the last year, and I was able to release a lot of it. Thanks for taking the time."

The meeting was hard, but it was good. God had indeed given a good gift.

What are the good gifts God has given you? How will you share those gifts with others?

Jesus, help me recognize your good gifts today.

Remember, dear brothers and sisters, that few of you were wise in the world's eyes, or powerful, or wealthy when God called you.   1 CORINTHIANS 1:26

The Value of Packaging

We men have a tendency to look more at packaging than at the message within the package.

In one of his sermons, Pastor Roger Thompson illustrated that truth:

When I was in high school, I worked for a time at an armored-car company, Brinks Armored Co. in San Bernardino, California. My job was to take care of the coin that Brinks handles. We used to get forty tons of coin from Las Vegas. . . .

One day we got a call from Bank of America in downtown San Bernardino, and they were in a panic: "We've got to have some coin in the hour." Well, all the armored trucks were gone, and so Larry, my manager, backed his '49 Ford pickup into the bay. Now if Brinks ever finds out about this they're going to shoot this guy. We loaded $25,000 worth of coin in a '49 Ford pickup. That thing was dragging. That's over a ton. Larry said, "Hop in. We're going up to B of A."

We hopped. I'm in my T-shirt and blue jeans. We drove up to the front of the Bank of America, parked the truck, and Larry said, "Hang on, I'll go in and get the dolly, and we'll haul this stuff in." I'm whistling, standing against this truck for twenty minutes. I don't have a gun. I thought, *If anybody notices what is in this common looking pickup truck, I'm a dead duck!* Of course, you can't carry eighty pounds very far. The treasure that people were walking by! But they didn't see it for the commonness of the delivery system.[11]

Sometimes great messages come in simple human packages. We should never discount the value of a message because of the package.

Jesus, may I never doubt the value of the gospel because of my view of the messenger.

TO READ
James 3:13-18

If you are bitterly jealous and there is selfish ambition in your hearts, don't brag about being wise. That is the worst kind of lie. JAMES 3:14

The Folly of Bitterness

Two shopkeepers were bitter rivals. Their stores were directly across the street from each other, and both men spent their entire days keeping track of each other's business. If one shopkeeper got a customer, he would smile in triumph at his rival.

One night an angel appeared to one of the shopkeepers in a dream and said, "I will give you anything you ask for, but whatever you receive, your competitor will receive twice as much. Would you be rich? You can be very rich, but he will be twice as wealthy. Do you wish to live a long and healthy life? You can, but his life will be longer and healthier. What is your desire?"

The man frowned, thought for a moment, then said, "Here is my request: Strike me blind in one eye!"

Bitterness truly is the most relentless enemy we men can face. When it takes root in a man's heart, it creates a life of its own. It has an insatiable appetite. It takes over a man's thinking and his heart, hardening it to everything good in life. It takes over his decision making so that his desire to inflict pain and revenge orchestrates his entire life.

The apostle James tells us that jealousy, selfishness, and bitterness are from the devil and are therefore destructive to our lives, even our very souls. In short, bitterness can ruin an otherwise focused, productive life.

But the good news is that none of us has to allow bitterness to define our lives. Instead of living in bitterness, we can choose to "live a life of steady goodness so that only good deeds will pour forth" (James 3:13).

Bitterness or steady goodness? Which of these do you want to define your life?

Jesus, help me live a life of goodness to others, even my rivals.

TO READ
Hebrews 12:11-17

No discipline is enjoyable while it is happening—it is painful! But afterward there will be a quiet harvest of right living for those who are trained in this way.

HEBREWS 12:11

✳ A Matter of Perspective

In his perfect perspective, God always knows the right thing to do for us—or to us. An account recorded in *Leadership Journal* illustrates this point:

> A Norfolk-Southern train was rolling down the rails of Indiana at twenty-four miles per hour. Suddenly the conductor, Robert Mohr, spotted an object on the tracks roughly a city block away. Initially the engineer, Rod Lindley, thought it was a dog on the tracks. Then Mohr screamed, "That's a baby!"
>
> The baby was nineteen-month-old Emily Marshall, who had wandered away from home while her mother planted flowers in her yard.
>
> Lindley hit the brakes. Mohr bolted out the door and raced along a ledge to the front of the engine. He realized there was no time to jump ahead of the train and grab the baby. So he ran down a set of steps, squatted at the bottom of the grill, and hung on.
>
> As the train drew close to Emily, she rolled off the rail onto the roadbed, but she was still in danger of being hit by the train. So Mohr stretched out his leg and pushed her out of harm's way. Mohr then jumped off the train, picked up the little girl, and cradled her in his arms. Little Emily ended up with just a cut on her head and a swollen lip.[12]

Emily Marshall had no idea why she had to endure the pain of the cut on her head and her swollen lip. But there was no other way to save her from an almost certain death.

It's often that way in our lives. When we are tempted to believe that our pain has no purpose, we should ask ourselves if our pain is God's way of sparing us from something worse.

Jesus, teach me your perspective on my life.

September

TO READ
Hebrews 11:17–12:1

Therefore, since we are surrounded by such a huge crowd of witnesses to the life of faith, let us strip off every weight that slows us down, especially the sin that so easily hinders our progress. And let us run with endurance the race that God has set before us.

HEBREWS 12:1

Our Biggest Supporters

Today's verse follows on the heels of Hebrews 11, "the Hall of Fame of the Faithful." Hebrews 11 lists the great spiritual "athletes" who have gone before us. It proclaims the exploits of Abraham, Moses, David, and others in a victorious tone and tells us to remember them, emulate them, honor them, and pass on the memory of them to the next generation.

But there's more. This "huge crowd of witnesses," as today's verse calls them, are now in heaven, cheering us on as we run the race. They are filled with anticipation as we prepare for the starting gun to go off. They understand we must wear the lightest, simplest clothes in order to reach our potential, and they agonize with us as we "strip off every weight that slows us down." They root for us as we wrestle free from "the sin that so easily hinders our progress."

Those of us who want to successfully compete in life must simplify our lives and free ourselves of all distractions. We also must be willing to see the deficiencies and blemishes in our souls. That means finding coaches who will help us carry on the great tradition started by the heroes of the faith.

We will all make mistakes in our training, so we all need life coaches, men who will honestly and courageously point out the areas in our lives that need to change. We are all selfish and prone to organizing our lives for our own benefit, so we need bold men who will call us to a life of service. And we are all prone to falling into the "sin that hinders our progress," so we need men in our lives who are focused enough to call us to repentance.

We already have a "huge crowd of witnesses." And when we find the right kind of training, we are sure to run the race with success.

Lord, give me grace to run the race you've called me to run.

Since we have a great High Priest who rules over God's people, let us go right into the presence of God, with true hearts fully trusting him.

HEBREWS 10:21-22

Our Access to God

An article in the *Rocky Mountain News* in Denver, Colorado, described various Web sites to which people can submit their prayers. One site, Newprayer.com, says, "Simply click on the 'Pray' button and transmit your prayer to the only known location of God." The site claims "that it can send prayers via a radio transmitter to God's last known location," a star cluster called M13, which is believed to be one of the oldest in the universe. Here is more from the Web site:

> Crandall Stone, 50, a Cambridge, Massachusetts, engineer and freelance consultant, set up the site last winter after a night of sipping brandy and philosophizing with friends in Vermont. The conversation turned to Big Bang theories of creation, and someone suggested that if everything was in one place at the time of the explosion, then God must have been there, too.
>
> "It's the one place where we could be sure he was," Stone said. "Then we thought that if we could find that location and had a radio transmitter, we could send a message to God." After consulting with NASA scientists, the friends settled on M13 as the likely location. They chipped in about $20,000, and built a radio-wave-transmitting Web site.
>
> Stone reports that they transmit about 50,000 prayers a week from seekers around the globe."[1]

Fortunately, we don't have to go to some Web site or contact some distant galaxy in order for God to hear our prayers. Prayer is so much simpler than that. We who know Jesus Christ as our personal Savior have the privilege of going boldly and confidently into God's very presence and making our requests known to him.

Jesus, I'm thankful that you're willing to listen to me.

TO READ
1 Samuel 12:1-22

Samuel called to the Lord, and the Lord sent thunder and rain. And all the people were terrified of the Lord and of Samuel. 1 SAMUEL 12:18

❋ A Sense of Awe

Well-known philosopher, lecturer, and author Jacob Needleman remembers:

> I was an observer at the launch of Apollo 17 in 1975. It was a night launch, and there were hundreds of cynical reporters all over the lawn, drinking beer, wisecracking, and waiting for this 35-story-high rocket.
>
> The countdown came, and then the launch. The first thing you see is this extraordinary orange light, which is just at the limit of what you can bear to look at. Everything is illuminated with this light. Then comes this thing slowly rising up in total silence, because it takes a few seconds for the sound to come across. You hear a "WHOOOOOSH! HHHHMMMM!" It enters right into you.
>
> You can practically hear jaws dropping. The sense of wonder fills everyone in the whole place, as this thing goes up and up. The first stage ignites this beautiful blue flame. It becomes like a star, but you realize there are humans on it. And then there's total silence.
>
> People just get up quietly, helping each other up. They're kind. They open doors. They look at one another, speaking quietly and interestedly. These were suddenly moral people because the sense of wonder, the experience of wonder, had made them moral.[2]

When we have a sense of awe and wonder toward God, our lives will also be changed for the better. We will begin living lives that please God as we help others toward a personal relationship with Jesus.

Jesus, teach me to live in awe of you.

TO READ
Hebrews 11:1-16

All these faithful ones died without receiving what God had promised them, but they saw it all from a distance and welcomed the promises of God. They agreed that they were no more than foreigners and nomads here on earth. HEBREWS 11:13

Our Real Citizenship

In the nineteenth century, many people who wanted to see how the upper class lived would pass by the famous Rothschild Mansion in the fashionable quarter of London. Lord Rothschild was incredibly successful and had a very nice home. In amazement, some of the people noticed that the end of one of the cornices was unfinished. They couldn't help but ask the question, "Why would the richest man in the world not finish his house?" The explanation was very simple but said a lot about Lord Rothschild himself. Rothschild was an orthodox Jew, and Jewish tradition says that every pious Jew's house must have some part unfinished. This was to bear testimony to the world that its occupant is, like Abraham, only a pilgrim and a stranger upon the earth.

Life is so full of hard work that it is sometimes difficult to remember that we are, in reality, citizens of heaven. We focus on making a living, building corporations, and raising children. We service our cars, mow our lawns, and manage our money. We seek enough success to take care of those we love, hoping that we don't get so carried away with it that pride takes hold of us.

But no matter who we are or how successful we may become, we must remember that we are but visitors on this earth. Our real citizenship is with Jesus, who has gone ahead to prepare a home for us to live in for all of eternity.

Lord, remind me often that I am only a visitor on earth and that my real home is with you in heaven.

The Spirit of the Sovereign Lord is upon me, because the Lord has appointed me to bring good news to the poor. He has sent me to comfort the broken-hearted and to announce that captives will be released and prisoners will be freed. ISAIAH 61:1

The Choice to Live Free

Frederick Douglass grew up as a slave in Maryland in the early nineteenth century. He suffered all the worst of a life of slavery. He was separated from his mother when he was an infant. For years he worked in the hot fields from before sunup until after sundown. He was kicked and beaten by his master and whipped many times with a cowhide whip until blood ran down his back. A few times he almost died.

Despite the harshness of life as a slave, Frederick Douglass had second thoughts about escaping to freedom. He struggled with the decision because he had grown to love so many people who had become part of his life.

He wrote in *Narrative of the Life of Frederick Douglass, An American Slave*: "I had a number of warm-hearted friends in Baltimore—friends that I loved almost as I did my life—and the thought of being separated from them forever was painful beyond expression. It is my opinion that thousands would escape from slavery, who now remain, but for the strong cords of affection that bind them to their friends."

It is difficult when life makes you choose between freedom and the people you are attached to. But it's a decision that must be made, for it will determine the state of your heart and life for years to come.

Consider Mr. Douglass's joy when he chose freedom: "I have been frequently asked how I felt when I found myself in a free State. . . . It was a moment of the highest excitement I ever experienced."

There is no more joyous moment than when we first discover true freedom—the freedom that comes through a personal relationship with Jesus Christ. And once we make a choice to walk in that freedom, we'll never want to return to the bondage of our old ways.

Jesus, thank you for showing me and giving me a life of freedom.

TO READ
Job 16:18-21

My intercessor is my friend as my eyes pour out tears to God. Job 16:20, NIV

Friends Who Intercede

Job endured many setbacks without knowing why. He took comfort in the fact that others prayed for him and there was a friend in heaven who would someday explain it to him.

Lloyd John Ogilvie, former chaplain of the United States Senate, tells a story about the value of a friend who will intercede:

Senator Max Cleland, who lost both of his legs and his right hand in Vietnam, came to the Bible study withdrawn and tired. Another senator said, "Max, are you all right?"

"Not really," he said. "I've been having the same dream for 30 years. I accidentally drop that grenade, and I leap on it, and it explodes and blows my legs off."

That night, the study group gathered around Max and prayed that the Lord would heal that memory.

Two days later the *History Channel* broadcast his story just as he remembered it. A man from Annapolis saw it and phoned Max: "Senator, you have the story all wrong. That wasn't your grenade. It was a young recruit behind you who had opened the pins on his grenades before jumping out of the helicopter. One of them popped out of the belt and rolled on the ground. You leaped on it to save us all. I wrapped you up myself and got you to the hospital. I was on the helicopter; I know how it happened."

Max came to the next Bible study a new man. He said a gigantic load had been lifted off his shoulders.[3]

Jesus, make me the kind of friend who will remind others of what is true.

TO READ
Romans 12:3-8

Just as our bodies have many parts and each part has a special function, so it is with Christ's body. We are all parts of his one body, and each of us has different work to do. And since we are all one body in Christ, we belong to each other, and each of us needs all the others. ROMANS 12:4-5

A Time for Teamwork, a Time to Labor Alone

One of my heroes growing up was UCLA basketball coach John Wooden. I was a big fan of Bruin basketball and even dreamed of playing for the legendary coach.

When I was in high school, Coach Wooden held a basketball camp in my hometown and was considering making a training video. He asked my head coach to provide some players for the video, and I was chosen. I was so excited I couldn't sleep for days.

Meeting the great coach was a fascinating experience. I was surprised to find out that he was only five feet six inches tall. He worked in a land of giants, but he was the shortest person in camp.

I have often reflected on that experience and have been amazed at how John Wooden was able to accomplish what he did. He could not have won the ten national championships on his own. He was a brilliant coach, but he also needed talented players to make it happen.

Coach Wooden was interviewed as part of the celebration of his ninetieth birthday on October 14, 2000. He talked about the memorabilia he has from his years as a coach—the photos, trophies, and plaques. But then he said, "There is one I treasure above the others. When I graduated from Purdue, I received the Big Ten medal as the senior athlete with the highest grade-point average. I did that. The other awards, my teams won."[4]

There are times when we need the help of others to accomplish great things for God. But God sometimes calls us to stand alone in our work for him.

Remind me, Jesus, that life is a team sport. But also remind me that there are some things you call me to do on my own.

TO READ
Job 13:1-12

Oh, how I long to speak directly to the Almighty.
I want to argue my case with God himself. JOB 13:3

✿ *Arguing Your Case*

Like many Americans, I watched the live courtroom arguments for the O. J. Simpson and Danielle van Dam cases. The lawyers on both sides of these cases presented evidence and arguments—on behalf of the victims and on behalf of the defendants.

Some days we feel like the accused, pleading for grace and mercy from a loving God. Other days we feel like the victim, arguing for justice and demanding our "pound of flesh" for the injustice done to us.

Either way, God wants you to argue your case before him, just as Job wanted to argue his case. He wants you to contend for truth and understanding. However, there are a few things you need to keep in mind as you approach the bench of God:

1. He is God. He is all-knowing. He sees the whole story.
2. He is God. He is perfect, holy, and righteous. He does not make mistakes.
3. He is God. He is all-powerful, merciful, and patient.
4. He is God. He is sovereign. He has the ability to make all things work together for your good, even when your situation looks bad.
5. He is God. You are not. He deserves your respect and praise, even if you don't feel like giving it.
6. He is God. And he loves you more than you can know.

So make your case. Just remember who the Judge is, how much of the evidence he already knows, and how much he really loves you.

Dear Jesus, thank you that you are the one who will judge me when I plead my case.

TO READ
Acts 27:33–28:2

The people of the island were very kind to us. It was cold and rainy, so they built a fire on the shore to welcome us and warm us. ACTS 28:2

Unusual Kindness

In the wake of the September 11, 2001, terrorist attack, hundreds of couples in New York City canceled divorces. It seems that in light of such a tragedy, what really matters—marriage, family, supportive friends, and faith—comes to light.

Pam and I have tried to live out our marriage of twenty-four years according to today's verse. We try, in every way we can, to treat one another with what the New King James Version of this verse calls "unusual kindness."

People are watching to see how we treat our wives. Our friends are watching, and our spouses are definitely watching. But most importantly, our children are watching and taking mental notes, because they look to us as role models of marital kindness.

Recently, Pam and I saw firsthand the results of our efforts to treat one another with unusual kindness. Our son Brock was a record-setting high school quarterback, and he was interviewed after breaking a passing record. *The San Diego Union Tribune*, the largest newspaper in the city, asked him, "Who is the most influential person in your life?" Brock replied: "My mom and dad. My dad is a great example of what a real man should be. I can tell he loves my mom very much. My mom tells me to be an upstanding citizen. She keeps me focused in terms of what's important in life."

Reading my son's quotation thrilled Pam and me because we realized that Brock had gotten a main message of our marriage: be unusually kind!

Do you treat your spouse with unusual kindness? Are your words so kind that others notice? Are your actions so gentle and gracious that people stop to watch?

Lord, make me unusually kind so others will notice you in me.

TO READ
2 Timothy 4:6-8

As for me, my life has already been poured out as an offering to God. The time of my death is near.

2 TIMOTHY 4:6

The Greatest Love of All

The apostle Paul understood the need for rescue workers. Physically, people find themselves in all kinds of predicaments, and it takes rescue workers to lead the survivors to safety. At times, the rescue work itself takes the life of the rescuers and soberly reminds us of their importance.

Ganelle Guzman was the last survivor found among the rubble of the World Trade Center following the disaster of September 11, 2001. She had fallen from the thirteenth-floor stairwell when the building collapsed and was trapped among the concrete and steel for twenty-six hours.

As rescue workers searched for survivors at great danger to themselves, Ganelle clung to hope. She was able to do so through the power of her own prayers and because of the presence of another individual.

Laying amidst the hard debris, Ganelle felt something soft near her. Before long, she realized that it was the body of a New York firefighter who had perished trying to rescue others. She tried not to think too much about the fact that she lay near a dead body.

Shortly after noon on September 12, 2001, Ganelle was found. Rescue workers told her that they never would have found her if it were not for that fireman. Her civilian clothes had blended in with the debris, making her virtually invisible. The firefighter's uniform, however, had reflective tape on it, and that drew the rescue workers to the spot where Ganelle had been trapped. His death had literally saved her life.

Are you willing to lay down your life for others? Are you willing to make yourself vulnerable, even put yourself in peril to save another?

Lord, make me willing to lay down my life for others who need to be rescued.

In a great chorus they sang, "Holy, holy, holy is the Lord Almighty! The whole earth is filled with his glory!" Isaiah 6:3

Holiness: A Better Way

Holiness is the attribute of God that is the most elusive in our understanding because we all fall so short of it. At the same time, it is the attribute that makes all his other attributes trustworthy. In his book *The Names of God*, Nathan Stone explains, "Power without holiness would degenerate into cruelty; omniscience without holiness would become craft; justice without holiness would degenerate into revenge."[5]

Holiness demands our obedience. The Bible tells us, "If you do anything you believe is not right, you are sinning" (Romans 14:23). Or as Bing Hunter writes, "Sin is the failure to live congruently with God's holiness."[6]

Holiness demands humility of us. Bill Bright, president and founder of Campus Crusade for Christ, wrote of the relationship between our sin and God's holiness:

> When I think of God's holiness, I am convicted by the sinful nature of my own being. We are all like a man wearing a beautiful white suit who was invited to go down into the depths of a coal mine. In the darkness of the mine, he was not aware that his suit was becoming soiled. But when he resurfaced into the dazzling light of the noonday sun, he was fully aware that his suit had become sooty and dirty. The light of God's holiness reveals the darkness of our sin.[7]

When the contrast between God's holiness and your own imperfection hits home, you will simply cry out with the angels, "Holy, Holy, Holy!"

Today, think about the ways God's holiness makes your life better. As you focus on those ways, use them as motivation to seek a life of holiness.

Jesus, renew my appreciation for your holiness, and give me the ability to live a life that pleases you.

TO READ
1 Corinthians 9:27–10:11

I discipline my body like an athlete, training it to do what it should. Otherwise, I fear that after preaching to others I myself might be disqualified.

1 CORINTHIANS 9:27

Can You?

One of my son Zach's favorite quotations is, "Whether you think you can or think you can't—you are right." What you think about your chances of success goes a long way in determining whether you will enjoy it.

Recently, Zach was on a team competing in the National Cheerleading Association competition in Anaheim, California. The team had looked forward to the competition and practiced hard for it.

As the team warmed up, one of the key members, a boy named Andre, dislocated his shoulder. Andre's part in the team's routine included lifting a cheerleader above his head several times. Andre's injury made the difficult maneuver even harder.

The team was worried about Andre. They knew the pressure he felt—and the pain. I laid my hand on his shoulder and prayed that God would give him strength and would send help. Right after I prayed, another coach saw Andre in pain and offered medical help.

Somehow, Andre managed to pop the shoulder back into place, but he was still in intense pain. Every time he lifted his arm over his head, the pain was so excruciating that tears would run down his cheeks.

We all held our breath and prayed as the team performed. Still hurting badly and with tears in his eyes, Andre pushed through and performed his stunts to near perfection. The team won the national competition.

Are you facing obstacles or pain as you push through to do the things God has placed before you? Whether you think you can overcome the pain or think you can't—you are right.

Jesus, remind me that despite the obstacles and pain, I can accomplish what you set before me.

TO READ
Jeremiah 24:1-10

I will give them hearts that will recognize me as the Lord. They will be my people, and I will be their God, for they will return to me wholeheartedly.

JEREMIAH 24:7

✳ *People, Places, and Passages*

Handling big decisions or stressful life experiences can raise some questions. Where do I go from here? Who do I tell? What does a plan look like? Where can I go for help? How do I handle roadblocks, obstacles, and opposition? How can I move the dream further? How can I move myself forward?

When I need answers to questions like these, I go back to the "three Ps"—People, Places, and Passages—that first helped me understand the truth about God and myself.

People: I go back to the people who best explained to me the plan of God. Sometimes those people are my friends, mentors, professors, or disciplers. But sometimes I go back and reread books by people I respect, books that were pivotal in my growth.

Places: Pam and I have had some wonderful experiences at Christian conference centers and at some of our favorite vacation spots. Sometimes when we have a big decision or need some clarity, we head back to those same comforting places to seek God. There's something comforting about going back to the same chapel, the same campground, or the same conference center where you first heard the call to follow Jesus Christ. Yes, God can speak to us anywhere, but it seems there are just some places where we hear better.

Passages: When I am seeking God, I often open my Bible and reread the verses or passages I have underlined or highlighted in the past. It brings a sense of security to remember how God has led me in the past. By going back to those verses, I often get what I need to go forward.

Are you facing a big decision today? Try going back to the people, places, and passages that helped you hear God more clearly in the past.

Lord, guide me to the people, places, and Bible passages that have clarified your will in the past.

TO READ
Luke 12:33-48

And the Lord replied, "I'm talking to any faithful, sensible servant to whom the master gives the responsibility of managing his household and feeding his family." LUKE 12:42

✳ *Consistency Means Credibility*

The one trait most workers say they desire in a boss or leader is integrity. I think that's true of anyone who wants to make a difference in the lives of others. Integrity gives you credibility. Credibility will help you build a team. It may even help you secure financing for your dream. It will be the honey that draws people to you. But how do we build credibility with others?

Consistent Work Ethic: A proven track record is vital when it comes to building credibility. Jesus pointed this out when he said, "You have been faithful in handling this small amount, so now I will give you many more responsibilities" (Matthew 25:23). Do the "small things" well—no matter how insignificant and mundane they may seem—and God will give you larger and greater things to do.

Consistent Behavior: I have talked with the children of many high-profile Christian leaders, and I always ask them, "What did your parents do right?" The number one answer of these second-generation leaders is usually along the lines of, "My parents had integrity. They were the same at home as they were in the pulpit." Being dependable and having self-restraint, self-control, and self-respect are vital to building credibility. Therefore, before you make a choice, ask yourself if the choice you are about to make builds up your reputation or tears it down.

Credibility is absolutely essential in the life of any man who wants to lead and do great things for God. If you are consistent in how you approach the work God has already given you and consistent in your personal behavior, you will have taken two major steps toward building credibility.

Jesus, make me consistent enough in my work and in my personal life to make me credible.

TO READ
Matthew 6:24-34

Your heavenly Father already knows all your needs, and he will give you all you need from day to day if you live for him and make the Kingdom of God your primary concern. MATTHEW 6: 32-33

Timely Provision

When Pam and I were called from youth ministry into the senior pastorate, there were about six months when I ran my own drafting business, just to help make ends meet. We didn't have a large savings, and when clients were late paying their bills, we were between the proverbial rock and a hard place.

We decided to put a list of needs on the refrigerator—real needs such as groceries, money for the electric bill, gas for the car, diapers for the babies, and so forth—and each day we prayed, "Give us this day our daily bread."

It was then I realized that I had not been satisfied with God's daily provision, that I expected him to provide for us ahead of time. I wanted a surplus in the bank so I could see his provision before I needed it.

While I know that the New Testament clearly teaches the value of hard work in providing for your family (2 Thessalonians 3:10; 1 Timothy 5:8), I have learned that life's storms sometimes last longer than the savings. I began to pray, *Lord, help me not feel the need until it really is a need* and *God, give me faith to believe you will provide right on time*. On the days I felt particularly needy, I even prayed, *Just let me go one more day and trust your provision*.

As Pam and I prayed, we kept a journal of God's provision. Later, as we looked back on how he had provided for us, we found some beautiful examples of God meeting our needs—right on time! There was the unexpected job that paid cash, the diaper rebate check that bought milk the day we ran out, and many other incidents we knew God had orchestrated in order to provide for us.

We learned a lesson at that time, and we've never forgotten it: God always meets our needs, and he always does it right on time.

Jesus, give me faith to believe that you will meet my needs on a daily basis.

| TO READ
Mark 9:14-29 | So He said to them, "This kind can come out by nothing but prayer and fasting." MARK 9:29, NKJV |

❉ The Power of Prayer and Fasting

A group of us sat around the lunch table sharing our personal testimonies. When it was Mark's turn, he told us the story of how a group of his friends had consistently fasted and prayed for him to come to Jesus for salvation.

"My girlfriend in high school came to me and said, 'I can't keep dating you. I can't be unequally yoked,' " Mark recalled.

Mark told us how he accompanied his girlfriend to church that week, where he heard a clear presentation of the gospel. Later that night, he prayed, "God, I don't know everything . . . I don't know much of anything. But I do know that if all the stuff I heard today is true, and I think it is, I need you."

Later, Mark called his girlfriend and said, "Hey, I'm one of you."

"What do you mean?" she asked.

"You know that prayer? Well, I prayed it," Mark announced.

Later that week, Mark went to the church's youth group. When he walked in, his girlfriend announced, "Mark received Christ!"

"Hey Mark!" one of his friends said. "What took you so long?"

Mark thought, *Took me so long? I just heard this God stuff a few days ago.*

Mark learned that his friends had been praying and fasting one day a week for months for his salvation. They knew God was what he needed, so they sacrificed food—and they prayed.

There is great power in fasting and prayer. Is there someone or something God has laid on your heart to fast and pray for? When you combine fasting with prayer, you demonstrate the kind of passion God wants to see as you approach him. It is just that kind of passion that produces results.

Lord, give me the passion it takes to approach you in prayer and fasting.

TO READ
Psalm 145

Let each generation tell its children of your mighty acts. PSALM 145:4

Role Model Love

Dan is a leader in his church in Kansas City, Kansas. His family's devotions are in three parts: First, they choose a passage to read from the Bible. Second, someone in the family explains what the passage means and how it applies to their lives. Third, they take prayer requests and ask God to work in their lives.

In February Pam and I were in Kansas City to lead a marriage conference. We were scheduled to speak in all three services at Dan's church on Sunday morning, but an ice storm moved in on Saturday night. Church was cancelled.

I had lunch with Dan that Sunday. Dan had decided that the family devotions would take the place of church that morning. His eleven-year-old son asked if he could preach. With a sense of pride in his voice, Dan told me, "It was really neat. My oldest daughter read from the book of Matthew. My son then spoke on the passage. He went line by line in an expository manner and explained to us what it meant. I know I am biased, but it was pretty good. My youngest daughter then led us in prayer, and she made sure we prayed for everyone who had traveled on the roads because they didn't hear about church being cancelled."

Dan then added, "You know, most of the family devotions we have are kind of boring. I wonder quite often if my kids are listening or if they are bored. I find myself hoping they don't resent my wife and me for making them do this. Yesterday pretty much made me glad I stayed at it."

How are you passing on what you believe to the next generation?

Jesus, give me the endurance to keep sharing what I believe even when it looks like no one is listening.

TO READ
Matthew 6:19-21

Don't store up treasures here on earth, where they can be eaten by moths and get rusty, and where thieves break in and steal. MATTHEW 6:19

Who Would You Call?

As a pastor, I have received some phone calls that I will never forget. One came from a woman by the name of Marjorie.

"Pastor, my house is burning to the ground!" Marjorie screamed.

Our church's associate pastor and I rushed to Marjorie's house and stood by her side as the firemen tried desperately to save her home. But it was to no avail. Her house was destroyed.

I called my wife. "Honey, Marjorie only has the clothes on her back, and she wants to know if you'll take her shopping."

Pam drove Marjorie to our local discount chain store. As the two women walked to the checkout, something on their faces must have broadcast their emotional state. The checker said, "Cheer up! It's almost Christmas! It can't be that bad."

"Actually, it could be," Pam replied. "My friend's home just burned to the ground."

In embarrassed silence, the checker rang up the purchases. When he finished, he reached across and touched Marjorie's hand as he looked at her. "Ma'am, I am so sorry," he gently said. "I will pray for you."

That caring gesture meant a great deal to Marjorie. As she and Pam stepped outside, Marjorie said, "Pam, the Bible says that in the end everyone's stuff will burn—mine just went up sooner than yours! I'll hang on to God and I'll survive." Then she smiled.

If your world were to come apart today, who would you call? Where is your hope? In stuff or in God?

Prepare me, Lord, for the sometimes-difficult realities I will face in life.

TO READ
Proverbs 2:1-19

Wisdom will enter your heart, and knowledge will fill you with joy. Wise planning will watch over you. Understanding will keep you safe.

PROVERBS 2:10-11

Direction for Your Relationship

When Pam and I were dating, we lived in different cities two hours apart. On many weekends I would drive to her hometown and stay with friends so I could spend time with her. Each time we got together, I pulled out a notebook in which I kept a running list of relationship questions and issues I wanted us to talk through. I would then write down any relationship questions or issues our latest visit brought up.

None of my friends carried these notebooks, and it wasn't something I was trained to do. It was simply my desperate attempt to keep our relationship on the right track.

Now, nearly twenty-five years into marriage, I am more grateful than ever that I took the time to record those things in that notebook. I also recommend that other couples do the same.

Do you want your marriage relationship to have purpose? Start by making a list of five relationship questions or issues you would like to address. Make them questions you'd like to discuss or goals you'd like to achieve.

The goals will need to be ones you have a measure of control over. For example, it is counterproductive to write, "I want my wife to be more sexually attentive." You can't control her actions. It is, however, productive to write something like, "I will set aside three hours each Thursday to focus on my wife and our relationship," because that is something you can control.

Once you've established the five questions or issues, research one at a time using resources such as the Bible, people you respect, professionals, books, or the Internet, then write down what you learn.

As you do all of this, don't forget that learning a new relationship skill doesn't mean anything if you don't apply it daily.

Lord, teach me to be more deliberate in my marriage relationship.

TO READ
Luke 10:25-37

The man answered, "'You must love the Lord your God with all your heart, all your soul, all your strength, and all your mind.' And, 'Love your neighbor as yourself.'" LUKE 10:27

Overcoming the Relationship Deficit

My friend Mike was talking about discipling and training leaders. He said, "When I see people who have a deficit in their relationships with other people, I know they have a deficit in their relationship with God. When we are rightly relating to God, we gain the ability to rightly relate to others. The key is to discover what is missing in their relationship with God."

Are you consistently having problems in your relationships with people? Take a look at the following list and see if any of these apply to you:

- Short with people? Maybe you are angry at God about what you see as his wrong timing or lack of provision.
- Non-communicative? How much are you talking with God?
- Distant? Maybe you have a hurt you haven't allowed God to heal.
- Keep running away from commitments? Maybe you aren't doing well in keeping your commitments to God.
- Hiding behind drugs or alcohol? Maybe you're trying to hide a pain, disappointment, or trauma from God.
- Always nagging? How much do you trust God? Do you feel the need to "help him out"?
- Resentful? Your underlying anger will go deeper unless you let God meet the need that another person was unable to meet.

When you look at your relationships with other people, do you see an unhealthy pattern? Invest in your primary relationship—with God—and you will see improvement in all your secondary relationships—with people.

Lord, be the strength of all my relationships—with you first, then with the people in my life.

TO READ
1 Corinthians 12:1-6

There are different kinds of spiritual gifts, but it is the same Holy Spirit who is the source of them all. There are different kinds of service in the church, but it is the same Lord we are serving.

1 CORINTHIANS 12:4-5

Getting—and Staying—on the Right Path

Sometimes we ignore the directional signs God places along our path. One friend of ours—we'll call him Doug—was a perfect example of this truth. Doug wanted to be a senior pastor, but God had another plan.

Several seminary professors had told Doug that he had a gift for research and the talent and skills to be a graduate assistant or maybe a teacher. All of his friends saw that he lacked charisma and struggled with recruiting and leading people. For that reason, we suggested he pursue teaching. But Doug wanted to be a senior pastor, and he continued on that path.

Doug's first pastorate was on an interim basis, and it didn't go well at all. The church let him go early. His second attempt at pastoring—a church plant—never got off the ground.

In frustration, Doug took a position teaching a few Bible classes at a Christian school. His students loved him, and he was soon offered a full-time position at the school. Doug quickly established a reputation as a quality teacher, and other schools began contacting him, wanting him to train their teachers.

God was obviously blessing Doug as a teacher, but Doug still wanted to be a senior pastor. One day a wise, caring friend asked him, "Why would you want to go to a church when God has given you so much success teaching?"

"I want to teach the Word and impact lives."

"You are," the friend said.

The light came on inside Doug. He realized what all of us need to understand: God knows what abilities we have. In his wisdom, he has called each of us to serve him in ways that best use those abilities.

Lord, don't allow me to fight against your plan for my life.

> TO READ
> 1 Peter 1:1-9

These trials are only to test your faith, to show that it is strong and pure. It is being tested as fire tests and purifies gold—and your faith is far more precious to God than mere gold. 1 PETER 1:7

Testing Your Faith

"Adversity doesn't build character as much as it reveals it." Agree?

"What doesn't kill you makes you stronger." Agree?

I think both statements can be true *if* you don't waste your pain. Pain, obstacles, and adversity can be the anvil on which your character is forged. However, if you fail to learn from the pain but instead choose bitterness and anger, then the next adversity you face will reveal the shallowness of your character and your faith.

We see the same kind of testing in the life of Job, who lost his children, his livestock, his home, and his health. Yet through all of this, Job never sinned against his God, either in word or in deed.

Job's wife wanted him to curse God and die. But he refused. "You talk like a godless woman," he told her. "Should we accept only good things from the hand of God and never anything bad?" (Job 2:10).

Job's three friends came to his side, but the comfort they offered was, in many ways, in the form of misrepresenting the God Job had so faithfully served. Yet, while Job had a lot of questions for God, he refused to give in and sin against him.

The outcome?

"After the Lord had finished speaking to Job, he said to Eliphaz the Temanite: 'I am angry with you and with your two friends, for you have not been right in what you said about me, as my servant Job was.' . . . When Job prayed for his friends, the Lord restored his fortunes. In fact, the Lord gave him twice as much as before!" (Job 42:7, 10).

God can indeed use adversity to build your faith and make you a stronger man. But he can also use those life storms as a proving ground for your faith.

Jesus, use my setbacks to show me that my faith is strong and pure.

TO READ
Exodus 20:1-17

Do not worship any other gods besides me. . . .
You must never worship or bow down to them, for I,
the Lord your God, am a jealous God! . . . But I lavish my love on those who love me and obey my commands, even for a thousand generations.

EXODUS 20:3-6

❋ Our Own Commandments?

Satan wants your eyes off God. But in order to get you distracted, he doesn't draw your attention to himself; rather he subtly directs your focus to yourself. He does that by twisting the truth so that you, not God, are the object of worship.

To illustrate the point, let's see what would happen if we rewrote the first five of the Ten Commandments so you, not God, are the focus. We need to start by stating that you are the lord of your own life and that no one, not even God himself, can tell you what to do. Now it's time for your very own commandments:

- Create your own religion. Worship whatever god you think will get you ahead.
- Have as many idols as you want. Follow sports teams and movie stars, and do whatever you want.
- Swear whenever you want. In fact, say anything you want, whenever you want.
- Don't get hung up on going to church. After all, it's just a building. Besides, the people who go to church are just a bunch of hypocrites anyway. Be "spiritual" any way you feel like.
- Don't listen to your parents. Those old people will just hold you down. Family is like a noose around your neck.

If thoughts like these have ever crossed your mind, you're like pretty much all of humanity. But now you know that such thoughts originate from the mind of Satan himself. Be sure to read (or reread) today's Scripture passage, which contains the real Ten Commandments—the ones that honor God.

God, may there be no room in my heart for counterfeits.

TO READ
John 8:34-45

The Devil . . . was a murderer from the beginning and has always hated the truth. There is no truth in him. When he lies, it is consistent with his character; for he is a liar and the father of lies. JOHN 8:44

✳ *More Subverted Truth*

It is a common tactic of our spiritual enemy to complicate everything in life. Love between a husband and a wife should be relatively simple, but we are all tempted to believe lies about the ones we love. Accomplishing God's will should be relatively simple, but people who worship together are tempted to question each other's motives.

Satan loves to subvert the truth to accomplish our destruction and the destruction of those around us.

With that in mind, if we were to rewrite the last of the Ten Commandments to align them with our own sinful desires, they become somewhere between ridiculous and disastrous:

- Murder might be a gift. Death isn't really so bad. Is life really that great?
- Have sex with whomever you want. If it feels good, do it! Marriage is overrated. Hardly anyone is happily married anyway, so why bother? Fulfill all your desires right now, any way you want.
- Take what you want from others. If someone is stupid enough to leave it right there in plain sight, they are just asking for you to take it.
- "White lies" are all right. Say whatever you need to cover for yourself.
- If you want someone's house, car, girlfriend, wife, clothes, or status, go for it! Your needs are more important than theirs anyway.

God gave us truth in his written Word, and he did so for his own glory and for our benefit. We need to make sure we never allow the enemy to destroy us by subverting God's truth with the devil's lies.

Make the truth obvious to me, Lord, and give me grace to embrace it.

TO READ
Galatians 6:1-10

Don't get tired of doing what is good. Don't get discouraged and give up, for we will reap a harvest of blessing at the appropriate time. GALATIANS 6:9

Being a Hell Rescuer

As a leader, I have felt it. And as a leader, I have heard it:

"Why bother? It's just going to fail anyway."

"Why call? They won't come."

"Why try? It's like beating my head against a brick wall."

"This wasn't worth the work."

"All this effort—for this outcome?"

"I give up."

Giving up is easy. Giving in takes no effort. There is pain in the struggle—especially in the struggle to live holy and healthy lives. There is hard work involved in beating back darkness.

Our youth pastor calls himself a "hell rescuer," based on Colossians 1:13: "He has rescued us from the one who rules in the kingdom of darkness, and he has brought us into the Kingdom of his dear Son."

Have you ever seen a police officer after a shoot-out? a firefighter after he has carried someone out of a burning building? a search-and-rescue leader after she has rappelled down a cliff to save a stranded and injured person? a lifeguard after he or she has saved someone from drowning in the ocean? They look tired! Rescuing is hard work!

Rescuing yourself from Satan's grip each day takes concentration and focus. Rescuing others takes tireless prayer and an intense drive to "be there"—inviting, reminding, giving healthy options, and training. It is work. Exhausting? Yes! Rewarding? Yes! Necessary? Definitely!

Jesus, transform me into a hell rescuer!

TO READ
1 Corinthians 4:1-16

When the Lord comes, he will bring our deepest secrets to light and will reveal our private motives. And then God will give to everyone whatever praise is due. 1 CORINTHIANS 4:5

When Everything Comes to Light

One Saturday morning, I read a newspaper story about a man I'll call John Smith. He had been driving erratically, so the highway patrol pulled him over. They gave him a battery of sobriety tests—walk a straight line, touch your nose, and so forth. The officers were about to administer a breath test when an accident occurred on the opposite side of the freeway. So they said to John, "Stay right here!" and hurried to tend to the accident. But John got in his car, drove home, and parked in his garage.

John told his wife to tell anyone who might ask where he was that he had been at home all day, sick. A few hours later, a knock came at the door. Mrs. Smith answered it and saw two highway patrol officers standing there.

"Does John Smith live here?" they asked.

Mrs. Smith nodded to the affirmative, and the officers asked to see her husband. John came out of the bedroom, faking a cough.

"What can I do for you fine officers?" he greeted them.

"Were you pulled over in a highway citation today?" they asked

"Oh, no! I've been sick all day," John coughed.

"Well, someone using your identity and your address was pulled over today. May we see your car so we can clear this up?"

"Sure, officers," John answered. He walked to the garage thinking, *That engine is nice and cool. I'm going to get away with this!*

John threw open the garage door, and there it was—the patrol car with the lights still flashing.

Our sins will indeed find us out. Knowing that, we should never try to hide our wrongdoing but instead confess it as quickly as possible.

Oh Jesus, help me to be honest with you and with others when it comes to my own sin. May I never try to hide my wrongdoing.

Therefore, anyone who becomes as humble as this little child is the greatest in the Kingdom of Heaven. And anyone who welcomes a little child like this on my behalf is welcoming me. MATTHEW 18:4-5

Who's the Greatest?

Part of being a man is being competitive, and part of being competitive is wanting to know who is the greatest—the greatest athletes, the greatest businessmen, the greatest politicians, the greatest friends, and so on. We men measure greatness based on what someone does—for us, in their own field, or for the world around them.

When Jesus' disciples asked him, "Which of us is the greatest in the Kingdom of Heaven?" they probably expected him to base his answer on performance or productivity. They probably even had some people in mind—maybe John the Baptist or David or Abraham . . . maybe even one of them.

But Jesus surprised them with his answer: "anyone who becomes as humble as this little child . . . "

The word *humble* in this context literally means "to depress." It suggests one voluntarily placing himself lower than another. In this regard, a child is the perfect example of humility.

A small child has more questions than answers. He has energy but lacks wisdom and must receive instruction from others. He cannot meet his own needs and must depend on another to provide for and protect him. And he makes mistakes because of his limited life experience and therefore must rely on those who are in charge to love him, accept him, forgive him, and reassure him.

A man enters the path of greatness when he humbles himself and seeks God for answers, wisdom, provision, protection, and forgiveness.

Jesus, give me the courage to humble myself like a child.

TO READ
1 Kings 17:1-7

Elijah did as the Lord had told him and camped beside Kerith Brook.   1 KINGS 17:5

✤ *Time for a Battery Change*

A series of television commercials from a few years back showed a pink battery-operated bunny beating a drum and traveling through different settings while a voice announced the battery company's slogan: "It keeps going and going and going and going . . . "

Many of us men feel just like that bunny. We feel driven to keep going and going and going. But while hard work is admirable and diligence is necessary, so is stopping once in a while. Even the Energizer Bunny needed to stop for a battery change!

My favorite biblical example of the need for rest is that of Elijah, the prophet who constantly battled Israel's evil kings: "The Lord said to Elijah, 'Go to the east and hide by Kerith Brook at a place east of where it enters the Jordan River. Drink from the brook and eat what the ravens bring you, for I have commanded them to bring you food' " (1 Kings 17:2-4).

God told Elijah to stop, so he stopped. He completely "unplugged," while the ravens provided what today would be considered "room service." He got away from all people and stopped all activity. The only things he was to do in this isolated spot were eat, drink, rest, and worship.

In the midst of all the stress of life—when work demands too much, when the pace of life wears you out, or when you are going through significant changes—you need to take time for your own battery change.

Give me the wisdom, Lord, to know when I need a battery change.

TO READ
Proverbs 18:1-24

There are "friends" who destroy each other, but a real friend sticks closer than a brother.

PROVERBS 18:24

Great Friends

It was one of those years. My career had gone through a difficult transition. The routine I had been doing for twenty years was replaced by a whole new set of activities. I had not been feeling well for months and was diagnosed with high blood pressure. This was a huge thing for me because my dad suffered a stroke when he was forty-eight years old and my grandfather died of a stroke when he was forty-seven. I was forty-four, so this news got my attention, to say the least. I had to refocus my life to lower stress and discipline my diet even further.

As a result, I went through a grieving process that struck deep in my soul. There were days when I was numb and days when I couldn't get focused.

It was on one of those dark days that Jim called. He simply said, "Hi, Bill. I just called to tell you that God loves you. He is not surprised by any of the circumstances you have gone through, and he knows it hurts. He will be with you every step of the way, so feel free to tell him how you are really doing. Oh, and by the way, I love you too."

Jim's call was just what I needed. The tone of his voice convinced me he was sincere and reminded me that he was a great friend. More importantly, he pointed me to the friend who could really help. Jim cared, but Jesus could be there always. The best friends in life offer whatever support they can, but then they point us in the direction of Jesus, the friend who is greater than all of us.

Which of your friends needs to hear from you this week?

Jesus, thank you for being such a great friend. Give me wisdom to know how to point my friends to you.

TO READ
Lamentations 3:22-33

It is good for the young to submit to the yoke of his discipline. LAMENTATIONS 3:27

A Test of Our Resolve

Pam and I received our call to ministry at the young age of nineteen. We were both trying to finish our educations and were convinced that part of our calling was to get married. We were wed at the age of twenty.

Neither of us owned much when we got married. Our apartment that first year was sparsely furnished. We had only one car—a green Chevy Vega with a blue back door.

After a year of marriage, Pam and I decided that I should go back to school full-time while she worked full-time. We knew it was going to be a tough go financially, but we believed it was what God wanted us to do. We wanted me to finish my degree and go on to seminary, and if we had to eat tuna casserole and macaroni and cheese every day, then so be it!

About a month after we made that decision, the Vega's engine overheated and cracked the block. We were now without transportation—except for bicycles.

I remember praying, "God, did I miss something? I was so convinced you were leading me back to school so I could fulfill this call to ministry. And now I have no car. Do you really want us to ride bikes everywhere?"

That is precisely what we did. During my senior year in college, I rode my bike to school while Pam rode her bike to work. It was strenuous and humbling, but we made it through. I finished my degree, bought a car, and started my career, but I could not have done it without Pam's willingness to endure a tough year.

Sometimes when God reveals his plan, he tests your resolve. That might mean running into obstacles, be they financial, physical, emotional, or otherwise. Are you willing to follow him anyway?

Jesus, give me a dream for my life, then give me the strength to live it out.

October

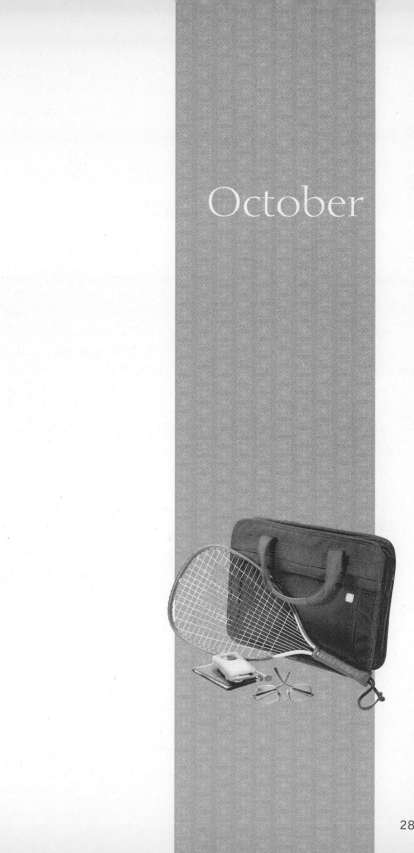

TO READ
Proverbs 9:1-18

Teach the wise, and they will be wiser. Teach the righteous, and they will learn more. PROVERBS 9:9

❋ When One Door Closes

My oldest son, Brock, wanted to play Division I college football after he graduated from high school.

Even though Brock had a successful senior year in high school, we found out during the recruiting process that he didn't fit the "formula" for a Division I college quarterback. Brock is slightly under six feet tall, but most Division I quarterbacks are at least six feet two and about two hundred pounds.

A number of schools contacted Brock, but because of his height, they all put him second or third on their quarterback recruiting lists.

With the door to playing Division I football closed, it was time to regroup and come up with another plan. Brock's long-term goal was to use football as a platform for sharing the gospel, so we sent Brock on a whirlwind tour of six colleges to look at as alternatives. He enrolled at Saddleback College, a junior college in southern California with a highly competitive football program.

Brock knew when he started his junior-college football career that he may never have an opportunity to play at a four-year school. But he also knew that the opportunity to play at the junior college could be the path to doing what is important to him: sharing Christ through football.

Brock led his team to junior college bowl games both years at Saddleback College. He is now on a scholarship at Liberty University in Lynchburg, Virginia—a Division I AA football program.

Has God given you a dream? How will you live out that dream?

Lord, help me choose your path as I live out my dream.

TO READ
Genesis 39:19-23

The chief jailer had no more worries after that, because Joseph took care of everything. The Lord was with him, making everything run smoothly and successfully. GENESIS 39:23

The Rewards for Faithfulness

When God rewards you for your faithfulness, often people around you are also rewarded. Joseph was an example of this truth:

> The Lord was with Joseph and blessed him greatly as he served in the home of his Egyptian master. Potiphar noticed this and realized that the Lord was with Joseph, giving him success in everything he did. So Joseph naturally became quite a favorite with him. Potiphar soon put Joseph in charge of his entire household and entrusted him with all his business dealings. From the day Joseph was put in charge, the Lord began to bless Potiphar for Joseph's sake. All his household affairs began to run smoothly, and his crops and livestock flourished. So Potiphar gave Joseph complete administrative responsibility over everything he owned. With Joseph there, he didn't have a worry in the world, except to decide what he wanted to eat! (Genesis 39:2-6)

Potiphar, Joseph's boss, saw that God was with this young man, so he basically turned over the running of his entire business to him. Joseph served Potiphar so faithfully and did such an outstanding job of running his business that all Potiphar was concerned with was what he ate. What a life that must have been! It was as if Potiphar had taken an early retirement.

When we serve with faithfulness in everything we do, it breeds trust. Does your boss or the people you work with have that kind of trust in you? If you don't think they have that kind of trust in you, or if you just want to breed further trust, ask yourself what you can do today to demonstrate your faithfulness.

Lord, may I serve so faithfully that others will benefit.

OCTOBER 3

TO READ
Titus 1:10–2:1

There are many who rebel against right teaching;
they engage in useless talk and deceive people.

TITUS 1:10

✳ Persuasive Arguments

The *Chicago Daily News* told of a lecture that was pure and simple nonsense. The master of ceremonies introduced the speaker as Dr. Myron L. Fox and gave him an ambiguous, high-sounding title. Fox, the emcee told the audience, was an authority on the application of mathematics to human behavior. His subject that day would be "Mathematical Game Theory as Applied to Physical Education." The speaker then stepped to the dais and gave the "lecture."

Actually, "Dr. Fox" was an actor hired by three medical educationists. It fooled the other forty-four educationists, school administrators, psychologists, and social workers in attendance that day. Although one of the attendees said the lecture was "too intellectual a presentation," not one of them realized it was a hoax.

The idea behind the setup was to prove this hypothesis: "Given a sufficiently impressive lecture paradigm, an experienced group of educationists, participating in a new learning situation, can feel satisfied that they have learned—despite irrelevant, conflicting, and meaningless content conveyed by the lecturer."[1]

This hoax proved its hypothesis true, but it also demonstrates something we men need to remember: Just because something sounds impressive or "intellectual" doesn't necessarily make it true.

As you travel the path called life, you will encounter some very professional-sounding people making some very persuasive—but very empty—arguments. You should be careful to never let those arguments take your focus away from the simple truth of the Word of God.

Lord, teach me never to be impressed with empty arguments but to cling to your truth.

290

The God of peace will soon crush Satan under your feet. May the grace of our Lord Jesus Christ be with you. ROMANS 16:20

❋ *Just a Few Steps*

We are engaged in an intense spiritual battle. Did you notice that the passage says the God of *peace* will be victorious? We might expect a reference to the God of *power* when we are talking about crushing Satan and winning battles, but here it is—the God of peace.

In Romans 16:17-20 Paul warns the readers about people among them who are causing division and creating unnecessary conflict. This is one of the enemy's favorite tactics. Disunity draws believers away from those outside the church who desperately need grace.

Like me, you have probably observed that those who are busiest doing the work of ministry tend to get the greatest criticism: "You are too busy"; "You make decisions too fast"; "All these people you bring to church are disrupting the way things used to be." These are comments often directed at the most productive people.

It will not always be this way. When Jesus died on the cross, he put in motion a plan for unity that would completely defeat Satan. All believers will spend eternity together in complete harmony. On the road to eternity, we will see glimpses of this unity, but it will not be complete. In this worldly realm, Satan and his demons are still free to operate and wage war with Jesus' followers. He knows his time is short, so he is putting up a furious fight, trying to look like an equal competitor with the God of the universe.

The reality is that we who have a personal relationship with God through Jesus Christ are on the winning team. We can create distance between ourselves and Satan's attempts to disrupt the spread of the gospel by seeking to focus more on our desire to reach the lost than our desire to be right.

Jesus, thank you for your victory. Lead me in the path of freedom.

TO READ
James 5:5-11

You, too, must be patient. And take courage, for the coming of the Lord is near. James 5:8

Hold the Fort!

During the American Civil War, the fort at Altoma Pass, which was held by General Corse, was besieged by the enemy. The attacking army, led by General Hood, waged an intense assault. General Hood called for the fort to surrender, but Corse courageously refused. There were many casualties on both sides during the long day of battle, but the defenders remained faithful, even in the face of a near-hopeless situation.

Then from across the valley—some twenty miles away—a white flag signaled the message, "Hold the fort, for I am coming." Much to the relief of the beleaguered defenders of the fort, General Sherman was marching toward them. And because the great general was on his way, the soldiers found new resolve to hold on until victory was secured.

We who follow Jesus Christ should feel that same kind of encouragement, knowing that he is coming for us. We can hang in there and face intense battles because we know that Jesus is on his way to rescue us and put down the enemy once and for all.

All of us will encounter opposition from those who don't want us to succeed. Some of us will have to suffer, maybe lose our lives in the battle. There will be times when the situation looks hopeless, times when options are limited and the path of success is impossible to see. All we may have to go on is the sense in our hearts that God wants us to stick to the task until he intervenes.

Through it all, we can see on the horizon our Savior. He's on his way, and that makes all the difference.

Make me fearless in the battle of life, Lord.

In the beginning God created the heavens and the earth. GENESIS 1:1

In the Beginning God Created . . .

The beginning of knowledge is embracing the fact that God has always existed and that he gave rise to everything else.

Knowing that God himself created us gives dignity to our existence and meaning to our decisions. Without that foundational knowledge, we lose consistency in our lives as our understanding tips out of balance, leaving us with nothing but speculation as to how we got here and why.

Throughout history, humans have attempted to replace God's revelation with their own speculation. The ancient Egyptians believed that the world was flat and that it rested on four pillars of stone. The ancient Hindus also believed that the world was flat but that it rested on the back of a huge elephant, which stood on the back of an enormous turtle, which stood on an immense coiled snake. And in an attempt to explain our existence, modern humanity has embraced evolution, leaving us with only a theory and no real evidence to back it up.

Instead of promulgating such foolish theories, Moses, who was educated in Egyptian schools, gave us the true, God-breathed account. In words of grand simplicity, matchless beauty, and exquisite accuracy he wrote: "In the beginning God created the heavens and the earth."

When you acknowledge that our universe, our world—you yourself—were created by God himself, it brings you to this question: What will you make of your created life?

Lord, let my life reflect the dignity of someone who is created in your image.

TO READ
Psalm 119:99-112

Yes, I have more insight than my teachers, for I am always thinking of your decrees. PSALM 119:99

God's Truth Is Sufficient

A good friend of mine oversees construction projects on the campus of a major university. He recently told me about a project that still has me shaking my head. A movement is on to create gender-neutral bathrooms. There is a group of people on the staff of the university who do not refer to themselves as either male or female. The group has grown large enough that it organized a committee to challenge the policies of the school, claiming their members are being discriminated against. They assert that it is offensive to have to use a bathroom that is designated by gender since they consider themselves to be transgender.

The group won its case. This university has made tremendous contributions in other areas to our society, and there are some truly remarkable things happening on campus. At the same time, there are some unbelievable conclusions coming from some of the most educated people in the country, the bathroom issue being just one of them.

In contrast, there is a group of staff members who meet weekly to study the Bible and pray for the campus. They have added the other group to their prayer list to compassionately ask God to work in their lives. The members of the Bible study recognize that such actions are symptoms of a life separated from God, and they earnestly want those individuals to discover the purpose and peace that is found in a vibrant relationship with Jesus.

You will encounter people who speculate on what life is about. They want to share their theories, but they do not want to subject their theories to the scrutiny of God's Word. Don't let such theories confuse your understanding of the truth.

Lord, give me confidence in the truth of your Word.

TO READ
1 Thessalonians 1:1-10

As we talk to our God and Father about you, we think of your faithful work, your loving deeds, and your continual anticipation of the return of our Lord Jesus Christ. 1 THESSALONIANS 1:3

Learning a Work Ethic

Charles W. Morton, an *Atlantic Monthly* editor, once told the story of a Harvard University freshman who came to Dean LeBaron Russell Briggs's office to explain his tardiness in handing in an assignment.

"I'm sorry, sir, but I was not feeling very well," he said.

"Young man," Briggs said, "please bear in mind that by far the greater part of the world's work is carried on by people who are not feeling very well."

Life's pursuits are characterized by hard work, and sometimes that hard work must be done in less-than-ideal life situations.

Churches and companies are built because people are willing to work hard. Children are raised because parents are willing to exert enormous amounts of energy. Communities are established through long hours and persistent dedication. All of these things are successfully accomplished, even though there are times when the people accomplishing them weren't exactly at their best.

The apostle Paul wrote the words of today's Scripture to a church that had become very dear to him. He felt a sense of camaraderie with them and was impressed because they shared his work ethic. Paul worked himself to the bone. He suffered hardships, took burdens upon himself, and deprived himself of comforts—all to accomplish the work God laid on his heart.

Every generation needs to be taught the value of hard work and of perseverance in the face of difficulties. We men can have lazy tendencies, but life requires each of us to step up and joyfully give ourselves to the challenges of life.

Jesus, help me to find joy in the work you have given me to do.

TO READ
1 Corinthians 2:1-10

That is what the Scriptures mean when they say, "No eye has seen, no ear has heard, and no mind has imagined what God has prepared for those who love him." 1 CORINTHIANS 2:9

The Importance of the Mind

Dr. Mason Gross, the former president of Rutgers University, once shared this stirring observation:

> One of the important battles of today is the battle between books and television. Television presents a tremendous emotional impact, but a picture does not pre-sent a clear thought. Television depends upon an instant response, but you cannot turn your set back to go over what was said three minutes back. Television is making us descend "into something like the global village that Mr. Marshall McLuhan warns us about, where there will be no more sharpness or elegance to the life of human beings, but instead a great big blob of emotional reactions. This must never be."
>
> The only alternative is the printed word, the reading and thinking about what is written in books and periodicals. Books give us the tools with which to think, to resist the dehumanization of language and the remaking of words in propaganda. "So, for the sake of analysis, for the sake of reason, for the sake of study, for the sake of reflection, we've simply got to bring our kids and ourselves away from the television sets occasionally and back to books."[2]

There is no substitute for the exercise of your mind. That is why God has given us the Bible. You can read it, study it, review it, memorize it, go back and check on it—all because it is written. We need to make time in our day to read the Word of God, to let its truth seep first into our minds, then into our very souls.

But how do we find time in our busy lives to sit and read? For many of us, it might just be a matter of shutting off the television.

Jesus, stimulate my thinking today as I search your Word for truth.

TO READ
Acts 17:1-17

But the Jewish leaders were jealous, so they gathered some worthless fellows from the streets to form a mob and start a riot. They attacked the home of Jason, searching for Paul and Silas so they could drag them out to the crowd. ACTS 17:5

An Inspirational Legacy

Have you ever gone to great lengths in a pursuit only to later feel like it was a waste of time? Six enthusiastic basketball players from Livermore Falls (Maine) High School certainly feel that way. *Sports Illustrated* reported their story.

These young men had concluded that school spirit was low. In order to raise spirit, they decided to dribble a couple of basketballs the twenty-two miles between their town and Farmington, where the team was scheduled to play. In freezing rain, it was no easy job. Weary, wet, chilled—and dedicated—the six arrived at the Farmington gym, only to learn that the game had been postponed because of adverse traveling conditions.

The apostle Paul was often faced with situations much like the one those players faced—except his had life-and-death implications. Paul was eager to reach new people and start new churches. He was passionate in his desire for everyone he encountered to meet Jesus. As a result, he was willing to do anything it took to reach people.

A lot of the time, however, the people Paul most desperately cared about didn't want to hear his message. They argued with him, persecuted him, and ran him out of town. There were times in Paul's life and ministry when it looked like his work wasn't having much effect, but history has proven that his tenacity has inspired millions around the world.

I believe that is the main point of our lives on earth. None of us is going to live as long as we would like, and few of us will enjoy the level of success we had hoped for. But all of us can leave a legacy that will inspire future generations to follow Jesus, no matter what life throws at them.

Lord, never let me think that anything I do for your kingdom is a waste of my time.

TO READ
2 Corinthians 4:1-15

But this precious treasure—this light and power that now shine within us—is held in perishable containers, that is, in our weak bodies. So everyone can see that our glorious power is from God and is not our own. 2 CORINTHIANS 4:7

In Perishable Containers

The last week has been a stark reminder to me that we proclaim the treasure of the gospel from bodies that will perish.

Our friend, Cynthia, is a very talented businesswoman. She was on her way to a Bible study when she received a call from the local fire chief. Her house was on fire, and they wanted her to return so they could confirm that it was her house. Her kids had not been not home, but she lost three pets in the fire. She relocated to a rental house and began the tedious process of working with the insurance companies and contractors. As soon as she got settled in to her temporary home, she received another phone call and was told that her dad had a heart attack. As I am writing this, her dad is in the midst of a bypass surgery.

Another friend, Clay, is one of the finest Christian thinkers in southern California. He was recently diagnosed with a tumor in his back. It was located along the spinal cord and was creating consistent pain. He was operated on a week ago. The doctors had to remove one vertebra with the tumor but only had to sever one nerve. He has a long road ahead with radiation treatments and physical and occupational therapy. Through it all, he is grateful that it isn't worse.

Both of these individuals have had a very positive impact on the world around them, but both of their lives have been interrupted by the frail nature of human life. We live in a world that is overly concerned, even obsessed, with appearance and human abilities. But as men of God, we always need to remember that our bodies, no matter how strong or weak or beautiful or homely they may be, are just the containers for what's really inside us.

Oh Jesus, may my weak body never hide your presence in my life but instead be a tool to share the gospel with others.

TO READ
Colossians 1:3-14

We also pray that you will be strengthened with his glorious power so that you will have all the patience and endurance you need. May you be filled with joy.

COLOSSIANS 1:11

Beyond Yourself

I live in San Diego with my family. Late in the fall of 2003, San Diego County experienced the worst fire in its history. Thousands of homes were lost. There was so much ash in the air that people were encouraged to stay home if at all possible.

A local pastor was away on vacation when the fires ripped through an area of San Diego County called Harbison Canyon. While he was gone, his house burned down, the church burned down, and most of the people in his church lost their homes. We collected a truckload of supplies for the congregation and delivered them a few days after the devastation.

As we were unloading the supplies at one of the remaining homes, a man approached me and said, "Thank you." Then he pointed to a couple of plastic storage bins on the back porch of the house. "You see those two bins? They contain everything I now own in the world. I am just glad to have a place to put them."

A member of the family that was collecting supplies for the people who lost their homes told us, "This is so strange. I have never been a leader before, but my home is standing for some reason. I figure if God wants to use my house to help others, I need to be willing."

A month after the disaster, we met with the pastor's wife, whose attitude was remarkable. She said, "People are focused on each other more than their stuff. This event has shown us what is really important. We just value each other more than we used to."

I have watched as God gave these people patience and endurance beyond their own ability. We never know when we will need it, but we can rest assured that God will give us strength at just the right time.

Jesus, hold me tight and use me in whatever way you choose.

TO READ
1 Corinthians 7:1-24

God purchased you at a high price. Don't be enslaved by the world. 1 CORINTHIANS 7:23

The Cost of Heaven

Jesus claims ownership of our lives, not because he is greedy or possessive, but because he paid a high price for us. Long ago he recognized that we could not earn or buy our own redemption. But he wanted us to be with him forever, so he gave the most valuable thing he had—his blood—to buy our freedom. No one but Jesus is entitled to lay claim to our lives because no one has paid a higher price.

An old and often-quoted story illustrates this wonderful truth:

William Dixon lived in Brackenthwaite, England. He was a widower who had also lost his only son. One day he saw that the house of one of his neighbors was on fire. Although the aged owner was rescued, her orphaned grandson was trapped in the blaze. Dixon climbed an iron pipe on the side of the house and lowered the boy to safety. His hand that held on to the pipe was badly burned.

Shortly after the fire, the grandmother died. The townspeople wondered who would care for the boy. Two volunteers appeared before the town council. One was a father who had lost his son and would like to adopt the orphan as his own. William Dixon was to speak next, but instead of saying anything he merely held up his scarred hand. When the vote was taken, the boy was given to him.[3]

If you ever doubt Jesus' love for you or his commitment to you, stop and think about what his hands and feet look like because of his efforts to rescue you.

Jesus, thank you for carrying eternal scars so I can have eternal life.

TO READ
Hebrews 11:1-6

So, you see, it is impossible to please God without faith. Anyone who wants to come to him must believe that there is a God and that he rewards those who sincerely seek him. HEBREWS 11:6

Overcoming Criticism

One of the enemies of faith is criticism. Sadly, a lot of people will try to tear down our faith by criticizing us. They may see what God wants to do in our lives and say, "It's impossible"—just because they have never seen anything like it. Or they may laugh in disgust when they hear us speak enthusiastically about how God has inspired and gifted us to work for him.

When you feel the sting of criticism, take heart! Many have gone before you, doing great things only to be criticized for them. Here are a few examples:

- When the famous clergyman/abolitionist Henry Ward Beecher preached in Brooklyn, New York, he carried a handful of flowers into the pulpit one Lord's Day and placed them in a vase on the stand from which he spoke. The next day, local newspapers carried lengthy articles condemning Beecher for desecrating the pulpit with flowers.
- When Samuel Morse was trying to get money from Congress for a telegraph line from Baltimore to Washington, he had to endure the criticisms of the press for eleven years.
- When, in 1842, Adam Thompson set up the first bathtub in America, the newspapers said he was "going to spoil the democratic simplicity of the republic."
- And when Cyrus Field was trying to lay the first transatlantic cable, the newspapers denounced him as "a mad freak of stubborn ignorance."

When you allow criticism to hold you back and keep you down in your faith, you can do nothing for God. But when you stay optimistic with your faith, you join the company of the great.

Jesus, make my faith stronger than my critics.

TO READ
Colossians 2:1-15

God made you alive with Christ. He forgave all
our sins. He canceled the record that contained the
charges against us. He took it and destroyed it by
nailing it to Christ's cross. COLOSSIANS 2:13-14

A Tribute to Christ

Many beautiful words have been spoken and written paying tribute to those
who have given their lives in defense of their country.

Winston Churchill paid a great tribute to the young men in the Royal Air
Force who guarded England during World War II, saying, "Never in the
history of mankind have so many owed so much to so few."

A monument in Bastogne, Belgium, pays tribute to the heroism of the
U.S. 101st Airborne Division during the famous Battle of Bastogne. Its
inscription reads: "Seldom has so much American blood been shed in the
course of a single action. Oh, Lord, help us to remember!"

These tributes to the fallen were made because there is no way to repay
them for their heroic deeds. We are truly indebted to the men who gave
their lives so that we might enjoy the life we enjoy today.

But as much as we are indebted to some of the great war heroes of
the past, we are far more indebted to the Savior who gave his life that all
humankind may live.

We owe Jesus a debt we cannot even imagine repaying. The shedding of
his blood, the enormous act of humility that paid for our sins, is of such
value to us for all eternity that any attempt to repay it is an insult. It would
be like offering pennies to a billionaire.

While we can never repay Jesus for what he's done, we can certainly
honor him for it—in our hearts and through our words and actions. When
we do that, we show to the world a tribute that looks like this: Never in the
history of all humankind have so many people of every culture and every
generation owed so much to one Savior.

Jesus, since I can never repay you, I will honor you today with my words
and deeds.

TO READ
Romans 12:9-11

Love each other with genuine affection, and take delight in honoring each other. ROMANS 12:10

Honor Each Other

Derrick and Brian have formed a sort of strategic partnership with one another. Derrick used to play football at Colorado State University. He is now a staff member with the Fellowship of Christian Athletes. As part of his responsibilities, he teaches a Bible study for high school football players. They meet together once a week to discuss what it means to be a competitor who honors Jesus.

Brian is the father of two of the young men who attend Derrick's Bible study. Brian has a talent with food. He used to run a catering business and loves to cook. To encourage the young men, Brian makes food for the study and delivers it each week.

Brian told me the other day, "I so appreciate what Derrick does. I can make food, but I can't explain the Bible to my sons like Derrick can. My kids tune me out, while they hang on every word he says. After my sons spend time with Derrick, they are easier to get along with."

Derrick told me the other day, "I don't think the Bible study would work without Brian. These kids come because there is good food. After they eat, they are more content and willing to listen. I have taught enough Bible studies in my life to know that this one is different. The only thing I can give credit to is Brian's cooking."

It takes both of these men with different talents to make the greatest impact on these young men. Derrick and Brian have tremendous respect for one another because they cannot do what the other one can do. They live in wonder at the abilities of the other.

Who are the people in your world who fill the gaps you cannot? Give thanks to Jesus for surrounding you with people who do what you can't.

Jesus, show me how to help others succeed.

TO READ
Deuteronomy 4:1-14

But watch out! Be very careful never to forget what you have seen the Lord do for you. Do not let these things escape from your mind as long as you live! And be sure to pass them on to your children and grandchildren. DEUTERONOMY 4:9

The Little Things

Many things in life seem insignificant but are actually vitally important. These are the things we must watch over and tend to with great care. If we fail to do so, we may face remarkably complicated consequences that could have been avoided.

The New York Times reported:

> J. P. Morgan & Company, a bank worth $21 billion, was disconnected from the Internet on June 13, 2000 for failure to pay a $35 bill. The venerable Wall Street firm found itself without a Web site or an e-mail connection to the outside world because it had failed to renew the registration of www.jpmorgan.com, the domain name that serves as its address on the World Wide Web. Throughout the day, clients were unable to visit the Web site or exchange e-mail messages with the firm's bankers and traders. All that frustration could have been averted if Morgan had sent a check for $35 for the annual registration fee to Network Solutions, a domain-name registrar in Herndon, Virginia. It pulled the plug on Morgan six weeks after Morgan's bill came due and after sending the firm at least three bills, said Chris Clough, vice president for corporate communications at Network Solutions.[4]

Little things really can make all the difference, can't they?

That's true of life in general, and it's true of our walk with Jesus Christ. That's why God has instructed us to study and meditate on his written Word, the Bible. When we do that, we will learn to avoid those unpleasant situations that don't need to happen. And we won't miss out on one blessing, either!

Give me eyes, Lord, to see the little things that make all the difference.

TO READ
Romans 8:22-30

We know that God causes everything to work together for the good of those who love God and are called according to his purpose for them.

ROMANS 8:28

Inconvenience or Opportunity?

We men can get frustrated when things don't go our way. Yet inconveniences can become opportunities.

I had one of these moments during homecoming weekend of my oldest son's senior year in high school. Brock and his girlfriend went to dinner and then to the dance with a number of their other friends. Brock swapped cars with one of his best friends.

When they arrived at the dance, Brock asked his girlfriend to put the car keys in her purse, then they began to mingle. Brock noticed that something wasn't right between him and his girlfriend but didn't think much of it. At the end of the dance, he noticed his girlfriend wasn't there.

She had left with another young man, and the keys to Brock's friend's car were still in her purse. Brock had to get a ride home so he could get on the phone. He called his girlfriend's parents and told them what happened. Then he took another of our cars and went looking for her. An hour later, his girlfriend called with a weak apology and an assurance that she was coming to our house with the keys. It took about forty-five minutes for her to get to the house where Brock was now waiting for her.

Brock drove her home. When he got home at 2 A.M., he asked me, "Dad, why does homecoming weekend my senior year have to be the worst weekend of my life?"

It was a tough question for two in the morning, but it led to one of the greatest conversations I have ever had with my son. This "inconvenience" was one of my finest moments.

Jesus, help me to understand that what seems like an inconvenience—even a tragedy—can really be an opportunity for me to shine for you.

TO READ
Isaiah 38:9-20

Only the living can praise you as I do today. Each generation can make known your faithfulness to the next. ISAIAH 38:19

The Gift of an Example

The greatest desire in my life is for my sons to know and love Jesus in a real way. I have often wondered how I am doing setting an example for them that is attractive and realistic. I especially wondered this when my middle son, Zachery, got bored with church at the age of twelve.

I was on the platform one Sunday morning when I saw him sitting in the third row with his friends. He had an orange plastic straw wedged into his hair so that it stuck out the front of his head like a horn. He was bobbing his head up and down, showing off for his friends. When our eyes made contact, he quickly took the straw out and acted like he was listening.

A couple of weeks later I looked out at Zachery again. He had lifted his shirt up on his head so the neck of the shirt was buttoned around his forehead. His friends were laughing, and I couldn't make eye contact with him because his head was covered.

One Sunday he was leaning his chair against the back wall when the legs slid out from under him. It was a metal chair on a tile floor, so it made lots of noise.

I asked myself in my heart, *I wonder if this young man will ever be serious about Jesus?*

Now Zachery is in high school, serving as president of the Fellowship of Christian Athletes club. He prays with teammates at the fifty-yard line after every football game, and he prays with his coed cheerleading squad before every competition. I praise God daily that Zachery worked past the boredom and found his own faith in the Savior.

There truly is no greater gift you can give your children than helping them discover their own faith.

Jesus, work in my life to make me a good example for those I love.

TO READ
Psalm 78:17-39

He remembered that they were merely mortal, gone in a moment like a breath of wind, never to return.
PSALM 78:39

No Longer Around

Throughout my lifetime I have heard stories of evil men who had great power but who no longer exert any influence. Adolph Hitler had a devastating impact on Europe. He killed millions of Jews in the course of events we now call the Holocaust. But he is no longer around. Mussolini was a brutal dictator in Italy who partnered with Hitler in an attempt to dominate Europe. But he is no longer around.

Idi Amin was another brutal dictator in Uganda who wiped out huge numbers of his own population in his quest for power. Many feared him during his life, and he was the subject of many headlines in newspapers around the world. But he is no longer around. The former Soviet Union was established by the likes of Joseph Stalin, Vladimir Lenin, and Nikita Kruschev. In an attempt to spread communism to the entire world, they murdered millions, abused much of their population, and recruited evil men to join them in their conquest. But they are no longer around.

More recently, I have followed the rise of Pol Pot, the communist leader of the Khmer Rouge in Cambodia. He led the slaughter of approximately 15 million people. But Pol Pot is no longer around.

The same is true of all powerful human leaders. They rise. They exert their influence. Then they pass away. In contrast is Jesus. He was here at the beginning, and he will be in charge at the end. He has been around through every generation and has outlasted every ruler.

Today, as you interact with people and hear about the leaders of the world, remind yourself that each of them will pass away, while Jesus works in your life forever.

Lord, build in me a legacy that will outlast me.

TO READ
Mark 12:28-40

I know it is important to love him with all my heart and all my understanding and all my strength, and to love my neighbors as myself. This is more important than to offer all of the burnt offerings and sacrifices required in the law. MARK 12:33

A Deeper Kind of Love

Illustrator/painter Gustave Dore, one of the patron saints of the DreamWorks team of Spielberg, Katzenberg, and Geffen, was handed a painting of Jesus just finished by one of his art students. Asked for his critique, Dore studied it, his mind searching for the right words. At last he handed it back to the student.

"If you loved him more," he said, "you would have painted him better."

The same could easily be said for our lives as a whole: If you loved him more, you would live a life more like the one he lived.

The way we live displays the level of love we have for Jesus. If we love him casually, we are content with an "adequate" life. But if we love him deeply, we live for him with passion and intensity. We will be naturally motivated to improve the example of Christ's love that our lives set for others.

Following Jesus truly is a matter of the heart. You can follow him half-heartedly and just go through the motions. When you do that, you reap the minimum of benefits. But when your heart is wrapped up in him, you long to study his life and to spend time with him. When you fall in love with Jesus, you are fascinated with each new thing you learn about him, and you make decisions that give him an ever-increasing place in your life. When you do that, you receive every blessing he meant for you to have.

Oh Lord, give me a love for you deep enough to impact my life.

TO READ
James 1:1-6

Dear brothers and sisters, whenever trouble comes your way, let it be an opportunity for joy. For when your faith is tested, your endurance has a chance to grow. So let it grow, for when your endurance is fully developed, you will be strong in character and ready for anything. JAMES 1:2-4

When Obstacles Become Opportunities

Jacques Plante was a legendary goalkeeper in the National Hockey League. He once described being a goalie like this: "Imagine sitting at your desk. You make a mistake. A red light goes on behind you, a siren starts sounding and 18,000 people are yelling at you. That's what it's like to be a goaltender."[5]

Plante was arguably the most influential goaltender ever to play. He is credited with a number of innovations that are standard aspects of the game today. He was the first player to wear a face mask on a regular basis. It started as a habit during practice, but it became part of his standard equipment. He was criticized regularly for doing so, but now every goalie in the league wears a mask. He was the first goalie to come out of the goal to challenge shooters and to skate to the corner to retrieve the puck for his defensemen. His exploits were successful enough that he won the Vezina Trophy—given to the best goalkeeper in the NHL—six times, including five seasons in a row.

The most interesting part of his story, however, is that Plante did not begin playing hockey as a goalie. He started out as a defenseman, but he suffered with asthma and was not able to keep up with the pace of skating that defense required. Because he loved the game, he switched to goalie by the age of fifteen, and the rest, as they say, is history.

Sometimes realizing our potential in any part of life means overcoming obstacles and making adjustments. When we have the right perspective, our trials can lead us to a place where we discover skills, talents, and abilities we may never have thought we possessed.

Jesus, do what you must to help me live up to my potential.

TO READ
Psalm 71:1-18

Now that I am old and gray, do not abandon me, O God. Let me proclaim your power to this new generation, your mighty miracles to all who come after me. PSALM 71:18

Speaking with Clarity

The greatest privilege we have as men is passing on to the next generation what is most dear to our hearts. But it can be a challenge to communicate to the next generation the truth that has changed our lives. Here is one humorous illustration of that point:

> One Sunday morning, after a lifeless service, the pastor noticed little Alex was staring up at the large plaque that hung in the foyer of the church. It was covered with names, and small American flags were mounted on either side of it.
>
> The seven-year-old had been staring at the plaque for some time, so the pastor walked up, stood beside the boy, and said quietly, "Good morning, Alex."
>
> "Good morning, pastor," replied the young man, still focused on the plaque.
>
> "Pastor, what is this?" Alex asked.
>
> "Well, son, it's a memorial to all the young men and women who died in the service," the pastor said.
>
> They stood together staring at the large plaque. Little Alex shot back, "Which service did they die in—morning or evening?"[6]

There can be a "communication gap" between one generation and the next. As we take the time to pass on to our children and their children what it means to know Jesus, we must do it with clarity.

Jesus, build in my life the clarity necessary for the next generation to see you in my life.

I discovered that God created people to be upright, but they have each turned to follow their own downward path. ECCLESIASTES 7:29

Whose Plan Are You Following?

The story is told about a truck driver whose job was to haul canaries. It was a tough and sometimes frustrating job, so he had to come up with a plan to make it easier on him and his truck.

One day another driver noticed that the trucker had a curious habit of stopping every two blocks and beating on the rear of the truck with a hefty piece of lumber. The driver flagged the canary-hauling trucker down and asked him why he beat on the truck every block or two.

The trucker explained, "Well, I've got two tons of canaries and a one-ton truck, so half of the birds have to stay in the air all of the time!"[7]

We men often get in over our heads in life. We make career decisions that force us to work too much. We involve our families in the community to the point that we can hardly manage our schedules. We add one deadline after another until our lives are nothing but deadlines.

It is very easy to overcommit, and it is just as easy to create schemes to try to manage that overcommitment. But rather than turning to God for wisdom to reprioritize our lives, we make up our own plans, implement them, then hope God in his mercy and grace will bless them.

I've learned that my life is a lot more manageable when I just take the time to go to God first and find out his plan, then do what I have to do to make his plans a reality in my life.

Whose plans are you following? Are you living a "cart before the horse" kind of life? Here's my suggestion: Go to God daily and ask him what he wants of you, then make the needed plans to make his will your own.

Lord, teach me to rely more on your plans than on my own.

TO READ
Colossians 4:1-10

Let your conversation be gracious and effective so that you will have the right answer for everyone.

COLOSSIANS 4:6

Effective Communication

The Wisconsin State Journal recently asked vice presidents and personnel directors of some of the nation's largest corporations to share their most unusual experiences interviewing prospective employees. Their stories included the following:

- A job applicant who challenged the interviewer to arm wrestle
- A balding candidate who excused himself, then returned wearing a full hairpiece
- A prospect who wore earphones to the interview, and when asked to remove them, explained that she could listen to the interviewer and the music at the same time
- A candidate who said she didn't have time for lunch, then started to eat a hamburger and fries in the interviewer's office
- An applicant who interrupted the questioning to phone her therapist
- A candidate who muttered, "Would it be a problem if I'm angry most of the time?"

These people have issues with communication, don't they? Yet it is not a stretch to say that many of us have the same kinds of shortcomings when it comes to communicating with our families, with our friends, with our coworkers, and even with God.

We need to make sure that we learn to effectively and clearly communicate what is on our hearts in a way that blesses the people around us. Start today by going to God and asking him what he would have you say and how he would have you say it.

Lord, teach me to think before I talk. Help me to be an effective communicator of your truth.

TO READ
Philippians 2:1-11

Then make me truly happy by agreeing whole-heartedly with each other, loving one another, and working together with one heart and purpose. Don't be selfish; don't live to make a good impression on others. Be humble, thinking of others as better than yourself. PHILIPPIANS 2:2-3

Repaying Kindness by Being Kind

Vernal E. Simms, the Senior Pastor of Morris Brown African Methodist Episcopal Church in Philadelphia, wrote of his experiences with someone who reached out and helped him get through college and seminary:

> I grew up in a rough Boston housing project called Columbia Point in a family of nine children. Although I'd been a hardworking student, paying for college seemed impossible. But my mother's favorite expression was "Pray, and the Lord will make a way somehow." I viewed that as good advice for other people. But when I decided to go to college and seminary because I believed the Lord had a call on my life, I had no other choice!
>
> I packed for college and even went to orientation, but still didn't have any money. I'd have to pack up my belongings and make the 100-mile trip back home. But an heir to a corporate fortune heard about my plight and paid for my college and seminary education. After I graduated, I went to my benefactor's office to thank him for all he had done for me and asked him what I could do to pay him back.
>
> Imagine my saying to a multimillionaire, "What can I do to repay you?" The man responded, "Help somebody."[8]

The greatest tribute we can pay to those who have helped us is to help others. Many people—especially people who love God and want to please him—don't reach out and help you just so you can pay them back. They gave of themselves because it brought joy to their hearts to do so. The best way to multiply their joy is to allow their influence to be multiplied in your life by helping others the way they helped you.

Jesus, make me more concerned about multiplying influence than about balancing accounts.

TO READ
1 Timothy 4:1-9

Physical exercise has some value, but spiritual exercise is much more important, for it promises a reward in both this life and the next.

1 TIMOTHY 4:8

A Big Enough Reason

My three sons are all athletes and work out regularly and intensely.

My oldest son is a quarterback. When he entered college, he stayed after practice two or three times per week during the summer, throwing footballs into trash cans that were spread out around the field. I asked him why he was doing it. His answer was, "I want the starting job. I am going to work as hard as I need to because I want to be the best."

My middle son is a defensive back in football and a "stunter" in coed cheerleading. That means he is the one who does lifts with the girls and launches them into the air. He lifts weights four days per week in the off season. I asked him why he works so hard at getting stronger. His answer was, "I don't want anyone else to get hurt because I wasn't strong enough."

My youngest son is just thirteen and plays basketball and baseball. He spends hours shooting the basketball and swinging a bat in the batting cages. He would rather do this than anything else. I asked him why he spends so much time practicing rather than watching television. His answer was, "It's fun, and I know I can get better. Besides, I like to win."

They all work hard without reminders because they have a big enough reason to do so. In our spiritual lives, the same principle applies. If we have a big enough reason, we will work hard at our development. This is Paul's point when he says that spiritual exercise has benefit for this world and the world to come.

Do you have a big reason for following Jesus? If not, ask Jesus to give you a goal that will make you willing to work hard at your spiritual growth.

Jesus, give me a big enough reason to work hard at knowing you.

<table>
<tr><td>TO READ
Mark 6:1-13</td><td>[Jesus] called his twelve disciples together and sent them out two by two, with authority to cast out evil spirits. MARK 6:7</td></tr>
</table>

Working Side by Side

God has a habit of commissioning people to work side by side in accomplishing his will.

In the days of Nehemiah, the wall around Jerusalem was down and had been for almost a century. Nehemiah led the charge to build it up again, thus providing the city much-needed protection from enemies on all sides. However, rebuilding the wall was no easy task. To accomplish it, he divided up the wall and gave families charge of sections of the wall.

Nehemiah found that the builders felt safer and worked better when they worked side by side, as these passages show.

Nehemiah 3:19-20: "Next to them, Ezer son of Jeshua, the leader of Mizpah, repaired another section of wall opposite the armory by the buttress. Next to him was Baruch son of Zabbai, who repaired an additional section from the buttress to the door of the home of Eliashib the high priest."

Nehemiah 3:24-25: "Next was Binnui son of Henadad, who rebuilt another section of the wall from Azariah's house to the buttress and the corner. Palal son of Uzai carried on the work from a point opposite the buttress and the corner to the upper tower that projects from the king's house beside the court of the guard. Next to him were Pedaiah son of Parosh . . . "

Nehemiah 3:27: "Then came the people of Tekoa, who repaired another section opposite the great projecting tower and over to the wall of Ophel."

Do you have a big task to tackle or a big obstacle to overcome? Does it feel like the challenge before you is insurmountable? Then divide up the project and work with those who are like-minded until it is completed.

Lord, surround me with people who are willing to work together.

TO READ
Nehemiah 1:1-11

O Lord, please hear my prayer! Listen to the prayers of those of us who delight in honoring you. Please grant me success now as I go to ask the king for a great favor. Put it into his heart to be kind to me.

NEHEMIAH 1:11

Official Approval

Sometimes when God gives you a task to accomplish, you need to get approval from someone in authority.

Nehemiah, a cupbearer to King Artaxerxes of Persia, was heartbroken over the state of Jerusalem. He wanted to be released to go back and rebuild the wall.

Nehemiah was careful to protect his emotions, but one day the king asked him why he was so sad. Nehemiah 2:2-12 tells the full story. When Nehemiah explained his concern, not only did the king release him, he offered to help.

This biblical story teaches something we need to understand today: Don't fear getting the stamp of approval from those in authority.

I saw that demonstrated in my own church during a building program.

We located an empty storefront building that had been home to a pet store. Our plan was to buy it and turn it into a church. But before we could move forward, we needed the approval of our city's planning commission. The review committee recommended a rejection, and the local newspaper printed an article that made our case look hopeless.

In the middle of all this, we gathered as a church to pray. The next night at the planning commissioners' meeting, each commissioner listened as community members and leaders told them how our church would benefit the community. Then each commissioner gave speeches encouraging our church, and we won unanimous approval.

If you are starting a ministry or business enterprise, follow the proper channels and get the approval of those who are in authority over you.

Give me wisdom, Lord, to know whose approval I need in order to accomplish your will.

TO READ
Acts 2:41-47

They worshiped together at the Temple each day, met in homes for the Lord's Supper, and shared their meals with great joy and generosity. ACTS 2:46

The Benefits of Togetherness

We can find the word *together* used more than twenty times in the book of Acts. Apparently the early church felt a need to be together.

One positive impact of togetherness is *synergy*. The *American Heritage Dictionary* defines *synergy* as "the interaction of two or more agents or forces so that their combined effect is greater than the sum of their individual effects."

That's exactly what the book of Acts is all about. Out of the efforts of a small band of fearful and mostly undereducated people came a belief system based on the truth of the gospel.

Not only does the togetherness that comes from being in the body of Christ create a synergy wherein we can do great things for him collectively, it also adds to the wellness of the individual. Gregg Easterbrook of *The New Republic* underscored this truth when he wrote:

> Recent studies indicate that men and women who practice in any of the mainstream faiths have above-average longevity, fewer strokes, less heart disease, less clinical depression, better immune-system function, lower blood pressure, and fewer anxiety attacks, and they are much less likely to commit suicide than the population at large. These findings come from secular medical schools and schools of public health.[9]

In the most striking finding, Dr. Harold Koenig of Duke University Medical Center has calculated that, with regard to any mainstream faith, "lack of religious involvement has an effect on mortality that is equivalent to 40 years of smoking one pack of cigarettes per day."[10]

Is working together with other believers a priority for you?

Lord, help me to see clearly the benefits of being together with other believers.

TO READ
Deuteronomy 5:22-31

Oh, that they would always have hearts like this, that they might fear me and obey all my commands! If they did, they and their descendants would prosper forever. DEUTERONOMY 5:29

A New Family Heritage

Avoidance of issues can be a learned behavior, passed down through generations of families. Take Abraham and Isaac, for example. Abraham was afraid, and it put others in danger:

> As he was approaching the borders of Egypt, Abram said to Sarai, "You are a very beautiful woman. When the Egyptians see you, they will say, 'This is his wife. Let's kill him; then we can have her!' But if you say you are my sister, then the Egyptians will treat me well because of their interest in you, and they will spare my life." And sure enough, when they arrived in Egypt, everyone spoke of her beauty. When the palace officials saw her, they sang her praises to their king, the pharaoh, and she was taken into his harem. Then Pharaoh gave Abram many gifts because of her—sheep, cattle, donkeys, male and female servants, and camels. But the Lord sent a terrible plague upon Pharaoh's household because of Sarai, Abram's wife. (Genesis 12:11-17)

A generation later, how does Isaac handle fear?

> When the men there asked him about Rebekah, he said, "She is my sister." He was afraid to admit that she was his wife. He thought they would kill him to get her, because she was very beautiful. But some time later, Abimelech, king of the Philistines, looked out a window and saw Isaac fondling Rebekah. Abimelech called for Isaac and exclaimed, "She is obviously your wife! Why did you say she was your sister?" "Because I was afraid someone would kill me to get her from me," Isaac replied. (Genesis 26:7-9)

We men, no matter what our "family heritage" might be, must be willing to stand up and be counted when we are faced with challenges.

Jesus, use my life to start a healthy family tradition.

November

TO READ
Jeremiah 20:1-9

If I say I'll never mention the Lord or speak in his name, his word burns in my heart like a fire. It's like a fire in my bones! I am weary of holding it in!

JEREMIAH 20:9

What I Must Do!

Each of us has been blessed by God with numerous talents. Some of these talents help you run your home life. Some make your career possible. Others are utilized by God in the context of ministry. It is a privilege to have been created with these skills, but it also creates a problem. At some point in your life you have to decide between the things you can do and the things you must do.

For Jeremiah, the thing he "must" do is speak out in God's name. He has just been beaten and put in stocks for doing what God called him to do. In his prophecy, he foretells that the road will continue to be difficult. People are looking for mistakes in his words. They are looking for ways to discredit him because they don't like what he is saying. It appears from his words that Jeremiah would like to walk away from the continued conflict and do something easier, but he recognizes that this is his calling. God has put a need in his heart to be a public spokesman for truth.

Most men are not called to be public spokesmen, but we are all called to be something. Just like Jeremiah's responsibility, the calling is both exciting and heavy. We are honored to have been chosen and gifted to accomplish it. But the calling is lived out in an imperfect, critical world, and we soon find there are many activities that are easier on us than pursuing the place of service God has called us to. At these times, the only thing that will keep you at the task is the overwhelming sense that you were made for this.

What is it that you must accomplish in your lifetime? What activities seem easier but distract you from your real calling?

Jesus, give me wisdom to clearly see what I must get done in my lifetime.

TO READ
Genesis 5:2-32

He created them male and female, and he blessed them. GENESIS 5:2

Who Does What around Here?

Who is responsible for what around your house? In my home growing up, my father's domain was the garage, while my mother's was everything inside the house. However, just down the street lived a family whose dad loved to cook and whose mom liked to mow the lawn each week.

Expectations springing from gender stereotypes can be a real point of contention in any marriage. Do gender stereotypes factor into decisions on who does what around your house? If so, then check out what the Bible says in Galatians 3:28: "There is no longer Jew or Gentile, slave or free, male or female. For you are all Christians—you are one in Christ Jesus."

What freedom this verse gives us men! When we apply the apostle Paul's teaching to our own homes, we can free ourselves of the expectations that come from long-held gender roles.

Rather than just assuming that you fill certain roles because you are the man, and your wife will fill others because she is the woman, take time to talk to your wife about who does what—and who likes what—better in your home. To get the conversation rolling, talk about these questions: What unspoken, unwritten expectations did both of you bring into your marriage? Of the household chores that need to be done, which ones do you most enjoy and which ones does your wife most enjoy? Which ones do you dislike doing and which ones does she dislike doing? Which ones are you both willing to do, even if you don't especially like or dislike them?

Once you've talked through these questions, delegate tasks and responsibilities according to gifts, talents, and passions rather than stereotypes.

Jesus, teach me to lead my home with wisdom rather than with my notions concerning gender roles.

TO READ
Psalm 23

He lets me rest in green meadows; he leads me beside peaceful streams. PSALM 23:2

Finding a Quiet Place

God can speak to us and direct us in a variety of ways—through a meeting, through an overheard comment, or through an observed circumstance, just to name a few. But there is one thing God needs from us before he can direct us: a receptive heart.

A quiet heart is a receptive heart, so if we want to hear from God, we need to find ways to quiet our hearts before him. But how can we find a "quiet place" in a world where it's hard just to find a moment's silence?

It's not as hard as you might think. Sometimes it's just a matter of looking.

Look along the path of everyday life: There are quiet places to be found in our everyday routine, but we often fail to see them. A table in the corner of a coffee shop, a comfy chair in a hotel lobby, a bench in a park, or a path by the water can all be quiet places.

Look away from the crowd: You find quiet places away from the company of other people. So take a backpack and head to the hills, to a lake, to the beach, or to the rooftop. Walk the beach on a cloudy day or go to the zoo in the rain. Rise earlier in the morning than you usually do.

Look in your home: What robs your home of quiet? The TV? The radio? The stereo? Turn them all off! Fold up the newspaper and walk into your own backyard. Sit under a tree—or in one. Create a quiet place in your home. Hang a hammock or a front porch swing, and enjoy the quiet in those places.

Look at your schedule: Is someone always talking to you or at you? Is your every waking moment full? Take an eraser and remove 30 percent of your obligations for one week, and find a quiet place.

Once you've looked around and found yourself a quiet place, stay there for a while. Relax and listen. You just might hear the voice of God.

Jesus, show me how to schedule time to be with you in a quiet place.

TO READ
James 4:8-10

Draw close to God, and God will draw close to you. Wash your hands, you sinners; purify your hearts, you hypocrites. JAMES 4:8

❁ Getting to Know Him

Great things happen in our lives when we spend time with God. We get to know him better, find out his will for us, and learn what it takes to live a life that pleases him. Time with God is absolutely essential if we want to change. Conversely, when we don't spend time with God, we remain stuck in old lies, old habits, old unhealthy relations, and old thought patterns.

Right now you may be asking what steps you should take to cultivate your relationship with God. Sometimes it's a matter of taking some simple, practical steps. Here are some of the tools you can use:

A concordance. My favorite electronic concordance is WordSearch by NavPress. There are many other software options and book versions, including *Strong's Exhaustive Concordance* and *Young's Analytical Concordance.*

A Bible dictionary and encyclopedia. There are words, people groups, and customs recorded in the Bible that are new or different from the ones in your everyday life. You will gain more from a passage of Scripture if you understand its historical and cultural relevance. A Bible dictionary and/or encyclopedia will help you to understand those things.

A journal. It's a good idea to keep a personal journal as you seek God in prayer and in Bible study. Using a journal, you can write out your questions, impressions, and feelings. You can keep notes on what God is telling you through his Word, and you can write personal notes back to him.

Time with God never happens accidentally. You must be intentional in the pursuit of time with him. Filling your spiritual toolbox with the tools I've listed will help you do just that.

Lord, give me direction as I make the time to seek you.

TO READ
Isaiah 26:1-21

You will keep in perfect peace all who trust in you, whose thoughts are fixed on you! ISAIAH 26:3

Rekindling Your Determination

Determination is a key ingredient in living out the dreams God gives us. But determination can wear thin on those days when it seems everything is going wrong.

When a phone call or letter comes with bad news, or when my plans are forced to a screeching halt due to an uncooperative circumstance or person, my natural reaction is anger, fear, or depression. If life were a movie, dark foreboding music would be playing in the background to heighten the already strong sense of impending doom.

At those moments, it is easy to believe Satan's lies: "You're going to fail. This will never happen! What were you thinking?" So I choose to take those thoughts captive by asking three strategic questions:

What's the worst-case scenario? Usually the obstacles that lie before me are more inconveniences than reasons for failure.

Is God still in control? The obvious answer is yes! God has shown me over and over that he holds the affairs of the world—and of my own life—firmly in his hand.

What help is available to me here? The answer to this question is found in today's Scripture. When I keep my eyes fixed on Jesus, he gives me peace, and in the midst of that peace my determination to follow through on what he's called me to do is rekindled.

When I'm finished asking myself these three questions, God seems to whisper in my ear the words of Ralph Waldo Emerson: "A man is a hero, not because he is braver than anyone else, but because he is brave for ten minutes longer."

Lord, give me strength to keep my eyes on you, no matter what kind of obstacles come my way.

Oh, how I love your law! I meditate on it all day long. PSALM 119:97, NIV

Why We Meditate

In our church, we reward the children for memorizing Scripture. They are delighted when they receive little Bibles, pencils, or a cross that glows in the dark. But for us men, memorizing Scripture is its own reward.

Familiarity and need are the two key ways I memorize. By familiarity I mean reading the verse, posting it, saying it, and using it in conversation. When I do that, the verse is always handy. But to be honest, need has always been my greatest motivator when it comes to memorizing Scripture.

Early in my own "wellness" journey, meditating on Proverbs 3:5-6 kept me going forward. At that time, I couldn't trust my own feelings or my own ability to make wise choices. My flesh—the selfish side of me—wanted to try to deal with my insecurities by giving in to old patterns and old habits. But I found that meditating on God's Word produced in me a new way of thinking and making decisions. Through aggressively trusting in his understanding rather than my own, I gained the ability to fight against my flesh and courageously learn new skills and develop new habits.

Sure, it felt uncomfortable at first, but I kept reminding myself of the payoff: "He will direct your paths." This "path" of meditating on God's truth includes much more joy, hope, fulfillment, and blessing than I had before.

Dawson Trotman, founder of the Navigators ministry, wisely said, "After twenty-four hours, you may accurately remember 5 percent of what your hear, 15 percent of what you read, 35 percent of what you study, 57 percent of what you see and hear, but 100 percent of what you memorize."

So memorize God's Word. Meditate on it. Marinate in it. Pick a verse and stew on it for a while today.

As I meditate on your Word, Lord, change the way I think and live.

Listen to me and treasure my instructions. . . .
Then you will understand what it means to fear
the Lord, and you will gain knowledge of God.

PROVERBS 2:1, 5

God's Word: Our Priority

Sometimes spending time with God can seem like just one more item on an already long to-do list. It's easy to lose perspective on exactly why we need to spend time in God's Word daily. But as today's Scripture tells us, God promises that if we listen to him and treasure his instructions for life, we will know him and what it means to fear him.

Our relationship with Christ is to be at the very top of our list of priorities, and that should be reflected in our love for God's Word and in our striving to understand his truth.

In talking about his spiritual journey, Charles Lindbergh once said:

In my youth, science was more important to me than either man or God. I worshipped science. Its advance had surpassed man's wildest dreams. It took many years for me to discover that science, with all its brilliance, lights only a middle chapter of creation.

I saw the aircraft I love destroying the civilization I expected it to save. Now I understand that spiritual truth is more essential to a nation than the mortar in its cities' walls. For when the actions of a people are undergirded by spiritual truths, there is safety. When spiritual truths are rejected, it is only a matter of time before civilization will collapse.

We must understand spiritual truths and apply them to our modern life. We must draw strength from the almost forgotten virtues of simplicity, humility, contemplation and prayer. It requires a dedication beyond science, beyond self, but the rewards are great and it is our only hope.[1]

Do you want a life full of rewards? Then make learning, loving, and understanding the truth of God's Word your priority.

Jesus, help me to make understanding your Word my priority.

Those who wait on the Lord will find new strength. They will fly high on wings like eagles. They will run and not grow weary. They will walk and not faint. ISAIAH 40:31

Maxing Out for Christ

The October 2002 edition of *Spirit* magazine carried an interview with Jon Gruden, coach of the Super Bowl XXXVII champion Tampa Bay Buccaneers.

The article said that one of Gruden's favorite terms is *max out*. He asks his players to max out for him, and he's not afraid to do the same for them. He is very disciplined, so much so that he is up and in his office by four o'clock every morning. The results speak for themselves. He is the youngest coach in the National Football League and has enjoyed great success, both as the coach of the Buccaneers and as coach of the Oakland Raiders.

The article pointed out that Gruden believes in making the most of every day he has on earth: "At the end of the day, I just want to feel I have done everything I can to get the most out of [the] day," Gruden said.[2]

Most of the successful people I know live and work with a "max out" attitude. Leadership specialist John Maxwell has been quoted as saying, "successful people are willing to do what unsuccessful people are not."

I have taken some flak from friends who don't travel, live, or work at the same pace I do. As a result, I begin to second-guess myself. I wonder if I am working too hard. So in my quiet times with God, I pray, "Lord, confirm my pace and the plan." I have come to the conclusion that every man needs to find his own pace in life. My pace is quick, so I need to move quickly. There are other men, however, who don't move at the same pace I do. The key for men like me and for men who move at a slower pace is to find out what it means for them to max out.

Do you want an average life, or do you want to find the limit of your potential? Then find out what it means for you to max out for Jesus Christ.

Lord, let me max out for you.

TO READ
2 Thessalonians 1:1-10

In his justice he will punish those who persecute you. And God will provide rest for you who are being persecuted and also for us when the Lord Jesus appears from heaven. He will come with his mighty angels. 2 THESSALONIANS 1:6-7

※ *When You Feel like Quitting*

Pulling up short. Quitting. Throwing in the towel. Giving up. Walking away. Whether or not we admit it, all of us have wanted to do these things. We know what God has called us to do, but after facing one trial or setback after another, we begin to wonder if we can carry on and finish.

The apostle Paul faced opposition, persecution, and trials unlike anything most of us will ever face. And what did he do about it? Read on!

- "Yet what we suffer now is nothing compared to the glory he will give us later." (Romans 8:18)
- "So we don't look at the troubles we can see right now; rather, we look forward to what we have not yet seen. For the troubles we see will soon be over, but the joys to come will last forever." (2 Corinthians 4:18)
- "I once thought all these things were so very important, but now I consider them worthless because of what Christ has done. Yes, everything else is worthless when compared with the priceless gain of knowing Christ Jesus my Lord. I have discarded everything else, counting it all as garbage, so that I may have Christ." (Philippians 3:7-8)
- "No, dear brothers and sisters, I am still not all I should be, but I am focusing all my energies on this one thing: Forgetting the past and looking forward to what lies ahead." (Philippians 3:13)

Do you see the pattern here? Paul didn't look at the task. He didn't look at the work. He didn't look at the suffering and trials. Instead, he looked beyond what was happening in his present life and focused on what was ahead: the finish line God had put in front of him.

Jesus, help me to focus on the finish line and not on the obstacles in my path.

TO READ
Psalm 119:57-72

I pondered the direction of my life, and I turned to follow your statutes. Psalm 119:59

A Matter of Choice

"We just drifted apart." This is the most common excuse a man gives when he wants out of a marriage. It's also the foundation for no-fault divorce, or what is legally called *irreconcilable differences*.

I don't believe that couples "just drift apart." Rather, they distance themselves from one another through a series of bad decisions and attitudes.

Do you feel stressed in your relationship with your wife? Then retrace your steps and see where you lost your closeness.

Once you've identified what has changed in your lives, then you can take steps—through prayer, counseling, intensive communication, and so forth—to make new changes that need to be made.

Pam and I went through a time in our marriage when everything each of us did seemed to irritate the other. As I retraced my steps, I observed that we had each taken on a full plate of responsibility, but that had been a characteristic of our entire married life. So what was different?

I realized that until the previous year, we had carried much of the load of our responsibilities together and that our current ministry and work responsibilities too often had us functioning independently of each other.

We made choices to bring about change. We moved our offices next to each other, scheduled different kinds of ministry we could do together, and delegated to others ministry responsibilities that would have kept us apart. It wasn't long before we had recaptured that closeness we once enjoyed.

Pam and I are examples of what I always say about having a happy marriage: It's all about the choices.

Lord, help me to make the choices that will strengthen my relationship with my wife.

TO READ
James 1:5-8

If you need wisdom—if you want to know what God wants you to do—ask him, and he will gladly tell you. He will not resent your asking. JAMES 1:5

Just Ask!

Ask why people don't lead bigger lives, for lives with greater impact and influence start with one simple step: asking God for it.

Ask because he knows you need it: "Your Father knows exactly what you need even before you ask him!" (Matthew 6:8).

Ask, especially if it will bring glory to God: "You can ask for anything in my name, and I will do it, because the work of the Son brings glory to the Father" (John 14:13).

Ask and remain in God's Word for the answer: "If you stay joined to me and my words remain in you, you may ask any request you like, and it will be granted!" (John 15:7).

Ask with right motives: "You want what you don't have, so you scheme and kill to get it. You are jealous for what others have, and you can't possess it, so you fight and quarrel to take it away from them. And yet the reason you don't have what you want is that you don't ask God for it. And even when you do ask, you don't get it because your whole motive is wrong—you want only what will give you pleasure" (James 4:2-3).

Ask, and if it's in God's will, he will say yes: "We can be confident that he will listen to us whenever we ask him for anything in line with his will. And if we know he is listening when we make our requests, we can be sure that he will give us what we ask for" (1 John 5:14-15).

Just ask! The worst God will say is no. But he just may, and most likely will, say yes!

Lord, give me the confidence to ask.

TO READ
2 Peter 2:17-20

They promise freedom, but they themselves are slaves to sin and corruption. For you are a slave to whatever controls you. 2 PETER 2:19

Moving out of a Cycle

In the movie *Groundhog Day* TV weatherman Bill Connors, the character played by Bill Murray, finds himself living the same day over and over again. At first he thinks he is going crazy. But when he figures out what is going on, he realizes he can use it to his advantage. The first thing he does is venture into self-destructive, cynical behavior. He overeats, mistreats people, and manipulates his environment for selfish gain.

Bill Connors thinks he is free, but the power quickly gets boring. He longs for real relationships and meaningful endeavors, so he decides to work on improving himself and helping others. As others benefit from his power, he finds himself much more satisfied. Only then can he move on to the next day.

Does your life feel like a series of endless cycles? Has your career reached a plateau? Are your relationships not working as well as you'd like? Are you repeatedly making spiritual and moral errors that keep tripping you up?

If you want to move on from this place in your life, start by making a simple change. Once you accept Christ, you are redeemed, but you are still a work in progress. In Christ you have more potential than you know. God wants to fill your life with satisfying relationships and meaningful pursuits. Once you take that first step, then you can move on to a new life with him.

Abraham Lincoln was fond of saying, "I will prepare myself and prepare myself and then my opportunity will come."

When God comes in and changes you, he will give you opportunities to do great things for him. It's just a matter of taking that first step.

Jesus, thank you for redeeming me and preparing me for the new life you have for me.

TO READ
2 Corinthians 13:1-13

> Our responsibility is never to oppose the truth,
> but to stand for the truth at all times.
>
> 2 CORINTHIANS 13:8

The Simple Truth

Jesus says "I tell you the truth" about eighty times in the gospels. Over and over again he says it. Why? Because telling the truth, the whole truth, and nothing but the truth builds trust.

The leaders of Jesus' day had overworked their knowledge and come up with a system that was so complicated, people got lost in it. In contrast, Jesus made it simple. He challenges us to do the same. The truth tends to be simple, straightforward, and action-oriented. When you know the truth, you know what to do. One of the comical aspects of human nature is our tendency to overwork the analytical process and miss the simple truth. Consider the following scenario:

Sherlock Holmes and Dr. Watson were on a camping and hiking trip. They had gone to bed and were lying there looking up at the sky.

Holmes said, "Watson, look up. What do you see?"

"I see thousands of stars," Watson replied.

"And what does that mean to you?"

"Well, I guess it means we will have another nice day tomorrow. What does it mean to you, Holmes?"

Holmes replied, "To me, it means someone has stolen our tent."

What simple truth do you need today? Ask Jesus for insight that will lead you to the simple, practical conclusions you need. When you find yourself overthinking and overanalyzing, stop and ask God to show you the truth.

Lord, rescue me from speculation when the truth is evident.

TO READ
Proverbs 22:16-29

Do you see any truly competent workers? They will serve kings rather than ordinary people.

PROVERBS 22:29

✳ *Remember Who You Work For*

As an employer and leader, I keep my eye open for people with both talent and a strong work ethic. I also watch for people to whom I can delegate an assignment and walk away knowing the task will be done. When people earn my trust and do well the jobs I assign them, I invest in and encourage that person so that he or she rises up the ladder.

Nothing, however, frustrates a leader or employer more than finding out that he or she has been paying for work that isn't being done well or done on time. And nothing causes more stress for a leader than finding out at the last minute that someone has dropped the ball.

Each of us, no matter what kind of work we do or for whom we do it, should strive to be the kind of worker a boss can trust, the kind of worker a boss wants to move up in his or her organization, the kind of worker who works hard at our assigned tasks.

But just how hard are we to work? Colossians 3:22 addresses slaves—those who were indentured to serve—at the time of the early church, but it contains good advice for workers in all callings and professions today: "You slaves must obey your earthly masters in everything you do. Try to please them all the time, not just when they are watching you. Obey them willingly because of your reverent fear of the Lord."

Let pleasing Jesus be the standard in everything you do. Your boss may not be your best friend, but Jesus is, and you should work to please him. Your boss may not be good and godly, but when you work to please Jesus, you will please your boss in the process. Your boss may not even be reasonable, but if you work to please Jesus, your conscience will be clean.

Jesus, I work for you. Please guard my steps.

TO READ
Psalm 90

Satisfy us in the morning with your unfailing love,
so we may sing for joy to the end of our lives.

PSALM 90:14

A New Morning Routine

The annoying alarm, the shower, and the quick stop at Starbucks for coffee and a bit of breakfast—if you are lucky! Does this sound like most of your mornings? If you could, would you trade it in for a new routine? Check out these options:

- "The next morning Abraham was up early and hurried out to the place where he had stood in the Lord's presence." (Genesis 19:27)
- "Listen to my voice in the morning, Lord. Each morning I bring my requests to you and wait expectantly." (Psalm 5:3)
- "But I cry to you for help, O Lord; in the morning my prayer comes before you." (Psalm 88:13, NIV).

Here are some things you can do to make your time with him in the morning a satisfying experience and not just a routine:

- Wake to the sound of a Christian radio station rather than the buzz of an alarm.
- Before you even get out of bed, pray about your day and ask for God's help.
- Read a Psalm or a Proverb. Write down a phrase from the passage you read and post it on your mirror or desk so you can meditate on it all day.
- Read a devotional.
- Record your prayers in a journal.

If you begin your day with God, if you make the very first moments of the morning your time to spend with him, you will see results, namely a heart that rejoices and sings throughout the day.

Lord, I will see you in the morning.

TO READ
John 12:20-28

The truth is, a kernel of wheat must be planted in the soil. Unless it dies it will be alone—a single seed. But its death will produce many new kernels—a plentiful harvest of new lives.

JOHN 12:24

Time in the Cocoon

A caterpillar on its journey to becoming a butterfly goes through an amazing metamorphosis. What's most incredible about this change is that it requires the caterpillar to go dormant for a time. The caterpillar spins itself into a cocoon and stays there—seemingly dead to the world.

Sometimes as God moves us from one place to another in our lives, he takes us through "cocoon" times. We usually don't like them. They seem boring, and we may start to think that God isn't moving fast enough. We may even be tempted to ask him, "If you gave me this plan, why don't you do something to move it forward?" We may even be tempted to take matters into our own hands, ripping the cocoon apart ourselves and running ahead of God. But the cocoon time is all part of the plan.

Science tells us that if you were to tear open a cocoon and set the butterfly free, its wings would be underdeveloped. That's because the very act of struggling to get out of the cocoon strengthens the butterfly's wings, allowing it to fly. Likewise, if we try to escape God's cocoon before he's done transforming us, we may delay or even nullify what he's trying to do.

So when you are going through your time in the cocoon, relax! For it is in the stillness that you hear God. It is in the waiting that your character is formed. If you wait and nuzzle close to God, when he finally releases you from the cocoon, you will be strong and beautiful and able to fly in ways you never could have if you had struggled free too soon.

Make it obvious to me, Jesus, when I need to stay in the cocoon.

TO READ
Matthew 17:1-13

Jesus came over and touched them. "Get up," he said, "don't be afraid." MATTHEW 17:7

✿ *What Would You Do?*

Rudy Giuliani was named *Time* magazine's Person of the Year in 2001. In some quarters, there was controversy around his selection for the honor, but to me it was a clear choice. As I watched the mayor of New York, America's largest city, run for his life at the site of the World Trade Center disaster on September 11, then give directions for steps to save the city, it just seemed right to give him an award for his clarity and compassion under pressure. Giuliani mobilized millions on a day when the impact of his own personal losses could have immobilized him emotionally.

I had to wonder how I would have responded to that kind of loss.

What do you do in the face of loss? loss of a job? loss of a dream? loss of hope? Many freeze, seemingly unable to move, think, or function. Others spiral into self-pity or self-destruction. But some rise above their own losses and do great things for God and for others.

When you have suffered a loss, I recommend that you turn the pain into positive energy. But how do you do that? How do you turn something that on the surface is a horrible, painful loss into a gain?

Frustration, anger, and grief all have emotional energy behind them. Start by turning that negative energy into a positive in your life and in the lives of others. Get about doing something—anything—constructive or helpful to yourself and others. Make the bed, clean the house, gather friends to pray, or go help another hurting person. Make a list of things you can do, then work your way from the easiest tasks to the most difficult ones.

When you take your pain and turn it inside out, it becomes a platform for doing good, and that is the first step out of despair.

Lord, help me to transform the painful circumstances of my life into positive energy.

TO READ
Psalm 121

I look up to the mountains—does my help come from there? My help comes from the Lord, who made the heavens and the earth! PSALM 121:1-2

Look Upward, Not Inward

As a pastor, I have the opportunity to hear many people's life stories. Sometimes the pain they tell me about is unimaginably difficult. And, sadly, these people's friends and family have compounded that pain at times.

Job knew exactly how these people feel.

Job's righteousness made him an appealing target for Satan. One day Satan approached God, and God pointed out Job to him. God was confident in his servant, so he granted the devil permission to test Job (see Job 1:8-12).

Satan took Job's possessions, livestock, livelihood, even his children. And if that weren't bad enough, he afflicted this righteous man by covering his body with horrible sores. The devil spared Job's wife, but she was no comfort to him. Instead, she told him to "curse God and die" (Job 2:9). Job still had his friends, but one by one they came to him and said what many might say to a hurting friend today: "All of this must be because of some secret sin."

My wife and I know a couple who had to endure just that kind of accusation. They had pulled away from a legalistic, guilt-ridden, self-righteous church so they could attend one that taught biblical truth. They had been gone just one week when they received news that their baby daughter had a terminal illness. The pastor of the church they had just left visited them but offered no comfort. Instead, he told them that their daughter's illness was a judgment from God for leaving his church. Fortunately, this couple knew the truth, and for that reason they understood that what the pastor had told them was completely wrong.

If you are walking with God and tough times come, don't look inward for a "hidden" sin. Instead, look upward and find hope.

Jesus, grant me the insight to know when I am simply battling life and not being punished for something I didn't do.

TO READ
Luke 22:39-46

"Get up and pray." LUKE 22:46

Pray, and Pray Often

The Bible tells us many times to pray, and to pray often. But we men, being the task-oriented creatures we are, need a good reason to pray.

What do you think God finds important enough for us to pray about? He wants us to pray about the areas in our lives he sees as vital for success:

So pray often . . .

- for your enemies and those who persecute or mistreat you (Matthew 5:44; Luke 6:28)
- for strength not to fall into temptation (Matthew 26:41)
- for reconnected relationships (Romans 1:10)
- that you are rescued from unbelievers (Romans 15:31)
- that your heart will be enlightened to the hope in God's promises (Ephesians 1:18)
- that you'll be strengthened by the Holy Spirit (Ephesians 3:16)
- that you'll be rooted and established in love (Ephesians 3:17)
- that you'll be given words to fearlessly and clearly share the gospel (Ephesians 6:19; Colossians 4:4)
- that God would count you worthy of your calling and would help you to fulfill every good purpose he has given you (2 Thessalonians 1:11)
- that you will actively share faith and have a full understanding of every good thing in Jesus (Philemon 1:6)
- that you have a clear conscience (Hebrews 13:18)
- when you have trouble or sickness (James 5:13-14)
- to confess sin (James 5:16)

Lord, never let me forget to pray, and pray often.

TO READ
Revelation 17:1-14

Together they will wage war against the Lamb, but the Lamb will defeat them because he is Lord over all lords and King over all kings, and his people are the called and chosen and faithful ones.

REVELATION 17:14

When Life Just Seems Too Hard

The apostle John must have heard a few complaints. Indeed, the believers under his leadership faced very real issues. The government was against them—taking their businesses, separating their families, even killing some of them. It must have been a temptation for them just to pull back and pull up short. But John goes beyond a pep talk and reminds them—and us—of the surpassing value of knowing Christ.

Indeed, there are times in life when doing God's will seems like it's too hard, maybe even impossible. But we can be encouraged in knowing that there is eternal hope that is worth sacrificing everything for.

Here is an example of a man who understood that truth:

George Atley, a young Englishman with the heart of a hero, was engaged in the Central African Mission. He was attacked by a party of natives. He had with him a Winchester repeating rifle with ten loaded chambers. The party was completely at his mercy. Calmly and quickly, he summed up the situation. He concluded that if he killed them, it would do the mission more harm than if he allowed them to take his life. So, as a lamb to the slaughter he was led; and when his body was found in the stream, his rifle was also found with its ten chambers still loaded. [3]

What happens on earth is never the end of the story. The people thought they had silenced the influence of George Atley. But his example has encouraged millions throughout history.

When life seems too difficult to bear, when it seems that God is calling you to sacrifice beyond what you think you can, just remember the eternal hope you have in Jesus Christ.

Lord, never let me forget the eternal hope I have in you.

TO READ
Colossians 2:1-12

My goal is that they will be encouraged and knit together by strong ties of love. I want them to have full confidence because they have complete understanding of God's secret plan, which is Christ himself. COLOSSIANS 2:2

❋ Bound Together in Christ's Love

It was the darkest day of my life. My youngest son, Caleb, then a kindergartener, asked if he could play at his friend's house until his brothers were out. I agreed.

An hour later I got a call from the friend's mom. "I don't know where the kids are. I looked for them, but I can't find them."

I jumped in my car and drove to the friend's house as fast as I could. When I got there, we called the police, and the search was on. Soon there were two helicopters in the air, circling the neighborhood and broadcasting the boys' names over loudspeakers. Eleven sheriff's deputies were driving the streets, calling out the boys' names. During the five hours of searching, almost one thousand people got involved in the search.

After the fourth hour, when the sun was starting to go down and I had looked everywhere I could think to look, I dropped to my knees in a vacant field and prayed, *God, you know I can't find him, but you know where Caleb is. Please bring him home safely. And no matter what happens, I will praise you.*

At the end of the fifth hour, we got word that the two boys were found. They had disappeared into a storm drain, where they were on a "great adventure." Because they were below ground, they hadn't heard any of the commotion. When we asked them what made them come up, they said, "We got hungry."

When the boys came to the surface, someone recognized them and had them wait while the sheriff came to get them. I will forever be grateful for the team of people that responded in our time of need.

Lord, thank you for making me part of a team of caring believers.

TO READ
John 18:31-37

Jesus answered, "I am not an earthly king. If I were, my followers would have fought when I was arrested by the Jewish leaders. But my Kingdom is not of this world." JOHN 18:36

A Piece of Heaven on Earth

When you come to know Christ as your personal Savior, you are given a sort of dual citizenship. You are still a member of the community of people on earth, and you have responsibilities to that community. But you have also received citizenship in heaven. Your name is written in the Lamb's Book of Life (see Revelation 3:5), and you have all the rights and privileges of eternal citizenship in heaven.

While you are still living on earth, you are an ambassador for Christ to the world around you, and there are heavenly embassies for you to take refuge in. Each church that teaches the truth of God's Word and offers fellowship for believers is like a little piece of heaven on earth.

When American citizens need help while they are in a foreign country, they go to an embassy. This is because an embassy is actually a part of America on foreign soil. Inside the embassy there are pictures of U.S. presidents on the walls. An American flag is prominently displayed. The people speak English and are familiar with American customs and policies. They celebrate the same holidays and live under the same laws as people who live in the fifty states. For this reason, an American citizen in a foreign land can find refuge and get the help they need because, for a brief period of time, they experience a little bit of home.

Do you want to see a little spot of heaven on earth? You can find it in fellowship with other believers, and you can find that fellowship in churches that teach and preach the Word of God.

Jesus, thank you for my citizenship in heaven, and thank you that I can find a piece of heaven here on earth.

<table>
<tr><td>
TO READ
Romans 8:15-22
</td><td>
We know that all creation has been groaning as in the pains of childbirth right up to the present time.

ROMANS 8:22
</td></tr>
</table>

The Wonder of God's Kingdom

About all that remains of the so-called Seven Wonders of the Ancient World are as follows:

- The only remains of the Tomb of Mausolus, built in 350 BC, are now exhibited in the British Museum.
- The Temple of Artemis at Ephesus, once the center of the fertility cult of Diana, was probably destroyed in AD 262.
- The Hanging Gardens of Babylon grow no more. Babylon's ruins have been found along the Euphrates River, about fifty-five miles south of modern Baghdad.
- The magnificent statue of Zeus was dragged off and burned.
- King Ptolemy's famous Lighthouse of Alexandria, in Egypt, crumpled during a fourteenth-century earthquake.
- The Colossus of Rhodes was also destroyed by an earthquake in 224 BC. It was originally a giant hundred-foot statue of Apollo that spanned the harbor on the isle of Rhodes.
- Only the pyramids of Egypt, built between 2700 and 2500 BC, before the time of Moses, have survived the ravages of time.

All of these ancient "wonders" were impressive, to be sure. But none of them—even the pyramids, the only ones still standing—will last forever. Only the things God himself builds last for eternity. That includes the kingdom of heaven, the ultimate destination of everyone who believes in Jesus Christ for salvation. That's more impressive, more magnificent than words can describe!

Lord, help me not to be too impressed with the things that will not last and more impressed with what will last for eternity.

TO READ
Psalm 139:19-24

O Lord, shouldn't I hate those who hate you?
Shouldn't I despise those who resist you?

PSALM 139:21

A Healthy Disgust

Life is competitive. We compete in our careers. We compete for our kids' growth and development. We compete for the ideologies we believe in. We compete with our sinful desires, and we compete with the one who wants those desires to rule our lives.

Part of the process of a man's life is to kindle an awareness of what is really going on in this world. We need to keep our hearts soft toward God, but we need to develop thick skin toward deception and false teaching, and we need to have a level of disgust toward those who want to lead us astray.

There is a true story of a Republican political leader in Vermont who always showed up at Democratic rallies. He seemed to take grim pleasure in attending these gatherings, somewhat to the discomfort of the assembled Democrats. His presence made their parties seem less "homey."

One day a Democratic leader asked the old fellow why he came to their meetings: "Is it in your mind that you might get converted or something?"

"Oh, no," said the Republican, "Nothin' like that. I'll tell ye, I jes' come aroun' t' yer meetin's so's t' keep my disgust fresh."[4]

We need to keep our disgust fresh toward Satan, his demons, and anyone who wants us to build our lives on lies. As followers of Jesus Christ, we are in a spiritual war with the devil and his minions. They have limited power and can lie very persuasively. But our Savior has ultimate power and is the very source of truth.

God, help me to see my spiritual enemies the way you see them. Remind me daily that ultimate victory is mine.

TO READ
James 1:12-18

Temptation comes from the lure of our own evil desires. These evil desires lead to evil actions, and evil actions lead to death. JAMES 1:14-15

Habits That Strangle

In South America there grows a strange species of vine known as the matador. Roughly translated, the Spanish word *matador* means "killer," and this little plant has certainly earned that name. The matador begins its life growing at the foot of a tree. At first it looks like a harmless little plant. But as it grows, the matador relentlessly winds its way around the tree and makes its way to the top, slowly strangling the tree. When the matador reaches the tree's top, it sends forth a flower, as if it is crowning itself.

Many habits in men's lives are very much like the matador. Left unchecked, any one of them can slowly entangle a man's life and render him helpless. It usually starts slowly. A little lust here, a small indiscretion there, then a little white lie to hide the sin. Before he knows it, the man is strangled by the habit that once seemed so harmless.

I have never met a man who set out to ruin his life through a sinful habit. The man who loses his wife and family because of his addiction to pornography doesn't do so on purpose. The man whose family no longer trusts him because of his anger and rage never put this on his goal sheet. And the man who depends on alcohol just to get him through the rigors of life didn't decide ahead of time that it would be a good idea to become an alcoholic.

No, these habits form gradually, and they subtly entangle our lives. We are usually not even aware we have a problem until we have done significant damage to ourselves or to the ones we care about most. These consequences are like the matador's flower—they bloom to our disgrace.

Is there some "vine" of a habit winding its way into your life right now? Ask God to identify it, cleanse you of it, and forgive you. Then prayerfully make it your purpose never to return to that habit again.

Jesus, point out the bad habits in my life that can strangle me.

TO READ
1 Peter 2:16-25

Once you were wandering like lost sheep. But now you have turned to your Shepherd, the Guardian of your souls. 1 PETER 2:25

An Overwhelming Desire to Follow

Jesus often referred to people as sheep because we humans have a tendency to follow. "The crowd" has a very powerful effect on us, and popular opinion is far too effective in shaping our thoughts and behavior. We prefer consensus to conviction, tolerance to truth. We can even be persuaded to be critical of some of the most impressive things on earth.

Consider how people responded when a magnificent 6,942-carat diamond was put on display in Cartier's Fifth Avenue store in New York City. Cartier had purchased the flawless gem for a record $1.05 million at an auction. He decided to put the diamond on display so people could file through the jewelry salon to get a glimpse of it in person.

The responses of some people were nothing short of incredible.

A short, bald man peered condescendingly at the big diamond in the small glass case and told his wife, "I see a flaw there, but I wouldn't want to say anything."

"It isn't really that beautiful," concluded a well-dressed lady, "but I wouldn't mind having it."

"It's too large," said one woman in rhinestone-studded glasses.

"I think it's vulgar, but I just had to see it," commented another woman.

Said Joe Whitehead, a guard at the store, "I've heard more sour grapes in the last two days than in my whole life."[5]

How do you tend to look at and think about life? Do you tend to "follow the crowd," or do you hold to your own convictions and beliefs?

Jesus, help me to hold to my own convictions and beliefs, no matter what "the crowd" wants me to believe.

TO READ
Psalm 133

How wonderful it is, how pleasant, when brothers live together in harmony! PSALM 133:1

✳ *True Unity*

Unity happens when people's hearts are knit together for a common purpose and when each person's contribution to that purpose is valued.

One American monument in Kissimmee, Florida, is an illustration of this truth. It was built out of fifteen hundred stones from the lower forty-eight states and twenty-three foreign countries. It was completed in 1943 and is called the Monument of the States. The idea behind the structure was to use stones from many different places, cultures, and belief systems in order to symbolize friendship among the states of the union and among the nations of the world.

Conceived by Dr. Charles D. Bressler-Pettis, the structure itself took years to materialize. On a twelve-year tour of the States and the rest of the world, the doctor collected many unusual stones with unusual stories. For example, he found a fragment of rock from the original foundation of the Washington Monument and stones from the walls of former President Franklin D. Roosevelt's Hyde Park estate.[6]

Just as Dr. Bressler-Pettis collected an amazing diversity of stones to include in his monument, our God has "collected" an amazing diversity of people to make up his kingdom. Each of us brings into the kingdom our own unique set of skills and gifts, and for that reason, each of us has something to offer.

The exciting task before each of us is to find out what kind of "stone" we are to be in the wall we call God's kingdom.

Oh Lord, help me to neither undervalue nor overvalue my worth in your kingdom.

TO READ
Proverbs 10:1-15

A wise child brings joy to a father; a foolish child brings grief to a mother. PROVERBS 10:1

The Wisdom of a Mother

Andrew Jackson, the seventh president of the United States of America, owed much of his success to his own wisdom and to that of his mother, Elizabeth Hutchinson Jackson. As a member of the army at age fourteen, Andrew was captured by the enemy and put in prison where he contracted smallpox. His mother arranged for his release and nursed him back to health. After taking care of her son, she responded to the urgent need for nurses in the war. She lost her life while serving her country, but before she died she spoke these words to Andrew, which became some of the guiding principles of his life:

> Andrew, if I should not see you again, I wish you to remember and treasure up some things I have learned in life: In this world you will have to make your own way. To do that, you must have friends. You can make friends by being honest, and you can keep them by being steadfast. You must keep in mind that friends worth having will in the long run expect as much from you as they give to you.
>
> To forget an obligation or to be ungrateful for a kindness is a base crime—not merely a fault or a sin, but an actual crime. Men guilty of it sooner or later must suffer the penalty. In personal conduct always be polite, but never fawning. None will respect you more than you respect yourself. . . .
>
> Never wound the feelings of others. Never brook wanton outrage upon your own feelings. If you ever have to vindicate your feelings, or defend your honor, do it calmly. If angry at first, wait till your wrath cools before you proceed.[7]

All of us should be grateful for fathers and mothers who passed their wisdom along to us. What parental wisdom do you treasure?

Lord, thank you for the wisdom of my parents.

TO READ
1 Timothy 6:1-10

These people always cause trouble. Their minds are corrupt, and they don't tell the truth. To them religion is just a way to get rich. 1 TIMOTHY 6:5

Should I Help?

People are capable of anything in an effort to gain an advantage in life.

Early in my ministry, I was visiting a man in the hospital who had recently had surgery. As I walked into the hospital with my Bible under my arm, I was stopped by a mom and her twenty-year-old son.

"Are you a pastor?" she asked. I guess the Bible gave me away.

After I said yes, she asked, "Can you help us?"

"I have to go visit someone upstairs, but if you are still here when I come back, we can talk."

I went upstairs and took care of my visit, and of course they were still waiting for me when I got back. They asked me if I was going to church that evening and if they could ride along. I naively agreed to take them.

On the way to church they told me, "We have been doing this for about a year. We take the bus to the next town and then walk to the nearest hospital. We wait there until we meet a pastor to see if we can get some help. Do you think you can help us with a place to stay and some food?"

I was floored at their confession. When we arrived at church, I asked our business manager what I should do. He met with the mother and son and offered to get them to the local rescue mission but told them we would not be willing do anything else for them. They got upset, told us we were not doing God's will, and left the church on foot.

Unfortunately, there are many people who "work the system" just like those two. Those of us who are sincerely following Jesus need to be wise as we seek to help others.

Jesus, help me show compassion wisely.

TO READ
1 Peter 1:10-25

Remember that the heavenly Father to whom you pray has no favorites when he judges. He will judge or reward you according to what you do. So you must live in reverent fear of him during your time as foreigners here on earth.   1 PETER 1:17

✤ Travelers on Earth

An American traveled to Poland to visit the famous rabbi Hofetz Chaim. Noticing that the rabbi's room had only a table, a chair, and some books, the American asked, "Rabbi, where is your furniture?"

The rabbi replied, "My furniture? Where is your furniture, my friend?"

"But I am only a tourist, passing through," said the American.

"So am I," replied the rabbi.

Life becomes so much simpler when you realize that you, like Rabbi Hofetz Chaim, are a traveler on earth and not a permanent resident.

The lives and outlook of residents is greatly different from that of travelers. Residents spend enormous amounts of time taking care of their houses and their neighborhoods. Residents get very attached to their possessions and go to great lengths to protect them.

Travelers, on the other hand, like to keep their burdens light so they can travel as quickly and efficiently as possible. Travelers admire the scenery but do not own any of it. Travelers are fascinated with the ways people in different cultures live, but they are not "permanently" attached to any single culture. Travelers enjoy great freedom, for they know that the place they are visiting belongs to another and is his or her responsibility. As soon as you meet Jesus, you become a traveler here on earth. You still live in, work in, and minister in the world around you. But you know that everything about this world is temporary and that your real home is in the presence of God.

Lord, make me a traveler in this world. Teach me to love and give in this world, knowing that it is not my permanent home.

December

TO READ
Psalm 96

Let the fields and their crops burst forth with joy!
Let the trees of the forest rustle with praise.

PSALM 96:12

Singing Trees

One summer my son and I took a trip with several other fathers and sons to the Colorado River, where we were going to enjoy a good time camping, riding Jet Skis, and fishing.

The "camp rule" for riding the Jet Skis was to travel in pairs. That way no one would get lost or stranded alone. One late afternoon we were surprised to see one of the teenage boys riding his Jet Ski back to camp alone. He told us that his partner's Jet Ski had run out of gas and couldn't make it back to camp. I got on another Jet Ski and went after him. I found him about five miles from our base camp. It was close to dusk, and I had to tow him back. It was a long, boring ride.

In my frustration and boredom over having to perform this tedious task, I almost missed it: the trees seemed to be singing! When I looked closer, I could see that the trees lining the river banks were covered with what I found out later were cicadas. These bugs, which look a lot like bloated grasshoppers, gather in the trees in the early evening, and the males rub their wings together to produce their "mating call." Thousands of them produced a beautiful song.

What an awesome experience! With the sunset turning the sky a brilliant red and orange, with the fading daylight glimmering off the water, and in the relative quiet produced by the low speed of the Jet Ski, I heard the beautiful song of God's creation. I remember the sense of amazement I felt as I thought, *The trees really do sing God's praises!*

The natural world is full of examples of God putting himself on display. Are you paying attention?

Show me today and every day, Lord, the ways you have put yourself on display.

TO READ
Psalm 144

Reach down from heaven and rescue me; deliver me from deep waters, from the power of my enemies.

PSALM 144:7

Our Father, Our Rescuer

When we enter into a relationship with the God of the universe, we enter into a relationship with a heavenly Father who will do whatever it takes to rescue us. It may not always be comfortable—at times it might be downright painful—but we can always count on him to deliver us.

Bryan Chapell shares this illustration of that truth:

> One of the most powerful images of my wife's childhood came when she and a neighbor girl were playing in some woods behind their homes. The neighbor girl wandered from the path and stepped into a nest of ground bees. As the bees began to swarm and sting, the girls began to scream for help. Suddenly, out of nowhere—like superman, my wife says—her dad came crashing through the woods, leaping over fallen logs, hurdling vines, and bushes. He swooped up a girl under each arm and tore through the woods at full speed to get away from the bees. As he ran, the father's grip bruised the children's arms, branches scratched their thighs, and thorns grabbed at their clothes and skin. The rescue hurt, but it was better than the bees.
>
> The image is not so unlike our heavenly Father's work. He sees the danger and, at times even before we call out, comes crashing into our worlds. From some throne above the universe, he hurdles galaxies and the infinite expanse of time to enter our realities and take us from spiritual danger. His rescue may hurt us, but the goal is always our safety, and the motive is always his love.[1]

We should never cease to thank God for protecting us and for rescuing us in times of trouble, even the times when we have brought it on ourselves. That is the picture of a God whose love is deeper than we can understand.

Thank you, Lord, for rescuing me, especially from my own stumbles and mistakes.

TO READ
Psalm 103:1-12

He fills my life with good things. My youth
is renewed like the eagle's! PSALM 103:5

Renewed Youth

Some time ago, I took my two oldest sons on a hiking trip in the Sierra
Nevada Mountains in California. As we walked along one of the paths near
the ten-thousand-foot summit, we were stopped in our tracks at the site
of an eagle. Its huge wingspan and majestic flight were spellbinding. It had
an obviously muscular physique, yet it appeared effortless in flight. As we
watched, the eagle suddenly swooped downward toward a large lake. As
it neared the surface, it reached out with its talons, scooped up a fish, and
soared off to enjoy its prey.

As I watched this eagle in action, I couldn't help but think, *I want to be
like that. I want to soar into God's will, swoop down on the challenges of life, and
majestically overcome any obstacles in my way.*

At that moment, it was easy for me to understand why God used this
powerful, beautiful bird as a picture of renewed strength. But there is
something more about the eagle I didn't know at that moment, something
that makes it a wonderful picture of the renewal of our youth the psalmist
wrote about in today's Scripture.

In his book *Sources of Strength: Meditations on Scripture for a Living Faith*,
former president Jimmy Carter points out another reason God uses the
eagle as a picture of renewed youth: "The eagle had an additional meaning
for the ancient Hebrews. Because it molts (sheds and regrows) its feathers
annually, they viewed the eagle as having a new life each year."[2]

There will be times in the life of every man when he longs for the exuberance and endurance of youth. But through a personal relationship with
Jesus, we can walk in his promise of the daily renewal of our strength.

Jesus, renew my strength today so I have the youthful endurance I need.

TO READ
Philippians 3:1-11

As a result, I can really know Christ and experience the mighty power that raised him from the dead. I can learn what it means to suffer with him, sharing in his death, so that, somehow, I can experience the resurrection from the dead! PHILIPPIANS 3:10-11

✳ The Reality of the Resurrection

In Barcelona, Spain, a truck carrying an empty coffin was rolling along when the driver stopped to pick up a farmer who was thumbing a ride. The farmer was bouncing around in the bed of the truck when it started to rain. He examined the coffin, found it empty, crawled inside to keep dry, then fell asleep.

Further on, the driver picked up two more hitchhikers. They were traveling along at a lively clip when the farmer inside the coffin woke up, pushed open the lid, stuck out his head, and observed: "Oh, it has stopped raining." The two other hitchhikers were so terrified that they leaped from the speeding truck.[3]

There's something other-worldly, even frightening, about the idea of the dead coming back to life, isn't there? But our hope for eternal life is the resurrection of Jesus Christ, who rose from the dead to prove that he had overcome death.

Jesus had promised numerous times that he would give his followers new life, that there would come a day when all who believe in him would receive new bodies in which they would enjoy eternal life without pain and sorrow.

Sadly, there are many who refuse to believe in a Savior who not only promised that those who followed him would overcome death but who also demonstrated his ability to defeat death by rising from the dead after three days in the grave.

For those who don't believe in the miracle of the Resurrection, the idea of someone rising from the dead is either patently absurd or overwhelmingly frightening. But for those of us who have put our faith in Jesus, overcoming death isn't just a dream but the precious promise of a future reality.

Risen Lord, thank you for dying, then rising from the dead. Thank you that because of your Resurrection, I too will be raised from the dead.

TO READ
Hebrews 2:14-18

Because God's children are human beings—made of flesh and blood—Jesus also became flesh and blood by being born in human form. For only as a human being could he die, and only by dying could he break the power of the Devil, who had the power of death.

HEBREWS 2:14

Putting Fear in Its Place

A World War II Japanese soldier by the name of Shoichi Yokoi lived in a cave on the island of Guam, to which he fled in 1944 when the tides of war began to change. Fearing for his life, he stayed hidden for twenty-eight years in the jungle cave, coming out only at night. During this long period of time, this self-made hermit lived on frogs, rats, snails, shrimp, nuts, and mangoes. All he had for clothing was an old pair of trousers and a jacket he had made out of tree bark.

One day two hunters found Yokoi and told him that he need not hide any longer, that the war had long been over and that there was nothing to fear. At last he was free, and with new clothes to wear and food to eat, he was taken by plane to his home. Incredibly, Yokoi said he had known that the war was over because of leaflets scattered throughout the jungles of Guam. But he was still afraid that if he came out of hiding, his own country would have him executed.[4]

It is amazing how many of us live in fear. There truly seems to be no end to the list of ways in which fear can run our lives. We are afraid of life and afraid of death. We are afraid of success and afraid of failure. We are afraid of boring lives and afraid of lives filled with excitement.

But over and over again in Bible, we are told that we are not to live in fear but are to live victorious lives in God's Son, Jesus Christ, who came to earth to live as a man, die as a man, and rise from the dead.

What do you fear today? Instead of clinging to that fear, cling to the promises of the God who tells us he is bigger than any fear this world puts in front of us and who proved it by raising his own Son from the dead.

Lord, give me a life bigger than my fears.

TO READ
Ephesians 6:1-18

We are not fighting against people made of flesh and blood, but against the evil rulers and authorities of the unseen world, against those mighty powers of darkness who rule this world, and against wicked spirits in the heavenly realms. EPHESIANS 6:12

Who Is Your Enemy?

When World War I broke out, the War Ministry in London dispatched a coded message to one of the British outposts in the inaccessible areas of Africa. The message read: "War declared. Arrest all enemy aliens in your district." The War Ministry received this prompt reply: "Have arrested ten Germans, six Belgians, four Frenchman, two Italians, three Austrians, and an American. Please advise immediately who we're at war with."[5]

It seems that we men don't always know just who we're fighting. We quarrel with one another and criticize one another, as though our battle is with our brothers in Christ and not against the forces of the devil. We argue over music styles because we elevate our own preferences to theological levels. We criticize others for the way they talk, the way they dress, and the way they spend their free time. We point out the shortcomings of others because it makes us feel victorious.

In doing those things, we lose sight of who the real enemy is, giving him a foothold in the spiritual battles we fight with him and his minions.

We need to understand that our real enemy is the devil, not one another. And we need to realize that Satan is constantly trying to confuse us by making it seem that our brothers and sisters in Christ are our enemies and by making even the most minor human conflict—at work, at church, with our friends, or in our families—look like the real problem.

The next time you encounter any kind of conflict, pray before you speak or act. Ask God to remind you who the real enemy is, and command Satan and his demons to be quiet. Then see if there is any conflict left to address.

Jesus, give me wisdom to know who the real enemy is.

TO READ
Proverbs 26:18-28

A quarrelsome person starts fights as easily as hot embers light charcoal or fire lights wood.

PROVERBS 26:21

Loving a Snapping Turtle

The snapping turtle is a surly creature who hatches from an egg not much smaller than a Ping-Pong ball. From the time it hatches, it is ready and willing to bite whatever or whomever comes near.

At the end of three years, the snapping turtle may have grown to the size of a saucer, but it is as ready to bite as ever. It is antisocial, has no friends but lots of enemies. By the time it is an adult, it may weigh as much as 150 pounds—depending on its habitat and species—and will have developed jaws big enough and strong enough to bite off a man's hand. At mating time, it engages in death struggles with other male snapping turtles and has been known to attack and eat females of his own species. It lives a good many years but never outlives its reputation for being a vicious snapper.

Sadly, some men are by nature just like the snapping turtle. They have a foul disposition and are prone to snapping at anyone who gets too close. They can be naysayers in our lives. When we talk about the things God is doing in and for us, they voice their doubt as to whether his blessings are real, and they try to knock us down. They seem to be threatened by our success and offended by the healthy balance in our lives. And if we get close to them, they bite.

One of my friends describes the "snapping turtles" in our lives as *E.G.R.*—Extra Grace Required—people. That means that if we are to love these people—and God calls us to love even the snapping turtles around us—we need an extra portion of his grace to do so.

Is there a "snapping turtle" in your life today? Is there someone in your world you just don't know how to love? Ask God today to give you an extra portion of his grace, and ask him to love that person through you.

Jesus, give me grace to love even the "snapping turtles" in my life.

TO READ
1 Timothy 4:10-16

Keep a close watch on yourself and on your teaching. Stay true to what is right, and God will save you and those who hear you. 1 TIMOTHY 4:16

The Benefits of Hanging in There

Life consistently throws challenges our way. We fall into predicaments we must outlast and face problems with no easy answers. We are thrust into confusing situations that seem beyond our ability to understand, let alone solve.

Often the only response we have to our challenges is simply to persevere.

Whenever I think about the benefits of perseverance, I think of this poem by T. C. Hamlet:

> Two frogs fell into a can of cream, Or so I've heard it told;
> The sides of the can were shiny and steep, The cream was deep and cold.
> "O, what's the use?" croaked No. 1. "Tis fate; no help's around.
> Good-bye, my friends! Good-bye, sad world!" And weeping still, he drowned.
> But Number 2, of sterner stuff, Dog-paddled in surprise,
> The while he wiped his creamy face And dried his creamy eyes.
> "I'll swim awhile, at least," he said. Or so I've heard he said;
> "It really wouldn't help the world If one more frog were dead."
> An hour or two he kicked and swam, Not once he stopped to mutter,
> But kicked and kicked and swam and kicked, Then hopped out, via butter![6]

When we are faced with an obstacle, we have two choices: either give up, give in, and face defeat; or keep our faith intact, wait for God to show us what to do, then enjoy the victory.

Which choice will you make?

Jesus, give me the strength to keep swimming until you deliver me.

TO READ
Job 25:1–26:14

God is powerful and dreadful. He enforces peace in the heavens. JOB 25:2

The Awesome Power of God

My wife and I visited some friends on the island of Kauai, Hawaii, the year after a hurricane had passed over the island. They had come face-to-face with the helplessness of mere humans when confronted with God's power.

Our friends took us downstairs to their first-floor garage and opened the garage door. From there we could see much of the neighborhood. They pointed to a parking canopy across the street and told us, "We watched that entire roof get pulled off by the hurricane. The sound of wood splintering was awesome." They pointed to the walls of their garage and said, "Do you notice there are no windows in the garage? We ran down here because all the windows in the house were breaking. The air pressure was such that the glass just shattered. There was nothing we could do so we just pulled up a couple of chairs and watched the storm."

As they spoke, I felt remarkably small and insignificant. I asked them, "Did this change your life?"

They immediately responded, "We will never be the same. The power of this storm left us helpless. As we reflected on the week, we realized this was just a small example of the kind of power God possesses. We have worried less and relaxed more ever since. The hurricane caused our view of God to get instantly bigger."

It always clarifies our place in relation to God when we come face-to-face with his power. Getting caught in a storm, surviving an accident, or having your plans interrupted by the forces of nature puts a new sense of humility in our souls. It causes us to fear God in a way that helps us worry less and relax more.

Oh Lord, may I always fear you enough to never let go of you.

TO READ
Exodus 15:1-18

With unfailing love you will lead this people whom you have ransomed. You will guide them in your strength to the place where your holiness dwells.

EXODUS 15:13

❊ *Just Listen!*

Erik Weihenmayer is blind, yet on May 25, 2001, he reached the peak of Nepal's Mt. Everest, more than 29,000 feet above sea level. A degenerative eye disease took Weihenmayer's sight when he was thirteen, but that didn't stop him from scaling this awesome mountain. Ninety percent of the climbers who attempt to scale Everest never make it to the top, and sixty-five climbers have died trying, just since 1953.

But Weihenmayer succeeded, in large measure because he listened well. He listened to the little bell tied to the back of the climber in front of him so he would know what direction to go. He listened to the voice of teammates who would shout back to him, "Death fall two feet to your right!" so he would know what direction not to go. He listened to the sound of his pick jabbing the ice, so he would know whether the ice was safe to cross.[7]

When we are in the perilous parts of our life journeys, listening well can make all the difference in whether we succeed or fail, whether we press on or fall. We won't always see what is ahead in our paths or where the path is taking us. But we press on, knowing God has led us to take the path we're on, knowing that he speaks as we persevere.

As we press on, we listen. We listen for God's "still small voice" inside us (see 1 Kings 19:12, KJV). We listen for what he is telling us through our circumstances. And we listen to what he is telling us in his written Word.

Are you wondering today where God is leading you or how he wants you to get there? Are you wondering how you're going to overcome the obstacle in your path? Then just listen, and God will tell you what you need to know.

Lord, give me ears that don't just hear your voice but actually listen.

TO READ
Psalm 119:129-140

Your promises have been thoroughly tested; that is why I love them so much. PSALM 119:140

Fans for Eternity

During the 2001 season, the Chicago White Sox held a Cancer Survivors Night at their home field, Comiskey Park. Before the game, Chicago slugger Jose Canseco spoke with four of the 450 cancer patients in attendance. Canseco told them he'd do his best to hit a couple of home runs for them in that evening's game. Incredibly, Canseco's first two at-bats produced home runs, true to his word.

When a reporter told White Sox second-baseman Ray Durham about the feat, he replied, "To say you'll hit a home run for someone and go out and do it, it had to have meant a lot [to him]. I'm pretty sure Jose's got fans for life."[8]

Any promise—let alone the promise of hitting two home runs in a major league baseball game—can be hard to keep. First, you must take your promise seriously enough to remember that you made it. Second, you must be willing to exert whatever effort is necessary to complete the provisions of the promise. Third, you must value the other person beyond the personal risk or cost involved.

When Jesus promised his followers eternal life, he was demonstrating his understanding of what it takes to keep a promise and he was expressing his deepest love. He knew that keeping his promise would come at great personal cost, and he understood that the benefits of keeping his promise would be ours, not his. He was willing to exert great effort to make sure that our eternities with him were secure.

In keeping his promise, Jesus gave us the privilege of being his fans not just in this life, but for all of eternity.

Jesus, you have a fan for life and for all eternity in me.

TO READ
Luke 12:1-21

Dear friends, don't be afraid of those who want to kill you. They can only kill the body; they cannot do any more to you. But I'll tell you whom to fear. Fear God, who has the power to kill people and then throw them into hell. LUKE 12:4-5

What—or Whom—Do You Fear?

All of us men fear one of two things: God or death. When we learn to properly fear God, we discover the secret to eternal life and realize that nothing on earth can take away our hope. But if we do not fear God, then we will fear death. We will see death as entering into the unknown or as an appointment to face God and give him an account of our lives.

What we fear, though, really is a matter of choice.

The following account demonstrates the kind of fear we who follow Jesus Christ should and shouldn't have:

A story is told about Rabbi Joseph Schneerson, a Hasidic leader during the early days of Russian Communism. The rabbi spent much time in jail, persecuted for his faith.

One morning in 1927, as he prayed in a Leningrad synagogue, secret police rushed in and arrested him. They took him to a police station and worked him over, demanding that he give up his religious activities. He refused. The interrogator brandished a gun in his face and said, "This little toy has made many a man change his mind."

Rabbi Schneerson answered, "This little toy can intimidate only that kind of man who has many gods and but one world. Because I have only one God and two worlds, I am not impressed by this little toy."[9]

Who do you fear more—men who don't care about you and can take your life, or the God who cares about you more than you can comprehend and holds your eternal destiny in the palms of his hands? If you fear God, then there is nothing or no one else for you to fear—either in this life or in the next.

Teach me, Lord, to fear you more than I fear death.

TO READ
1 Corinthians 9:1-23

When I am with those who are oppressed, I share their oppression so that I might bring them to Christ. Yes, I try to find common ground with everyone so that I might bring them to Christ.

1 CORINTHIANS 9:22

A Cause Worth Sacrificing For

There is nothing more inspiring than a man who is willing to make a great sacrifice to save other people. Many of us carry heroic dreams in our hearts but aren't willing to make the sacrifices it takes to make them reality.

When we read about someone who has paid a great price for a just cause, we are reminded of the noble pursuits in life. For example, most of us are impressed with the apostle Paul, who was so overwhelmed when Jesus chose him that he was willing to pay any price—even his own death, if it came to that—to take the gospel to all the world.

Throughout the history of Christianity, there are many examples of men who were willing to sacrifice everything in order to reach others for Jesus. Here is one lesser-known but incredible example:

During the nineteenth century a group of missionaries in what is now Surinam in South America wanted to reach the inhabitants of a nearby island with the gospel. Most of these islanders were slaves on the large plantations that covered the island. The plantation owners feared the gospel and its results and would not even allow the missionaries to talk with the slaves. They would only allow other slaves to talk with slaves.

So the missionaries sold themselves into slavery in order to take the gospel to the islanders. Working in bondage in the harsh conditions of a tropical climate, they reached many of them with the good news.[10]

Today, ask yourself what kind of sacrifices you are willing to make for the cause of Christ. Are you willing to give of yourself—your personal comfort and safety, even your very life—for the good of others?

Jesus, give me the courage to make a personal sacrifice for the benefit of those who need to know you.

TO READ
Romans 8:5-14

The Spirit of God, who raised Jesus from the dead, lives in you. And just as he raised Christ from the dead, he will give life to your mortal body by this same Spirit living within you. ROMANS 8:11

A Life of Spiritual Power

Pastor John Ortberg captures what it means to live a life of spiritual power:

> Significant human transformation always involves training, not just trying.
>
> Spiritual transformation is a long-term endeavor. It involves both God and us. I liken it to crossing an ocean. Some people try, day after day, to be good, to become spiritually mature. That's like taking a rowboat across the ocean. It's exhausting and usually unsuccessful.
>
> Others have given up trying and throw themselves entirely on "relying on God's grace." They're like drifters on a raft. They do nothing but hang on and hope God gets them there.
>
> Neither trying nor drifting are effective in bringing about spiritual transformation. A better image is the sailboat, which if it moves at all, it's a gift of the wind. We can't control the wind, but a good sailor discerns where the wind is blowing and adjusts the sails accordingly.
>
> Working with the Holy Spirit, which Jesus likened to the wind in John 3, means we have a part in discerning the winds, in knowing the direction we need to go, and in training our sails to catch the breezes that God provides.
>
> That's true transformation.[11]

Are you living a life of power in Jesus Christ, or are you just drifting along, waiting for your eternity in heaven? If you want that life of power, ask God daily to open you up to the influence and control of his Holy Spirit.

Jesus, grant me the will to submit to the Holy Spirit.

Commit everything you do to the Lord. Trust him, and he will help you. He will make your innocence as clear as the dawn, and the justice of your cause will shine like the noonday sun. PSALM 37:5-6

Power in Prayer

Over and over in Scripture, we are reminded of the incredible power of prayer. The following is an incredible testimony to that power:

Fifty Christian truckers got together to pray that somehow the sniper who was terrorizing the Washington DC area would be caught. Ron Lantz would be retiring as a driver in a few days and didn't even live in the area, but he felt sure that God would answer their prayers. In fact, he told the others there that God was going to use him to catch the sniper.

A few days later he was listening to the radio as he was driving through the region and felt compelled to pull off the highway to a rest stop. As he pulled in, he was shocked to see a car similar to what was being described on the radio right there before his eyes.

Carefully trying to read the license plate, a chill went up his spine as he realized the numbers matched. He quickly called 911 and remained there for what he said were the longest fifteen minutes of his life until the police arrived. He even pulled his truck across the exit so there would be no escape for the elusive murderers.[12]

The rest is now history—the snipers were taken into custody without incident.

Ron's testimony shows the power of prayer. When asked what he would do with the award money, he showed his true character: he said the half million dollars would be given to the victims' families.

In prayer, we men have a powerful weapon with which we can wage spiritual battle. It's a weapon we should never set down.

Sovereign Lord, remind me constantly that I have an overwhelming weapon for the spiritual battle: prayer.

TO READ
Proverbs 22:1-14

Choose a good reputation over great riches, for being held in high esteem is better than having silver or gold. PROVERBS 22:1

Establishing and Keeping a Good Name

A good name is difficult to establish but easy to lose. Building a reputation of dedication and integrity means establishing a consistent track record of sound decisions and hard work. In other words, we must prove ourselves dependable over and over again. The undoing of a good reputation, on the other hand, can be completed with just one mistake.

The following story demonstrates the importance of a good name:

[Sports columnist] Skip Bayless reports that Mark Cuban, owner of the NBA's Dallas Mavericks, recently offered WGN Chicago Radio sports-talk host David Kaplan $50,000 to change his name legally to "Dallas Maverick."

When Kaplan politely declined, Cuban sweetened the offer. Cuban would pay Kaplan $100,000 and donate $100,000 to Kaplan's favorite charity if he took the name for one year.

After some soul searching, and being bombarded by e-mails from listeners who said he was crazy to turn down the money, Kaplan held firm and told Cuban no. Kaplan explained: "I'd be saying I'd do anything for money, and that bothers me. My name is my birthright. I'd like to preserve my integrity and credibility."[13]

The name *Christian* is the birthright of every follower of Jesus Christ. We have a responsibility to live every day in a way that brings honor to that name.

Protecting your good name and your reputation as a Christian means giving Jesus control of your life so that you will do the things you should do—and you won't do the things you shouldn't do—that define for others who you are.

Lord, empower me to do the things that protect the value of my good name and identity of *Christian*.

TO READ
1 Peter 4:10-19

It is no shame to suffer for being a Christian.
Praise God for the privilege of being called
by his wonderful name!   1 PETER 4:16

❁ *What Is Your Name?*

The movie *Gladiator* tells the story of General Maximus Decimus Meridius. Maximus is about to be given reigning authority in Rome by the aging emperor, Marcus Aurelius. Before this can be accomplished, however, the emperor's son, Commodus, kills his father in order to establish himself on the throne. Out of jealousy, he orders the deaths of Maximus and his family. Maximus escapes, is sold into slavery, becomes a nameless gladiator, and finally seeks justice against the wicked Emperor Commodus.

The turning point comes late in the movie. After Maximus wins a great battle in the Coliseum, Emperor Commodus decides to meet this unnamed gladiator face to face. The crowd watches as the emperor in full pomp strides with his soldiers onto the sands of the Coliseum.

The emperor asks the simple question: "What is your name?"

Maximus, streaked with blood and dirt from the battle, takes off his helmet and says: "My name is Maximus Decimus Meridius, commander of the Armies of the North, general of the Felix Legions, loyal servant to the true emperor, Marcus Aurelius, father to a murdered son, husband to a murdered wife. And I will have my vengeance, in this life or the next."[14]

The crowd erupts with a deafening roar, while the emperor visibly shakes under the weight of the true identity of a man he thought was a mere slave. The emperor flees the Coliseum, only to later face defeat and death at the hands of Maximus.

How would you answer the question, "What is your name?"

Lord, thank you for giving me your name.

See, God has come to save me. I will trust in him and not be afraid. The Lord God is my strength and my song; he has become my salvation. ISAIAH 12:2

Clarity versus Simple Trust

We men often believe it is our right to have God clearly and specifically communicate what he has in mind for us before we move out and do it. But God tells us clearly and often in his written Word that our sole responsibility is to trust him and to have faith in him, then await his direction.

In his book *Ruthless Trust*, Brennan Manning relates this story:

When the brilliant ethicist John Kavanaugh went to work for three months at "the house of the dying" in Calcutta, he was seeking a clear answer as to how best to spend the rest of his life. On the first morning there he met Mother Teresa. She asked, "And what can I do for you?"

Kavanaugh asked her to pray for him. "What do you want me to pray for?" she asked.

He voiced the request that he had borne thousands of miles from the United States: "Pray that I have clarity."

She said firmly, "No, I will not do that."

When he asked her why, she said, "Clarity is the last thing you are clinging to and must let go of."

When Kavanaugh commented that she always seemed to have the clarity he longed for, she laughed and said, "I have never had clarity; what I have always had is trust. So I will pray that you trust God."[15]

Our human pride makes us believe that God owes us clear and detailed instructions—a road map, as it were—for our futures. But when we humble ourselves and place our faith in him, realizing he knows best how to direct our lives for our own good and for the good of his kingdom, we are content to obediently and completely trust him.

Lord, give me a heart that trusts you, even in those times when you don't give me clear and detailed instructions for my life.

I will guide you along the best pathway for your life.
I will advise you and watch over you. PSALM 32:8

Signs to Guide You

There are signs on the path of each or our lives. Over the course of your life, you will develop a track record that contains a history of where God blesses your life and where he withholds blessings. You will discover that there are certain activities you engage in that work consistently well. People are influenced, things get done, and you experience a high level of satisfaction. Conversely, there are other pursuits that tax your abilities, have little impact on people, and leave you frustrated and exhausted. These are all signs to help you discover the plan God has for your life.

I have noticed on the journey of my life that when I teach God's Word and when I engage in helping people grow at a personal level, things go pretty well. I feel a sense of deep satisfaction as I am energized by those activities. On the other hand, I have noticed that activities requiring executive leadership are much harder for me. It isn't that I can't do them. It is just that it takes a lot more effort than teaching and training individuals.

I have just been through a major career transition. In the process, I was privileged to be able to ask, "Where do I want to put my efforts?" I had opportunities to increase the amount of time I spend speaking publicly and working with individuals. I also had the opportunity to tackle a couple of positions in large ministries. As I looked at the signs God has placed along the path of my life, I concluded I needed to maximize the time I spend doing what I am best at.

What signs has God put in the track record of your life? What are the activities in your life that God consistently blesses? What steps can you take to maximize these areas in your life during the next year?

Thanks, Jesus, for filling my life with your directions.

We are the people he watches over, the sheep under his care. Oh, that you would listen to his voice today! The Lord says, "Don't harden your hearts as Israel did at Meribah, as they did at Massah in the wilderness." PSALM 95:7-8

Head toward His Voice!

When the now-infamous American Airlines Flight 77 barreled into the Pentagon on the morning of September 11, 2001, thirty-eight-year-old police officer Isaac Hoopii was nearby but outside the building. Immediately he began helping people out of the burning structure.

But Hoopii wanted to do more. Although he lacked protective gear, he ran into the Pentagon.

"Stop!" someone yelled at him.

"We gotta get people!" he shouted back. He knew people were in trouble, and he could not just sit by and be a spectator.

Nearly suffocating on the smoke, Hoopii heard the building cracking. He called out, "Is anybody in here?" From out of the darkness, he heard the cries: "Help me! Help me! I'm over here!"

Wayne Sinclair and five coworkers were crawling through rubble and had lost all sense of direction. Then they heard Hoopii's voice. When they cried out, Hoopii responded, "Head toward my voice." Sinclair and the others soon made their way out of the crumbling building.

By the time it was all over, Hoopii had saved dozens of lives.[16]

Jesus rescues his own in very much the same way. When we're stumbling around in the darkness of sin or doubt, we frantically cry out, "Jesus, help me!" Jesus hears us and calls out, "Head toward my voice!"

When we choose to respond to Jesus' voice, we find purpose, direction, peace, and safety, regardless of how lost we have been.

Lord Jesus, give me ears to hear your voice always, but particularly in those times when I feel lost.

TO READ
Isaiah 49:1-26

Then you will know that I am the Lord. Those
who wait for me will never be put to shame.

ISAIAH 49:23

Ironclad Promises

Vic Pentz, senior pastor at Peachtree Presbyterian Church in Atlanta,
Georgia, told this story:

> About a year and a half ago, I bought a new navy blazer at Nordstrom. It was
> one of those cases you may have gone through where you buy an item of cloth-
> ing and the more you wear it, the more you realize you don't like it. My blazer
> wasn't the right color, and to make matters worse, it attracted lint like it was
> going out of style. After wearing it pretty regularly for six months or so, I stuck
> it in my closet and didn't wear it for a long time.
>
> Tucked away in the back of my mind all the while was that famous
> Nordstrom unconditional-return policy. I thought, I've had this thing for a year
> and a half. I've worn it lots of times, and there's just no way they're going to
> take it back. About two weeks ago I . . . took it down to Nordstrom's men's
> department. I walked in, and immediately I felt nervous. I felt like I was about to
> pull a scam of some sort, but I played it straight. I walked right up to the
> first salesman I saw and gave this little prepared speech. I said, "I am about to
> put your famous unconditional-return policy to its ultimate test. I have here a
> blazer. . . . I don't like it. It's the wrong color, and it attracts lint like it's going
> out of style. But I want to return this blazer for another blazer that I like." Then
> I stood there.
>
> I couldn't believe it. This guy with a big handlebar mustache just looked at
> me and shook his head. He said, "For heaven's sake, what took you so long?
> Let's go find you a blazer."[17]

God's promises are much like Nordstrom's return policy. Is there a promise of God you would like to take him up on?

Lord, I depend on you.

TO READ
Psalm 90

Teach us to make the most of our time, so that we may grow in wisdom. PSALM 90:12

Growing in Wisdom

If life were like the movies, we would expect the following outcomes:

- The ventilation system of any building would be the perfect hiding place.
- The Eiffel Tower could be seen from any window in Paris.
- A man would show no pain while taking the most ferocious beating but would wince when a woman tries to clean his wounds.
- Persons knocked unconscious by a blow to the head would never suffer a concussion or brain damage.
- Any lock could be picked in seconds using a credit card or a paper clip— unless it's to the door to a burning building with a child trapped inside.
- All bombs would be fitted with electronic timing devices with large red readouts so you know exactly when they will go off.
- It would not be necessary to say hello or good-bye when beginning or ending phone conversations.
- Any person waking from a nightmare would sit bolt upright and pant.
- It would not matter if you are heavily outnumbered in a fight involving martial arts; your enemies will patiently wait to attack you one by one by dancing around in a threatening manner until you have knocked out their predecessors.

However, life doesn't play by the same rules as the movies. There all kinds of unexpected, non-cliché turns in real life. For that reason, we must continually seek after and grow in wisdom—the kind God gives us when we ask.

Lord, give me an ever-increasing hunger for your kind of wisdom.

TO READ	All have sinned; all fall short of God's glorious
Romans 3:9-31	standard. ROMANS 3:23

❋ Stewards of God's Truth

Billy Sunday, the great American evangelist of the early twentieth century, once told this chilling story:

A terrible blizzard was raging over the eastern part of the States making more and more difficult the progress of a train that was slowly facing its way along.

Among the passengers was a woman with a child, who was much concerned lest she should not get off at the right station. A gentleman, seeing her anxiety, said: "Do not worry. I know the road well, and I will tell you when you come to your station."

In due course the train stopped at the station before the one at which the woman wanted to get off.

"The next station will be yours, ma'am," said the gentleman.

Then they went on, and in minutes the train stopped again.

"Now is your time, ma'am; get out quickly," he said.

The woman took up her child, and thanking the man, left the train. At the next stop, the brakeman called out the name of the station where the woman had wished to get off.

"You have already stopped at this station," called the man to the brakeman. "No, sir," he replied, "something was wrong with the engine, and we stopped for a few moments to repair it!"

"Alas!" cried the passenger, "I put that woman off in the storm when the train stopped between stations!" Afterwards, they found her with her child in her arms. Both were frozen to death! It was the terrible and tragic consequence of wrong direction being given![18]

As a steward of God's truth, how are you directing the people around you?

Oh Jesus, remind me daily that I am surrounded by people who need you.

TO READ
Jeremiah 9:1-16

"They pile lie upon lie and utterly refuse to come to me," says the Lord. JEREMIAH 9:6

A Heart for Deception

One of California's most colorful stagecoach robbers was a man called Black Bart, whose domain was the rugged foothills of the Sierra Nevada mountains. Over a six-year period, from 1877 to 1883, Bart committed twenty-eight stage robberies.

Bart dressed in a long, linen duster and put a flour sack over his head. His weapon of choice was a shotgun, which he would aim at the stagecoach driver while demanding, "Will you please throw down your treasure box, sir?"

Finally, near Copperopolis, California, Bart was wounded while escaping a holdup and dropped a handkerchief with the laundry mark "FX07." Authorities were able to trace the mark to San Francisco, where police made one of the most surprising arrests in the city's history. Black Bart the highwayman turned out to be Charles E. Bolton, one of San Francisco's leading citizens, and one with close connections in the police department.

Bolton had a reputation as a nonsmoking, nondrinking, God-fearing man with big business interests in the gold mines. Amid much publicity, he confessed his crime and was sentenced to six years in San Quentin Prison.

We all live in a world of deception. Men deceive other men, not because they have to but because it is in their heart to do so. Black Bart had no reason to be a thief. He was intelligent, resourceful, well-respected, and resilient. But it was in his heart to deceive.

As men who follow Jesus Christ, we should be absolutely certain that there is not so much as a hint of deception in our words, actions, or attitudes.

Lord, guard my heart from its tendency toward deception.

TO READ
1 Thessalonians 5:14-22

No matter what happens, always be thankful, for this is God's will for you who belong to Christ Jesus.

1 THESSALONIANS 5:18

Giving Thanks through Everything

George Washington made the following proclamation in which he called the people of the United States to celebrate Thanksgiving as a national holiday:

> Whereas, It is the duty of all nations to acknowledge the providence of Almighty God, to obey His will, to be grateful for His benefits, and humbly to implore His protection and favor;
>
> Whereas, Both the houses of Congress have, by their joint committee, requested me "to recommend to the people of the United States a day of public thanksgiving and prayer, to be observed by acknowledging with grateful hearts the many and signal favors of Almighty God, especially by affording them an opportunity peaceably to establish a form of government for their safety and happiness"!
>
> Now, therefore, I do recommend next, to be devoted by the people of the states to the service of that great and glorious Being, who is the beneficent Author of all the good that was, that is, or that will be, that we may then all unite in rendering unto Him our sincere and humble thanks for His kind care and protection of the people of this country.

What circumstance in your life today requires thanksgiving? What has God done in the last year that would lead you to give him thanks? After you've answered those questions, consider this one: What circumstance in your life makes it difficult for you to give him thanks?

Your willingness to give thanks in the midst of all circumstances is the single greatest determiner of your attitude.

Lord, give me a thankful heart in every circumstance.

TO READ
James 4:8-17

When you bow down before the Lord and admit your dependence on him, he will lift you up and give you honor. JAMES 4:10

Unsung Heroes

The following article appeared in a Texas newspaper.

> Memo to a stranger:
>
> Mrs. Roy Alvarez didn't have a chance to thank you. Of course, being a father with seven children of your own (she remembered your remark to that effect), you understand. . . .
>
> Mrs. Alvarez saw her son, Roy Alvarez, Jr., 10, being swept to his death by a vicious riptide at Rollover Pass near Gilchrist Thursday. . . .
>
> Then a Boy Scout (Mrs. Alvarez recalls his name was "Rudolph" and she kissed and hugged him) ran out and grabbed Roy, trying to hold his head above water. But the scout was in danger of drowning himself.
>
> Then you sped into the surf, fully clothed.
>
> You took Roy from the Boy Scout, who, exhausted, began making his way back to shore. You held on to Roy when the riptide rolled you both under and into jagged underwater rocks.
>
> And you gave him back to his hysterical mother and trembling father, who came on back to Houston.
>
> The last they saw of you, you were limping along the beach, trailing blood.
>
> Mrs. Alvarez was calmer Friday. She called the *Houston Chronicle* and told the story, and she said: "He was hurt, and we didn't even get his name. Will you please tell him how grateful we are. Will you thank him for us—thank him for giving me back my son."[19]

Today, ask yourself what kind of hero you would want to be—one who quietly does what needs to be done or one who needs human recognition.

Thank you, Lord, for unsung heroes.

TO READ
Job 8:1-22

He will yet fill your mouth with laughter and your lips with shouts of joy. JOB 8:21

✻ Take Time to Laugh!

Laughter is one of the great gifts God has given mankind. We often take life too seriously. We think too hard about our jobs. We overanalyze our relationships. We get too intense about winning. And we come to church out of balance. We approach God with reverence, as we should, but we seem to see our God as being only serious and without a sense of humor.

Consider the following two stories and ask yourself if you think God enjoys stories like these:

After church on Sunday morning, a young boy suddenly announced to his mother, "Mom, I've decided I'm going to be a minister when I grow up."

"That's okay with us," the mother said, "but what made you decide to be a minister?"

"Well," the boy replied, "I'll have to go to church on Sunday anyway, and I figure it will be more fun to stand up and yell than to sit still and listen."

During the minister's prayer one Sunday, there was a loud whistle from one of the back pews. Gary's mother was horrified. She pinched him into silence, and after church she asked, "Gary, whatever made you do such a thing?"

Gary answered soberly, "I asked God to teach me to whistle . . . and He just then did!"

Approach God with the reverence due him. And take seriously the place he has given you in life. But don't forget to take time to laugh today.

Lord, fill my life with laughter.

TO READ
2 Timothy 3:1-17

All Scripture is inspired by God and is useful to teach us what is true and to make us realize what is wrong in our lives. It straightens us out and teaches us to do what is right. 2 TIMOTHY 3:16

What Does the Bible Mean to You?

Consider what the following influential men of history have said about the Bible:

- George Washington: "It is impossible to rightly govern the world without God and the Bible."
- John Quincy Adams: "So great is my veneration of the Bible, that the earlier my children begin to read it the more confident will be my hope that they will prove useful citizens of their country and respectable members of society."
- Charles Dickens: "The New Testament is the very best book that ever was or ever will be known in the world."
- Abraham Lincoln: "I believe the Bible is the best gift God has ever given to man. All the good from the Savior of the world is communicated to us through this book."
- Horace Greeley: "It is impossible to mentally or socially enslave a Bible-reading people. The principles of the Bible are the groundwork of human freedom."
- Woodrow Wilson: "I ask every man and woman in this audience that from this day on they will realize that part of the destiny of America lies in their daily perusal of this great Book."
- Douglas MacArthur: "Believe me, sir, never a night goes by, be I ever so tired, but I read the Word of God before I go to bed."
- Dwight D. Eisenhower: "To read the Bible is to take a trip to a fair land where the spirit is strengthened and faith renewed."

What do you have to say about the Bible? Do your actions back up your words?

Jesus, give me a greater respect for your Word.

TO READ
Hebrews 12:2-10

After all, you have not yet given your lives in your struggle against sin. HEBREWS 12:4

Our Approach to Sin

It is far too easy for many of us to make room in our lives for sin. We often feel as if we can get away with wrongdoing. After all, we reason, our sin doesn't really hurt anyone, so why shouldn't we make allowances for it?

When it comes to sin, many of us don't even struggle. We just give in without a fight. But the Bible tells us that we are to take sin very seriously because God takes it seriously.

While we will never attain sinless perfection this side of eternity, we must accept the fact that our sin killed our Savior. We must recognize that it was because of our selfishness he was crucified, because of our rebellion he was nailed to the cross, and because of our lack of character he was tortured.

These recognitions in themselves should motivate us and give us an intense desire to defeat sin.

Billy Sunday, the famous baseball player turned evangelist and reformer, never spared himself nor those he wanted to reach when it came to his vigorous attacks on sin. From the Gay Nineties through the Great Depression, he thundered against evil. Until his death in 1935, he preached Christ as the only answer to man's needs.

"I'm against sin," Sunday said. "I'll kick it as long as I've got a foot, and I'll fight it as long as I've got a fist. I'll butt it as long as I've got a head. I'll bite it as long as I've got a tooth. When I'm old and fistless and footless and toothless, I'll gum it till I go home to Glory and it goes home to perdition."[20]

How passionate are you when it comes to your struggle with sin? Do you tolerate sin in your own life and in the lives of those closest to you, or do you confront it the way Jesus confronted it—with gentleness but with passion?

Holy God, may I never fall asleep at the wheel when it is my turn to fight in the battle against sin.

Remember, it is a message to obey, not just to listen to. If you don't obey, you are only fooling yourself.

JAMES 1:22

Being Genuine

In London, England, there is a strange house. It looks like any other house on the block. But wait! Nobody ever comes out of No. 23 Leinster Gardens. There is neither a doorbell nor a letterbox. From the windows no one at all peers out. And nary a soul ever sits on one of the balconies.

Simply put, No. 23 Leinster Gardens, in the tree-lined Bayswater section of London, is "The House that Never Was."

Yes, No. 23 is a sham. It's a dummy house whose door and windows are merely painted on a cement wall. Behind this oddball facade there is nothing except a network of girders, some train tracks, and the entrance to a tunnel. Every so often a fresh coat of paint is applied to the facing wall to keep it looking exactly like the neighboring buildings.

"The House That Never Was" was put up by London's Metropolitan Railway (the so-called Underground), whose officials decided it would be the best way to hide the entrance to the subway tunnel and fill the gap in the row of houses so as not to spoil the harmonious look of the street.[21]

There is nothing more confounding to people than something that is not what it appears to be. That is true of men who claim to follow Jesus Christ. When we talk one way and live another, it confuses people and adds stress to our lives and to the lives of those around us.

When our talk about Christ doesn't match our walk with him, it will only be a matter of time before people see that we're not the genuine article, that there is something missing in our lives. But when we live every day in obedience to God's Word, our lives will be a testimony to the grace, love, and power of God.

Lord, let my life show others that I am the genuine article.

TO READ
Colossians 3:18-25

You husbands must love your wives and never treat them harshly. COLOSSIANS 3:19

Loving the Fairer Sex

Here's a shocking news development: Men and women are drastically different from one another! Consider these differences:

- *Nicknames:* If Laura, Suzanne, Debra, and Rose go out for lunch, they will call each other Laura, Suzanne, Debra, and Rose. But if Mike, Charlie, Bob, and John go out they will affectionately refer to each other as Fat Boy, Godzilla, Peanut-Head, and Useless.
- *Money:* A man will pay $2 for a $1 item he wants. A woman will pay $1 for a $2 item that she doesn't want.
- *Bathrooms:* A man has six items in his bathroom: a toothbrush, toothpaste, shaving cream, razor, a bar of soap, and a towel from the Holiday Inn. The average number of items in the typical woman's bathroom is 337. A man would not be able to identify most of these items.
- *Arguments:* A woman has the last word in any argument. Anything a man says after that is the beginning of a new argument. . . .
- *Offspring:* Ah, children. A woman knows all about her children. She knows about dentist appointments and romances, best friends and favorite foods, secret fears and hopes and dreams. A man is vaguely aware of some short people living in the house.[22]

We men have a tendency to become frustrated with the differences between us and the "fairer" sex. That's why God instructed us to treat our wives with love and understanding rather than impatience.

How do you typically respond when your wife does or says something you see as irrational, hypersensitive, or overly emotional? Do you become frustrated, or do you simply throw more love and understanding her way?

Jesus, give me the grace it takes to truly and unconditionally love the woman in my life!

NOTES

January

1. Paul Lee Tan, "More Knowledge, Less Liberty," in *Encyclopedia of 7,700 Illustrations* (Rockville, Md.: Assurance, 1979).

March

1. W. Bingham Hunter, *The God Who Hears* (Downers Grove, Ill.: IVP, 1986), 18–26.
2. Hunter, *God Who Hears*.

May

1. Clark Cothern, *Detours: Sometimes Rough Roads Lead to Right Places* (Sisters, Ore.: Multnomah, 1999).
2. Bob Jones, "It's Good to Be King," *World*, July 28, 2001.
3. James M. Kouzes and Barry Posner, *Encouraging the Heart: A Leader's Guide to Rewarding and Recognizing Others* (San Francisco: Jossey-Bass, 1999).
4. Adapted from "Teamwork Helped Miners Survive Underground," *CNN.com*, July 28, 2002, http://www.cnn.com/2002/US/07/28/mine.accident/.
5. Vesper Bauer, *ChristianReader.net*, September–October 1998, quoted in *Leadership* (Summer 2000): 67.
6. John C. Maxwell and Dan Reiland, *The Treasure of a Friend* (Nashville: J. Countryman, 1999), 27–28.
7. Brian Harris, *PreachingToday.com*, 2004.
8. Adapted from Jim Congdon, "Beauty's True Source," *Leadership* (Summer 2000): 67.
9. Zig Ziglar, *Something Else to Smile About: More Encouragment and Inspiration for Life's Ups and Downs* (Nashville: Nelson, 1999).
10. Kevin Miller, "Train to Persevere," *PreachingToday.com*, 2004.
11. Bill Gates, *Business @ the Speed of Thought: Succeeding in the Digital Economy* (New York: Warner, 1999), quoted in *Leadership* (Summer 2000): 67
12. Chris Peterson, "Optimism and By-pass Surgery," *Learned Helplessness: A Theory for the Age of Personal Control* (New York: Oxford University Press, 1993).
13. Howard Mumma, "Conversations with Camus," *Christian Century*, June 6–7, 2000, 644.
14. Adapted from Mark Moring, "My Dad, My Hero," *Campus Life*, May–June 1999.
15. Michael Bamberger and Don Yaeger, "Over the Edge," *Sports Illustrated*, April 14, 1997, 60.

June

1. "Walt Disney," *Leadership* 8, no. 2, quoted in *Preaching Today.com*, 2004.

2. Bob Welch, *A Father for All Seasons* (Eugene, Ore.: Harvest House, 1998).

3. Robert Andrews, Mary Biggs, and Michael Seidel, eds., *The Columbia world of Quotations* (New York: Columbia University Press, 1996), http://www.bartleby.com/66/67/28167.html.

4. "A Local Hero: A Dream in the Midst of a Nightmare," *Disaster in America, September 11, 2001* (New Rochelle, N.Y.: Cross-Cultural Solutions, 2001).

5. Paul Lee Tan, "Parable from a Plane," in *Encyclopedia of 7,700 Illustrations* (Rockville, Md.: Assurance, 1979).

6. Adapted from "Four of a Kind," *Sports Illustrated.com*, September 24, 2001.

7. *Pastor Tim's CleanLaugh*, http://cybersalt.org/cleanlaugh/, quoted in *Preaching Today.com*, 2004.

8. Tan, "Quaker Oats," in *Encyclopedia of 7,700 Illustrations*.

9. Geoffrey Colvin, "Think about This as You Don Your Tuxedo," *Fortune*, December 18, 2000, quoted in Alan Wilson, "Corporation Chooses Charity over Party," *Preaching Today.com*, 2004.

10. *Newsday.com*, 2001, http://www.newsday.com.

11. William Wimmer, "Purpose of the Law," *Preaching Today.com*, 2004.

12. Thomas Cahill, *The Gifts of the Jews: How a Tribe of Desert Nomads Changed the Way Everyone Thinks and Feels* (New York: Doubleday, 1998).

13. Jeff Arthurs, "Life Goals," *Leadership* (Summer 2000): 71.

July

1. Paul Lee Tan, "Go Easy!" in *Encyclopedia of 7,700 Illustrations* (Rockville, Md.: Assurance, 1979).

2. Tan, "New York's Realistic Demonstration," in *Encyclopedia of 7,700 Illustrations*.

3. Adapted from Barbara and David P. Mikkelson, *Urban Legends Reference Pages*, http://www.snopes.com/humor/jokes/fbipizza.htm.

4. Adapted from Dale Bruner, "Is Jesus Inclusive or Exclusive?" *Theology, News and Notes*, October 1999, 3.

5. Adapted from Jerry White, *Dangers Men Face: Overcoming the Five Greatest Threats to Living Life Well* (Colorado Springs: NavPress, 1997).

6. Dave Goetz, *Preaching Today.com*, 2004.

7. Mark Galli, "The Right Risks," *Leadership* (Winter 2000): 75.

8. C. S. Lewis, *The Screwtape Letters* (San Francisco: HarperSanFrancisco, 2001), 155.

9. Tan, "Pastors' Sons in Successful Industries," in *Encyclopedia of 7,700 Illustrations*.

10. Colin Powell with Joseph E. Persico, *My American Journey* (New York: Random, 1995).

11. Greg Asimakoupoulos, "Forgiveness," *Preaching Today.com*, 2004.

12. Adapted from Bill Myers and David Wimbish, "The Dark Side of the Supernatural," *Leadership* (Winter 2000): 77.

13. Tan, "Soviet Astronaut Denies God," in *Encyclopedia of 7,700 Illustrations*.

14. Keith Todd, "Woman Tells Man He's Going to Hell," *SermonFodder.com*, quoted in *PreachingToday.com*, 2004.

15. Adapted from RiShawn Biddle, "Interview with an Unlikely Hero," *Forbes.com*, September 13, 2001, http://www.forbes.com/2001/09/13/0913hero.html.

16. "Strange World," *Campus Life* 56, no. 8.

17. Stan Toler, *God Has Never Failed Me, but He Sure Has Scared Me to Death a Few Times!* (Tulsa: Honor, 1995).

18. "Evangelism: Its Theology and Practice," *Christianity Today*, October 26, 1992.

August

1. Paul Lee Tan, "Do Not Be Overawed by Satan," in *Encyclopedia of 7,700 Illustrations* (Rockville, Md.: Assurance, 1979).

2. Tan, "Worry Chart," in *Encyclopedia of 7,700 Illustrations*.

3. Tan, "Walking 500 Miles Blindfolded," in *Encyclopedia of 7,700 Illustrations*.

4. Calvin Miller, "Liberty Demands Responsibility," *PreachingToday.com*, 2004.

5. Michael Blakley, "Thankful for Freedom," *PreachingToday.com*, 2004.

6. LTD Enterprises, a Berra Family Corporation, "Yogi-isms," *Yogi Berra: The Official Web Site*, http://www.yogi-berra.com/yogiisms.html.

7. "Christus Imperator," *Preaching Today*, audiocassette no. 55.

8. Lewis Smedes, "Keeping Promises," *PreachingToday.com*, 2004.

9. Carl D. Windsor, *On This Day* (Nashville: Nelson, 1989).

10. John Medina (lecture, Multnomah Bible College, Portland, Ore., 1995).

11. Roger Thompson, "Treasure in a Brown Bag," *PreachingToday.com*, 2004.

12. Charles Kimball, "God's Loving Kick," *Leadership* (Summer 2000): 75.

September

1. Judith Gaines, "Tapping into God," *Rocky Mountain News*, March 12, 2000.

2. Alan W. Steier, "Wonder Brings Morality," *PreachingToday.com*, 2004.

3. Lloyd John Ogilvie, "Pastoring the Powerful," interview by the editors, *Leadership* (Fall 2000).

4. "John Wooden's Individual Achievement," *The Tennessean*, November 9, 2000, quoted in Rubel Shelly, *PreachingToday.com*, 2004.

5. Nathan Stone, *Names of God in the Old Testament* (Chicago: Moody, 1944), 97.

6. W. Bingham Hunter, *The God Who Hears* (Downers Grove, Ill.: IVP, 1986), 23.

7. Bill Bright, *God: Discover His Character* (Orlando: NewLife Publications, 1999), 131.

October

1. Paul Lee Tan, "Learning about Nonsense," in *Encyclopedia of 7,700 Illustrations* (Rockville, Md.: Assurance, 1979).

2. Tan, "From Television Back to Books," in *Encyclopedia of 7,700 Illustrations*.

3. Tan, "He Merely Showed Hands," in *Encyclopedia of 7,700 Illustrations*.

4. Patrick McGeehan, "For Want of Thirty-five Dollars, J. P. Morgan Loses Its Web Site and E-Mail," *New York Times*, June 14, 2000.

5. Hal Bock, "The Puck Stops Here," *Triumph Books*, http://www.triumphbooks.com/Without%20Fear-APstory.htm.

6. *Great Stories*, July–September 2000, 15.

7. Adapted from Rick Warren, *Great Stories*, July–September 2000, 13.

8. "Blessing Boomerang," *Preaching Today.com*, 2004.

9. Gregg Easterbrook, "Faith Healers: Is Religion Good for Your Health?" *The New Republic*, July 19 & 26, 1999, quoted in "Worshippers Live Longer," *Leadership* (Winter 2000): 77.

10. Easterbrook, "Faith Healers."

November

1. Paul Lee Tan, "Lindbergh on Truth," in *Encyclopedia of 7,700 Illustrations* (Rockville, Md.: Assurance, 1979).

2. Jim Morrison, "Necessary Roughness," *Spirit,* October 2002, 66.

3. Tan, "His Unused Rifle Was Loaded," in *Encyclopedia of 7,700 Illustrations*.

4. Tan, "To Keep on Being Disgusted," in *Encyclopedia of 7,700 Illustrations*.

5. Tan, "I See a Flaw," in *Encyclopedia of 7,700 Illustrations*.

6. Tan, "Monument of the States," in *Encyclopedia of 7,700 Illustrations*.

7. Tan, "Precepts from Jackson's Mother," in *Encyclopedia of 7,700 Illustrations*.

December

1. Bryan Chapell, *Holiness by Grace* (Wheaton, Ill.: Crossway, 2001), 180.

2. Jimmy Carter, *Sources of Strength: Meditations on Scripture for Daily Living* (New York: Random, 1997), quoted in "Live Like an Eagle," *Leadership* (Summer 2000): 73.

3. Paul Lee Tan, "Voice from Coffin in Truck," in *Encyclopedia of 7,700 Illustrations* (Rockville, Md.: Assurance, 1979).

4. Tan, "Fear without Basis," in *Encyclopedia of 7,700 Illustrations*.

5. Tan, "Who Is Enemy?" in *Encyclopedia of 7,700 Illustrations*.

6. Tan, "Two Frogs in Cream," in *Encyclopedia of 7,700 Illustrations*.

7. Bill White, "Listening Well Leads to Success," *Preaching Today.com*, 2004.

8. Adapted from "Canseco Homers for Kids," *The Goodland Daily News*, August 2, 2001.

9. Philip Yancey, *The NIV Student Bible* (Grand Rapids: Zondervan, 1996).

10. Ray Hoo, "Turn Your World Upside Down," *Discipleship Journal* (July–August 1982).

11. John Ortberg, "True and False Transformation," *Leadership* (Summer 2002): 104.

12. Adapted from "Sniper's Arrest Is the Answer to Truck Driver's Prayers," *The Presidential Prayer Team*, October 25, 2002, http://www. presidentialprayerteam.org/?id=9.

13. "Radio Host Prefers Class over Crass," *Chicago Tribune*, January 10, 2001, quoted in *Leadership* (Summer 2001).

14. *Gladiator*, directed by Ridley Scott (DreamWorks, 2000).

15. Brennan Manning, *Ruthless Trust: The Ragamuffin's Path to God* (San Francisco: HarperSanFrancisco, 2000).

16. Angie Cannon, "The 'Other' Tragedy," *U.S. News & World Report*, December 10, 2001, 24–32, quoted in Steve Gertz, "God Calls Us to Him," *Preaching Today.com*, 2004.

17. Vic Pentz, "A Twinge of Nostalgia," *Preaching Today*, audiocassette no. 88.

18. Tan, "Wrong Direction into Blizzard," in *Encyclopedia of 7,700 Illustrations*.

19. Tan, "She Didn't Even Get Name," in *Encyclopedia of 7,700 Illustrations*.

20. Tan, "Billy Sunday Fights Sin," in *Encyclopedia of 7,700 Illustrations*.

21. Tan, "House That Never Was," in *Encyclopedia of 7,700 Illustrations*.

22. "Men and Women: The Differences," *Jokes-Quotes.com*, February 9, 2003, http://www.jokes-quotes.com/contentid-220.html.

REFERENCE INDEX

John 4:1-39	January 11	John 11:33-35	May 29
John 4:27-38	April 24	John 11:36-42	May 30
John 4:46-54	January 18	John 11:38-46	April 2
John 5:1-15	April 8	John 11:44-48	May 13
John 5:1-17	January 10	John 11:45-54	May 31
John 5:16-47	April 25	John 12:1-8	June 1
John 5:18-46	April 10	John 12:9-11	June 2
John 6:1-14	April 26	John 12:12-15	June 3
John 6:16-29	January 8	John 12:16-18	June 4
John 6:22-32	April 27	John 12:17-19	June 5
John 6:33-40	April 28	John 12:20-27	June 6
John 6:34-58	January 5	John 12:20 28	November 16
John 6:35-58	April 29	John 12:27-30	June 7
John 6:60-66	April 30	John 12:31-41	June 8
John 6:61-69	March 28	John 12:42-50	June 9
John 7:1-11	May 1	John 13:1-5	June 10
John 7:12-24	May 2	John 13:1-17	January 15
John 7:25-36	May 3	John 13:18-30	June 11
John 7:37-44	May 4	John 13:31-35	June 12
John 7:45-49	May 5	John 13:32–14:1	March 26
John 7:50-53	May 6	John 13:36-38	June 13
John 8:1-11	March 6	John 14:1-7	March 13
John 8:1-20	May 7	John 14:6-11	June 14
John 8:21-24	May 8	John 14:7-29	June 15
John 8:25-29	May 9	John 14:12-15	June 16
John 8:30-38	May 10	John 14:16-21	June 17
John 8:31-35	January 6	John 14:22-31	June 18
John 8:34-45	September 24	John 15:1-8	June 19
John 8:39-53	May 11	John 16:1-15	June 23
John 8:54-59	May 12	John 16:16-22	June 24
John 9:1-5	March 11	John 16:25-33	June 25
John 9:6-12	May 15	John 17:1-12	June 26
John 9:24-36	May 17	John 17:13-16	June 27
John 9:37-38	May 18	John 17:17-26	June 28
John 9:39-41	May 19	John 18:1-27	June 29
John 9:39–10:19	March 19	John 18:28-32	June 30
John 9:40–10:5	May 20	John 18:31-37	November 22
John 10:6-10	May 21	John 18:33-40	July 1
John 10:11-18	May 22	John 19:1-15	July 2
John 10:22-26	May 23	John 19:16-27	July 3
John 10:27-41	May 24	John 19:28-42	July 4
John 11:1-8	May 25	John 20:1-10	July 5
John 11:1-15	January 23	John 20:11-29	July 6
John 11:9-12	May 26	John 21:1-9	July 7
John 11:14-16	May 27	John 21:10-23	July 8
John 11:17-27	May 28	John 21:24-25	July 9